PEREGRINE BOOKS
Y66

HOBBES

RICHARD PETERS

HOBBES

Richard Peters

PENGUIN BOOKS

BALTIMORE · MARYLAND

Penguin Books Ltd, Harmondsworth, Middlesex, England
Penguin Books Inc., 3300 Clipper Mill Road, Baltimore, Md, 21211, U.S.A.
Penguin Books Australia Ltd, Ringwood, Victoria, Australia

—

First published in Pelican Books 1956
Reissued in Peregrine Books 1967

—

Copyright © Richard Peters, 1956

—

Made and printed in Great Britain
by Cox & Wyman Ltd,
London, Fakenham and Reading
Set in Monotype Baskerville

To J. P.

For when we calculate
the magnitude and motions of heaven or earth,
we do not ascend into heaven that we may divide it into parts,
or measure the motions thereof,
but we do it sitting still in our closets,
or in the dark.

THOMAS HOBBES

CONTENTS

PREFACE TO FIRST EDITION

THE texts of Hobbes' works used and referred to in this book are those edited by Sir William Molesworth.[1] *The English Works of Thomas Hobbes* (edited by Molesworth in eleven volumes and published in 1839) will be abbreviated to E.W. and the *Opera Latina* (edited by Molesworth in five volumes and published in 1845) will be abbreviated to L.W. Thus a reference to the tenth page of e.g. *Leviathan* will appear as E.W. III, 10. Readers who may be stimulated by this book to read *Leviathan*, at least, for themselves, will find Michael Oakeshott's edition in Blackwell's Political Texts most suitable. The editor has provided an imaginative introduction.

In my attempt in this book to reconstruct Hobbes' problems and to present his solutions to them, I have been most helped by G. C. Robertson's *Hobbes* (Blackwood, London, 1886), J. Laird's *Hobbes* (Ernest Benn, London, 1934), and F. Brandt's *Thomas Hobbes' Mechanical Conception of Nature* (Engl. Trans., Hachette, London, 1928). The last-mentioned book is an indispensable classic for all serious students of Hobbes. Readers who are more anxious for a general impression than for technicalities will find Leslie Stephen's *Hobbes* (Macmillan, London, 1904) stimulating as well as scholarly.

I am indebted to Miss Helen Hervey for lending me a copy of her Ph.D. thesis on *Hobbes' Theory of Truth and Knowledge*, which was a great help to me in gathering together the relevant material from Hobbes for my second chapter. I am also grateful to Ruth Saw, Maurice Cranston, and Professor H. B. Acton for reading and commenting on parts of the book, and to Professor A. J. Ayer, the editor of the series, for his detailed suggestions for improvements – especially on points of style. But my greatest debt is to John Watkins who has helped me enormously with his painstaking comments on the whole book.

1. In reproducing quotations from the text of the Molesworth edition the italics have been ignored except in one or two places where they seemed necessary to the sense of the passage. In one or two other places italics have been used by the author to stress some point he is making about Hobbes' own words. These passages are indicated by means of a footnote.

PREFACE TO SECOND EDITION

THE second edition differs only slightly from the original edition – in the main by the correction of a few errors which were pointed out by reviewers and others. There has been no attempt to take account either of recent works on Hobbes or of the further development in philosophical understanding of the matters which he discussed.

KEY TO HOBBES' MAJOR WORKS IN THE MOLESWORTH EDITION

E.W. I	*De Corpore* (English translation)
E.W. II	*Philosophical Rudiments concerning Government and Society* (the English translation of *De Cive*)
E.W. III	*Leviathan*
E.W. IV	*Human Nature*
	De Corpore Politico
	Of Liberty and Necessity
E.W. V	*The Questions Concerning Liberty, Necessity, and Chance*
E.W. VI	*A Dialogue between a Philosopher and a Student of The Common Laws of England*
	Behemoth
E.W. VIII, IX	*Translation of Thucydides*
L.W. I	*Vita* and *auctarium* (supplement)
	Vita carmine expressa (the verse autobiography)
L.W. II	*De Homine*

The Little Treatise or *A Short Tract on First Principles* is published as an appendix to *The Elements of Law* (ed. Tonnies, C.U.P., 1928).

The dates and contexts of the above works can be found in Ch. I.

CHAPTER I

LIFE AND PROBLEMS

THOMAS HOBBES was born prematurely on 5 April 1588, when his mother heard of the approach of the Spanish Armada. In spite of this somewhat unpropitious entry into the world Hobbes had the equivalent of two lives. For he lived cheerfully to the age of ninety-one, which was double the normal expectation of life in those times; his health greatly improved at about the age of forty and the melancholy and seedy mien, which, together with his jet black hair, earned for him in his youth the nickname of 'The Crow', gave way to a ruddy complexion; and although he was a competent classical scholar and stylist at forty, his bent for philosophy did not reveal itself till he was nearly fifty. He was thus a schoolboy during the closing years of Elizabeth's reign, an undergraduate, young tutor, and classical scholar under James I, a mathematician and aspiring philosopher under Charles I, a famous and suspect philosopher under Cromwell, and after the Restoration a fashionable historian, a poet, and almost an English institution.

Hobbes' father was vicar of Westport, an adjunct of Malmesbury in Gloucestershire. Aubrey referred to him as an ignorant man who 'could only read the prayers of the Church and the homilies, and disesteemed Learning . . . as not knowing the Sweetnes of it'.[1] However he had other ways of enlivening his parishioners. On one occasion, after a card party on a Saturday night, he went to sleep in the middle of the service and announced to the congregation, while dreaming, that clubs were trumps. He was a choleric man and, on being provoked by another parson at the church door, struck him and fled to London, where he died in obscurity. Thomas, however, was fortunate in having a rich,

1. J. Aubrey, *Brief Lives*, p. 147 (ed. O. Dick.).

respectable, and childless uncle who paid for his education. He was sent to school at four at Westport church and was learning Latin and Greek at six. At eight he was sent to a small private school in Malmesbury where a certain Mr Robert Latimer, 'a good Graecian and the first that came into our Parts hereabout since the Reformation',[1] took a great interest in him and used to instruct him and one or two other boys till nine o'clock at night. At the age of fourteen, having already attained sufficient competence in Latin and Greek to translate Euripides' *Medea* into Latin iambics, he was sent by his uncle to Magdalen Hall, Oxford, where he remained for five years before taking his bachelor's degree. At Oxford he was bored by his Aristotelian teachers, though he thought himself a good disputant at logic. His college had a strong Puritan tradition. This may well have perturbed him, though his later reflections on Oxford indicate that the prevalent drunkenness, wantonness, gaming, and other vices, which occasioned frequent commissions and campaigns for reform, impressed him more than the religious threats to peace. Later in his life he was to launch furious attacks on the Universities as hotbeds of sedition planted by the Roman Catholic Church in the Middle Ages to perpetuate the challenge to secular power, for which purpose they were also used later by the Puritans. But it is doubtful whether Hobbes was politically conscious enough to see them in that light while he was an undergraduate; rather, if we can trust Aubrey, his interests lay more in trapping jackdaws than in baiting Puritans. He also preferred going to bookbinders' shops and gaping at maps to poring over theories of senseperception. For at this time it was the new and strange worlds charted by Drake and Magellan that fired his imagination rather than the intellectual voyages of Kepler and Galileo out of the snug, earth-centred security of the Aristotelian cosmology.

On leaving Oxford in 1608 Hobbes was fortunate to become tutor to the young son of William Cavendish, Earl of Devonshire; for in this way he was introduced to influential people, foreign travel, and a first-class library. These were to be the three main stimulants that turned Hobbes first of all into an eminent classical

1. J. Aubrey, op. cit., p. 148.

scholar and stylist and later into a brilliant philosopher. The young Earl, who was about Hobbes' age, already had a wife aged twelve. One of Hobbes' duties was to keep the young man's purse. On occasions this necessitated borrowing money, in the course of which he often caught cold through standing about soliciting with wet feet. In 1610, however, the two young men were packed off to the Continent.

Hobbes' intellectual development can be conveniently related to his three visits to the Continent before he went to Paris as a voluntary exile. On this first occasion he discovered the disrepute into which the Aristotelianism, in which he had been nurtured, had fallen. Kepler had published his *Astronomia Nova* in 1607 and Galileo had just returned to Tuscany after his triumphant revelation of the satellites of Jupiter by means of his telescope. The foundations of Aristotelianism were cracking. Politically, too, France was in a turmoil after the assassination of Henry IV by Ravaillac, a lay Jesuit. Hobbes returned from Italy with his Greek and Latin vastly improved and with a determination to become a classical scholar. There were plenty of facilities for this in his master's library. He was also considerably helped by the access to prominent people which his position in the Cavendish family afforded him. Aubrey records that 'the Lord Chancellor Bacon loved to converse with him. He assisted his Lordship in translating severall of his Essayes into Latin. . . .'[1] Bacon seemed particularly appreciative of Hobbes' company because he was accustomed to dictate his thoughts 'in his delicious walkes at Gorambery', and Hobbes was the only companion whose notes gave evidence that the Chancellor's musings had been understood. These meetings probably took place between 1621 and 1626 when Bacon was in retirement, writing and dabbling in scientific research. It was Hobbes who told Aubrey that Bacon died of pneumonia after getting out of his coach in winter in order to buy a fowl from an old woman which would serve as a subject for experiments on the preservative powers of snow.

Not unnaturally this association with Bacon, while he was engaged on research and soon after the appearance of his *Novum*

1. J. Aubrey, op. cit., p. 149.

Organum in 1620 – his famous attack on Aristotelianism and outline of the new experimental method – has led to much speculation about Bacon's influence on Hobbes. It is usual to point out
that Hobbes expressed his contempt for the experiments of the
Royal Society which were conducted in the true Baconian spirit;[1]
that he hailed Copernicus, Galileo, and Harvey as the founders
of the new natural philosophy and did not mention Bacon;[2] that
Hobbes' inspiration came from the deductive method of mathematics of which Bacon knew little and which he regarded as being
of little importance compared with the method of induction. All
this is important and incontrovertible. But too much stress on
palpable differences can lead to the neglect of more profound
similarities. Already Hobbes had met with widespread contempt
for the Aristotelian tradition. Is it not probable that he would
have felt the wind of this climate of opinion more keenly when he
listened to and read the Lord Chancellor's pungent and self-
confident indictments of the wisdom of the past? This was an age
of shifting opinions and increasing social mobility. Bacon was the
mouthpiece of self-made men who thought that knowledge as well
as political office was obtainable by those who had ability and
wits. Bacon provided a book for them which would serve as a substitute for being brought up in the right families and colleges.
With this book in his hand a judicious man could emerge from
the barren wilderness of forms and species, tended by the relics of
scholasticism, and find a new heaven and a new earth. The book,
too, would enable him to improve this newly found paradise by
using Nature's secrets for his own ends. For to Bacon and his
followers knowledge meant power – power to use Nature for
human purposes. This conviction, shared by so many of the new
men of the seventeenth century and evidenced by the rapid development of experimentation and technology, is one of the keys to
understanding Hobbes' thought. Like Bacon, he was to coin some
of his most pungent epigrams for the discomfiture of the Aristotelians; like Bacon, he replaced reverence for tradition by belief in
method, albeit a different method; and, like Bacon, he believed
that knowledge was power. His hope was to devise a civil philo-

1. E.W. IV, 437.　　　2. E.W. I, viii.

sophy which would provide a rational ground-plan for the reconstruction of civil society by those who could penetrate the secrets
of human nature.

There is, too, another significant similarity between Hobbes and
Bacon. Both men used language to say things clearly, pungently,
and in order to convert. They believed that ambiguities in
language were intolerable. Bacon referred to them as idols of the
market place which lie at the source of much nonsense and mis-
understanding; Hobbes thought that society could almost be
saved by definitions and tracked down the various types of
ambiguity and vacuousness in scholastic terminology which he
regarded as potential sources of danger to the peace. 'Words,' he
says, 'are wise men's counters; they do but reckon by them; but
they are the money of fools.'[1] For both men the primary function
of language was to describe things clearly, words being 'signs' or
'notes' or 'marks' of things or of our thoughts about things.
Nature, for these self-confident adventurers, was no longer
haunted by mysteries to be suggested and conveyed by language;
she lay before them to read, to probe, to use. The medievals and,
to a large extent, the Elizabethans were involved in Nature; they
felt bound in a settled order by common ties issuing from a benign
protector. Their language of description did justice to this sense of
belonging and was therefore less clear because it expressed their
intimations of this secure relationship; their explanations, to our
more detached way of looking at Nature, systematically confused
their fears, hopes, and aspirations with how Nature in fact
behaved. Aristotelianism, which Hobbes attacked so savagely,
represented a sort of twilight world between animism and a more
detached mode of explanation. Even in the thoughts of Sir
Thomas Browne, Hobbes' curious contemporary, superstitions
and mysteries jostled higgledy-piggledy with rational explanations. But to Hobbes, Bacon, Descartes, and other representatives
of the new order, Nature was something apart from man to be
clearly and distinctly conceived, more like a machine to be understood and used than an abiding place to be endured and enjoyed.
To Descartes animals were machines; Hobbes even achieved the

1. E.W. III, 25.

17

detachment necessary for regarding both men and civil society as machines to be understood and manipulated. This was a great advance in detachment; for most men even today are as involved and non-detached in their thinking about society as Hobbes' predecessors were about Nature.

Surely this similarity in outlook expressed in their hostility towards Aristotelianism, in their denunciations of verbal ambiguities and their preference for plain, clear speech, in their belief in the efficacy of method or technique, and in their conviction that knowledge was power, owed something to these early meetings after Hobbes' return from the Continent? Surely from this didactic master of English prose Hobbes caught something of his inquisitive pragmatic attitude towards Nature? Hobbes never acknowledged any debt to Bacon. Indeed he prided himself, like many dogmatists, on avoiding stuffing his mind with other people's opinions. Sir William Petty reported that he never saw more than half a dozen books in Hobbes' chamber and Aubrey recorded 'He was wont to say that if he had read as much as other men, he should have knowne no more than other men.'[1] But these reports refer to a later period after Hobbes had emerged as a philosopher. Until at least the age of forty he read copiously in the Cavendish library and his friend Sorbière regarded Hobbes' style as a survival from Bacon, under whom he wrote in his youth and from whom he learnt a great deal. We know definitely from Aubrey that Hobbes helped to translate at least three of Bacon's essays into Latin. Hobbes' meetings with Bacon antedated his espousal of the rival deductive method. And, in general, few men are aware of the sources of their most deep-seated presuppositions or admit them gladly if perchance they light upon their traces. This is especially the case with those who pride themselves on their originality.

Hobbes' study of the classics lasted about fifteen years, a period which he refers to in his verse autobiography as the happiest in his life.[2] His purpose in turning to the classics was not merely to improve his style. In the supplement to his prose autobiography[3] it is indicated that he also did so in order to develop an adequate

1. J. Aubrey, op. cit., p. 154.   2. L.W. I, lxxxviii.   3. L.W. I, xxiv.

philosophy in view of the discredit into which the philosophy of the Schools had fallen. Their logic and metaphysics were distasteful because of their sophistry and contentiousness, their ethics because it rested on popular prejudice rather than on truth, and their Aristotelian physics because it smelt of the study, being based on the ingenuity of pedants rather than on investigations of nature. The literature of the Schools being, too, of little civil use, Hobbes turned to Greece and Rome in search of treasures which he could employ more profitably. The supplement then goes on to speak of Hobbes' friendship with Bacon, who thought so highly of him, and with Edward Herbert, philosopher and historian. It does not seem that Hobbes had no interest in philosophy during these years; on the contrary he seems to have been actively dissatisfied with the philosophy of the Schools and to be in search of other inspiration. This did not come till later when he discovered geometry. In the meantime, after reading through many poets and historians, Hobbes decided, for reasons both of style and of civil usefulness, to translate Thucydides.

Hobbes' choice was a significant indication of the trend of his thought. For, like Thucydides, Hobbes believed that the function of the historian was 'to instruct and enable men, by the knowledge of actions past, to bear themselves prudently in the present and providently towards the future'.[1] The historian, while remaining truthful, should select and record events which seem most significant for instructing mankind. Hobbes, in his introduction to his translation, described Thucydides as 'the most politic historiographer that ever writ'[2] who 'least of all liked democracy' and praised the government of Athens most when Peisistratus, the tyrant, reigned, and when at the start of the Peloponesian War 'it was democratical in name, but in effect monarchical under Pericles. So that it seemeth, that as he was of regal descent, so he best approved of the regal government.'[3] In his autobiographies Hobbes stressed that he published his translation because he wished to point out the unsuitability and danger of democracy to his fellow-countrymen. Had not Thucydides traced the downfall and degeneration of Athens to the time when representatives

1. E.W. VIII, vii.   2. E.W. VIII, viii.   3. E.W. VIII, xvii.

of the people like Cleon, the eloquent tanner, took the place of Pericles? In 1628, when Hobbes published his translation, Charles I had been on the throne for three years and was already at loggerheads with Parliament led by Eliot and Pym. In 1627 the King's favourite, Buckingham, had been decisively defeated at La Rochelle in trying to help the French Huguenots. In 1628 an election had returned a Parliament most hostile to the King; Sir Edward Coke, the great defender of the Common Law against James I, had introduced a Petition of Right to secure from the King a proper respect for the rights and liberties of the subject; Buckingham was assassinated. In 1629 the Commons launched an attack on the King's religious policy. When the Speaker, on the King's orders, tried to put an end to these attacks by adjourning Parliament, he was held in his chair while three further resolutions were passed. Truly it was a time when the fortunes of England abroad under 'regal government' were at a low ebb and when the democratic tide at home was rising ominously. What more appropriate for a supporter of 'regal government' like Hobbes than to publish the warnings implicit in the fate of Athens? Was not this wisdom from the past of more civil use than the wranglings of the Schools?

In 1628, at the age of forty, there occurred a radical change in Hobbes' health, in his fortune, and in his thinking. To quote Aubrey: 'From forty, or better, he grew healthier, and then he had a fresh, ruddy, complexion. He was *Sanguineo-melancholicus*; which the physiologers say is the most ingeniose complexion.'[1] His master died, and, as a temporary economy, the Countess of Devonshire dispensed with Hobbes' services. Hobbes transferred his services to Sir Gervase Clinton and, in 1629, accompanied his son on a journey to the Continent. It was on this second journey that Hobbes' inspiration came. 'Being in a Gentleman's Library, Euclid's Elements lay open, and 'twas the 47 El. libri I. He read the Proposition. By G——, sayd he (he would now and then sweare an emphatical Oath by way of emphasis), this is impossible! So he reads the Demonstration of it, which referred him back to such a Proposition; which proposition he read. That referred him back

1. J. Aubrey, op. cit., p. 153.

to another, which he also read. *Et sic deinceps* (and so on) that at last he was demonstratively convinced of that trueth. This made him in love with Geometry.'[1] The fascination of geometry for him lay in its method, which permitted important and indubitable conclusions to be drawn from premisses that no one could help accepting. For one who believed that knowledge was power and that divergent opinions were at the root of civil discord, it was a revelation to light upon a method for establishing conclusions with demonstrative certainty. Could not his convictions about the dangers of democracy be demonstrated in a similar manner? Could not his estimate of man's motives and of the causes of war, which he shared with Thucydides, be shown to follow from self-evident postulates like Pythagoras' theorem? Given knowledge of the axioms of human nature could not the rationale of society be constructed like a geometrical figure?

The feverish state of England provided Hobbes with his major problem; his translation of Thucydides indicated his rough and ready diagnosis; the method of geometry suggested a way of reaching an indisputable diagnosis which would end for ever the arguments of Arminians and contentious sectaries; the Baconian conviction that knowledge meant power, with geometry as the paradigm of knowledge, suggested as a manner of cure the reconstruction of society on rational lines like a geometer's figure. But this rehabilitation of the body politic required a vision of content as well as of form; for a new society could not be constructed solely out of a knowledge of lines, planes, and solids. And it was Hobbes' third journey to the Continent which provided him with the missing content for his geometrically conceived social equilibrium.

Hobbes had returned to the service of the Devonshires in 1630 and went with the next Earl to the Continent from 1634 to 1636. During his stay in Paris he became a member of the intellectual circle of the Abbé Mersenne, who patronized Descartes, Gassendi and other famous thinkers. He also made a pilgrimage to Italy in 1636 to visit Galileo, the great genius of the new natural philosophy. By the time of his return to England in 1637 he was ready to work out his own philosophical system and had established a

1. J. Aubrey, op. cit., p. 150.

reputation as a philosopher. His great imaginative idea had been born – the geometrical deduction of the behaviour of men in society from the abstract principles of the new science of motion. 'For seeing life is but a motion of limbs. . . . For what is the heart but a spring; and the nerves but so many strings; and the joints but so many wheels, giving motion to the whole body, such as was intended by the artificer?'[1]

Hobbes claimed originality for two main parts of his philosophy – his optics and his civil philosophy. Between the time of his discovery of geometry and his return to England in 1637 he wrote a *Little Treatise* in geometrical form in which he tried to give an explanation of the act of sense in terms of a general theory of motion. Whatever the exact date of the *Little Treatise* between 1630 and 1637 – and scholars are not agreed about this – it obviously represents an exercise in the newly discovered geometrical method in an attempt to solve a particular problem. But why this seemingly sudden interest in sensation? At the end of his prose autobiography[2] he relates how after his study of history and poetry, he found himself in the company of some learned men who were discussing the cause of sensation. One of them asked derisively what sensation might be and Hobbes was astonished to find that no one of them could say. From this time forward Hobbes was haunted by the problem of the cause of sense until he lighted upon the idea that if bodies and their parts were always at rest or always moved by the same degree of motion, the ability to make discriminations would no longer exist and consequently all sensation would be no more. He concluded that the cause of everything, including sensation itself, was in variations of motion. Unfortunately no date is given to this episode. We do know, however, from the same autobiography,[3] that while he was in Paris in 1634 he was investigating the types of motion that brought about sense, intellect, fancy, and other animal properties. In his verse autobiography,[4] too, he relates graphically how on his third journey he was obsessed by the omnipresence of motion. All this is evidence for Hobbes' great interest in sensation and motion at this

1. E. W. III, ix.   3. L.W. I, xiv.
2. L.W. I, xx–xxi.   4. L.W. I, lxxxix.

period; it also shows that he considered his originality to consist in applying a general theory of motion to the particular problem of the cause of sense. But it does not help us to explain the shift in interest from the political warnings of Thucydides to problems of optics.

An ingenious suggestion has been made[1] that Hobbes' early interest in sensation is to be seen in the context of his hostility to theological and scholastic doctrines, prominent amongst which was the scholastic doctrine of 'intelligible species' which was part of their theory of sense perception. Elsewhere Hobbes goes out of his way to attack this doctrine as a lynch-pin of the Catholic conspiracy against the state, and Hobbes mentions in a letter to Newcastle, when reporting on his fruitless attempts to find a copy of Galileo's *Dialogues* in London in 1633, that 'it is called, in Italy, as a book that will do more hurt to their religion than all the books have done of Luther and Calvin. . . .'[2] In the *Little Treatise*, too, Hobbes constantly considers, criticizes, and rejects, Aristotelian solutions to various problems before advancing his own theory. Whether Hobbes' own theory was as original as he claimed it to be, or whether he drew on Galileo's *Il Saggiatore*, on Bacon's theories, or on the atomic theories of the ancients, is a matter for conjecture; but there can be no doubt that the *Little Treatise* represents an explicit assault on the theory of sense that he had learnt from the Aristotelian teachers of his university days, the outlines of which are referred to in his verse autobiography.[3] It is therefore tempting to suggest that both his fascination for the method of geometry and his aroused interest in the theory of sense are explicable in terms of his desire to eliminate sources of civil unrest, and that his *Little Treatise* was a preliminary exercise in geometrical demonstration to show the folly of scholastic doctrines in contrast to the unassailable conclusions of the new theory of motion. This suggestion would provide an ingenious link between his translation of Thucydides and his later civil philosophy.

1. H. Hervey in *Hobbes' Theory of Truth and Knowledge*, Ph.D. thesis, University of London, 1952.
2. Historical Manuscripts Commission, Vol. XIII. Portland Papers, p. 124.
3. L.W. I, lxxxvii.

There is, however, no direct evidence for it, and in view of Hobbes' persistent preoccupation with the wonder of sense,[1] it is just as plausible to suggest that Hobbes became genuinely puzzled about the cause of sensation. It is not unusual for people to get excited in maturity about problems which bored them at the university; Hobbes very probably included a careful study of the ancient atomists in his search for new inspiration in the work of the ancients during his classical period; and, after all, there is something puzzling about the relationship between our subjective experiences, our bodies, and the world outside our bodies. No doubt Hobbes turned to such philosophical puzzles partly because of his fear of civil unrest and because of his anger at the mystery-mongering of the Aristotelians which he regarded as one of its main sources. But to suggest that this was the main cause of his turning to philosophy is to underrate the ferment of intellectual excitement on the Continent which Hobbes shared with other exponents of the new natural philosophy. It looks as if Hobbes tended to be caught up in the excitement of theoretical problems while he was on the Continent and to revert to predominantly political problems when in England or when his compatriots came later to Paris laden with English sorrows.

It is difficult for us, who inherit the world-view forged by thinkers from Copernicus to Newton, to picture the intellectual ferment of the seventeenth century which followed the gradual acceptance of the heliocentric theory of Copernicus and the law of inertia which was first formulated in rather a clumsy way by Galileo. And the intellectual excitement was not just the product of replacing one or two old conceptions by new ones; it was due also to the vast scope for new explanations which was opened up by these shifts in fundamental assumptions. Hobbes' inspiration came from the law of inertia as well as from the method of geometry which actually made possible its formulation.[2] What excited him was the possibility of deducing consequences from the law of inertia in spheres to which it had not yet been applied – sensation, psychology, and politics. When he speaks in his verse

1. In *Leviathan,* for instance, and *De Corpore.*
2. See *infra,* p. 63.

autobiography of his obsession with the omnipresence of motion, what he was in fact doing was acclimatizing himself to the fundamental shift in thought required by Galileo's law. For in the Aristotelian world-view rest had been regarded as the natural state for bodies. Things only moved when motion was imparted to them by a mover. As soon as this influence ended bodies relapsed into their normal state. But Galileo imagined motion as the 'natural state' for bodies. They continued in motion to infinity unless they were impeded. In other words everything was moving, including the world itself as suggested by Copernicus; the problem was to account for why things seemed to stop moving. Rest was a limiting case of motion. This was the imaginative idea which so excited Hobbes and which he applied to the problem of the cause of sense as well as to psychology and politics.

In 1637, the year in which Descartes produced his *Discourse on Method*, Hobbes returned home stimulated by his own venture in philosophy and by his contact with Mersenne's circle. Like Descartes he was fired by the thought of a universal system of philosophy. The first part on 'Body' would outline the general principles of magnitude and motion and deal with the behaviour of natural bodies; the second part on 'Man' would show how man's feelings, sensations, thoughts, and desires could be explained in terms of the peculiar internal motions in the human body in contact with other bodies; the third part on 'Citizen' would reveal the state as an artificial body to be constructed out of the movements of men towards or away from each other. But the course of political events necessitated postponing this grand design in favour of issuing abbreviated statements to influence the contemporary situation. He arrived home when the ship-money dispute was raging. The attempt, also, to impose a Book of Common Prayer upon the Scots caused a riot in Edinburgh in 1637 and led to the Covenant of 1638, the subscribers to which swore to resist to the death such religious innovations. War broke out soon after in Scotland and in 1640 Charles had to summon the English Parliament in order to raise the money to fight it. Before they would discuss the grant of subsidies by the King, Pym listed the grievances which had first to be redressed – attacks on parliamentary privilege, religious innovations, ship-money. The King insisted on the prior discussion of the grant of subsidies and, when it was clear that Parliament would not consider it, dissolved Parliament on 5 May.

Hobbes, on his return, was living with the young Earl of Devonshire, and mixed with Lord Falkland, Hyde, and other perplexed politicians. No wonder that he turned aside from his wider speculations and published *The Elements of Law* in 1640 during the assembly of Parliament. This book was circulated in manuscript form and dealt only with 'Man' and 'Citizen', the more theoretical questions about 'Body' being almost omitted. Later, in 1650, these two parts were published separately under the titles of *Human Nature* and *De Corpore Politico*. The work demonstrated the need for undivided sovereignty, but the arguments were taken from general principles of psychology and ethics rather than from assertions about Divine Right. Hobbes characteristically remarked later that his life would have been in danger because of this publication had not the King dissolved Parliament – an exemplification of his claim that he and fear had been born twins at the time of the Spanish Armada.[1] But Hobbes' fear was that of a self-made man whose feeling of insecurity and desire for esteem expressed itself in the flattering delusion that men were taking note of him and planning his decease; it was not an unreasoning panic. Similarly Hobbes' flight to the Continent six months later, when Parliament reassembled and impeached Strafford, was the well-calculated move of a man who sees events in terms of threats to himself. He was over fifty and confident of a friendly reception by Mersenne whose circle flourished under the approving eye of Richelieu, renowned for his patronage of the sciences. For a man with a major work to write and who, though favouring monarchy, must have been aghast at the ineptitude and foolhardiness of Charles I, Paris presented much better prospects than London. If he stayed at home, he might well, so he thought, have languished in the Tower. And his loyalty was not such that, at the age of fifty, he would contemplate taking up arms if civil

1. L.W. I, lxxxvi.

war broke out. Hobbes prided himself on being 'the first of all that fled'. As always his fear was mingled with an exaggerated sense of his own importance. On his arrival in Paris Hobbes was welcomed by Mersenne and was asked by him to compose some objections to Descartes' *Meditations* in advance of their publication. Hobbes gladly obliged with sixteen objections from an anonymous Englishman. Descartes replied, but the interchange became increasingly acrimonious; for Hobbes sent with his further objections a paper on optics, later published in 1644 in Mersenne's *Optique*, which was critical of Descartes' *Dioptric* (1637). Descartes accused the Englishman of plagiarism – an improbable charge in view of Hobbes' early fascination with the problem of sense. Hobbes dealt in a dignified way with these accusations, pointing out that some of the opinions, which he was accused of having taken from Descartes – for instance, the view that secondary qualities like sound and colour were subjective phantasms – had been publicly expressed by him as early as 1630. Hobbes and Descartes actually met in Paris in 1648[1] and discussed the cause of hardness, about which they disagreed. But the meeting seems to have been quite amicable and in later years Hobbes, according to Aubrey, spoke well of him. 'Descartes and he were acquainted and mutually respected one another. He would say that had he kept himself to Geometry he had been the best Geometer in the world but that his head did not lye for philosophy.'[2] It was Descartes' theological opinions that Hobbes could not stomach. He could not pardon him for writing in defence of transubstantiation to please the Jesuits, a doctrine in which Hobbes knew that Descartes did not believe. Descartes, who was a brilliant mathematician, was rather derisive about Hobbes' somewhat amateurish demonstrations but admitted, when his *De Cive* was published in 1642, that Hobbes had ability in ethics, though he found Hobbes' account of human nature pernicious. But, as Brandt has pointed out in his masterly

1. See H. Hervey, 'Hobbes and Descartes in the Light of Some Unpublished Letters of the Correspondence between Sir Charles Cavendish and Dr John Pell.' *Osiris*, Vol. X, 1962.

2. J. Aubrey, op. cit., p. 158.

unravelling of the relationship between Hobbes and Descartes,[1] the main cause of the enmity between Hobbes and Descartes was that they *agreed* on two doctrines which were basic to the new mechanical picture of Nature – *materia subtilis*, an imagined medium between non-contiguous bodies, and the subjectivity of sense-qualities – and that they arrived at their conclusions on these issues independently of each other. Both were self-made men and very conscious of points of prestige; the question of priority was therefore very important to them as they both regarded themselves as founders of a new philosophy, consciously discarding an old tradition and making a fresh start. Paternal pride made them both possessive of their ideas and blind to their indebtedness to others without whose intellectual labours their ideas would never have been born.

After writing his *Objections* Hobbes did not settle down to work straight away on his ambitious project for a complete philosophy of nature, man, and citizen, but issued another contribution to the English controversy. This was his *De Cive* published in 1642 in which he tried to demonstrate conclusively the proper purpose and extent of the civil power. The Long Parliament, after the impeachment and execution of Strafford, spent much time on a bill to exclude the clergy from participation in civil affairs and on the general reform of church organization and ceremonial. John Milton's tract *Of Reformation Touching Church-Discipline in England* had appeared in 1641 and the activities of the various sects opposed to the Church of England were greatly on the increase. England was seething with religious individualism. The *De Cive* was a Latin version of that part of the earlier *Elements of Law* which later appeared as *De Corpore Politico*; but it was expanded considerably so as to deal in more detail with the topical issue of the relationship between the church and the civil power. These religious controversies provided Hobbes with the occasion to express his life-long fear and hatred of religions which set up authorities above the civil power. Hobbes has the angry, aggressive style of an insecure man, and when he writes about religious organizations his furious pen seems almost to jab and lacerate the

1. F. Brandt, *Thomas Hobbes' Mechanical Conception of Nature*, Ch. 4.

paper as if it were a Puritan or a Catholic. He assigned great importance to the religious causes of the Civil War. In his later work on the causes and course of the Civil War[1] Hobbes made a list of those who corrupted and seduced the people and so brought about the war.[2] Presbyterians, Papists, and the various Nonconformist sects were mentioned first on his list before the city of London and other towns of trade, classical scholars, and spendthrifts. In his verse autobiography[3] Hobbes spoke of the interruption to his studies occasioned by a disease which swept England in 1640. Anyone affected by it thought that the laws of God as well as the laws of man were revealed to him personally. This remark epitomized Hobbes' attitude towards the Puritan conscience.

Though Hobbes considered his *De Cive* to be a fundamental and original work in which the grounds of natural justice were clearly set out, the fragment surviving of *A Minute or First Draught of the Optiques* – a treatise in English which he sent to the Marquis of Newcastle in 1646[4] – makes clear that he thought his optical theory equally important and original. The former he considered the most profitable, the latter the most curious of all his work. In 1644, too, he contributed a long section to Mersenne's *Ballistica* which amounted to an abbreviated statement of his psychological theory. This period between the publication of *De Cive* in 1642 and the completion of the optical treatise in English in 1646 was spent in the intellectual haven of Mersenne's circle. Hobbes, now an acknowledged leader of the new philosophy, was working continuously on the details of his natural philosophy, the first part of his trilogy which was later to appear as *De Corpore*. In his verse autobiography Hobbes recorded that for four years he pondered on the 'form' of *De Corpore* and that the material was all in order for writing[5] when the Prince of Wales came to Paris with other fugitives from Naseby. But perhaps because of his desire to establish himself as an equal of Descartes in optical theory,[6] he turned aside from the *De Corpore* to write his *A Minute or First*

1. *Behemoth*. Published posthumously in 1682.
2. E.W. VI, 167–8.   4. E.W. VII, 471.
3. L.W. I, xc.   5. L.W. I, xcii.
6. See Brandt, op. cit., p. 190 and Ch. 6 passim.

Draught of the Optiques and then external events interrupted his more ambitious project. For, at the end of 1646, when Hobbes was on the verge of accepting an invitation to retire to the peace of a friend's estate in Languedoc in the South of France, he was requested to act as tutor in mathematics to the future Charles II. Hobbes complied with this request. Newcastle had been his instructor for a time and had drawn up a brief advising that the boy should not be too devout and should be very civil to women. Charles found little difficulty in complying with these not very exacting instructions; but what influence Hobbes had on him is more difficult to discern, though many attribute his later patronage of the sciences to his initiation under Hobbes' guidance into the secrets of mathematics.

Hobbes' tutorship was interrupted, if not terminated, by a severe illness in 1647. Mersenne visited him on his sick bed at the request of a common friend who hoped that Hobbes might be converted to Roman Catholicism. Mersenne began tactfully on his bizarre enterprise by discoursing on his church's power to remit sins. Hobbes characteristically interrupted him in full flight. 'Father,' he said, 'I have long ago gone over the question in my own mind. You have something pleasanter to say. When did you see Gassendi?' This sick-bed scene reveals Hobbes' most endearing qualities – his hatred of humbug and his great capacity for close friendship. Aubrey says simply of Hobbes and Gassendi[1] that they loved each other entirely. A few days later, however, Hobbes consented to receive the sacrament from Dr Cosin, who later became Bishop of Durham, on condition that the English prayer-book was used. This occasion later stood him in good stead when he was accused of atheism and heresy; for he was able to refer his accusers to the testimony of the Bishop of Durham.

Hobbes recovered and contact with the exiled Royalists stimulated him to arrange for his views on church and state to be more widely known. A second edition of the *De Cive* appeared in 1647; but this was in Latin and had only a limited circulation.

1. Gassendi was professor of mathematics in the College Royal. He probably exerted great influence on Hobbes' thought. His materialism stemmed from Greek atomism, his *De Vita et Moribus Epicuri* being published in 1647.

Hobbes therefore decided to publish his views on 'Man' and 'Citizen' for all his contemporaries to read. He began work on his *Leviathan*, his masterpiece. Aubrey reports how he composed this work. 'He sayd that he sometimes would sett his thoughts upon researching and contemplating, always with this Rule that he very much and deeply considered one thing at a time (*scilicet*, a weeke or sometimes a fortnight). He walked much and contemplated, and he had in the head of his Staffe a pen and inke-horne, carried always a Note-book in his pocket, and as soon as a notion darted, he presently entreed it into his Booke, or els he should perhaps have lost it. He had drawne the Designe of the Booke into Chapters, etc., so he knew whereabout it would come in. Thus that booke was made.'[1]

Mersenne died in 1648 and Hobbes began to feel increasingly isolated in Paris. He was suspected of atheism and known to be a declared enemy of Catholicism. When his friend Sorbière proposed to describe Hobbes on the title page of the new edition of the *De Cive* as tutor to the Prince of Wales, Hobbes wrote him a brusque letter saying that the Prince might be harmed by the suggested connexion, that Hobbes himself might be accused of vanity as he was definitely not a member of the royal household, and that it would be difficult for Hobbes to return to England if it was suggested that he belonged to the exiled Court. This letter is indicative of Hobbes' uneasy situation in Paris after the death of Mersenne.

Political events provided a fitting prelude to the publication of Hobbes' *Leviathan*. The King was executed in 1649 after the abortive attempt of the Presbyterians to establish him in power. Up till 1653, when Cromwell was made Protector, there was constant discussion and experimentation to find an appropriate form of government to succeed the monarchy. The *Leviathan* was published in England in 1651 after the two parts of the earlier *Elements of Law* had been published separately in 1650 as *Human Nature* and *De Corpore Politico*; the *De Cive*, too, had been translated into English in 1651 with the title of *Philosophical Rudiments Concerning Government and Society*. The *Leviathan* was thus the culmination and

1. J. Aubrey, op. cit., p. 151.

definitive expression of Hobbes' convictions about the conditions necessary for social order.

In view of the controversy about Hobbes' intentions in publishing his masterpiece at this particular juncture, it is as well to indicate the contemporary significance of its main conclusions; for it was not really the conclusions of the *Leviathan* that were of outstanding importance but the way in which these conclusions were reached. There were at least four issues of philosophical interest about which there was much contemporary controversy. The first concerned the legitimate basis of government. Parliament and the army believed in forms of popular representation ranging from the radical democracy of the Levellers, who believed in full adult suffrage, to the mixed constitution of checks and balances introduced by Cromwell and the moderates; the Stuarts, on the other hand, believed in the Divine Right of Kings. Hobbes conceded popular representation but, by an ingenious twisting of the social contract theory, made it result in an absolute sovereign whilst rejecting the Divine Right of Kings. The doctrine of sovereignty which emerged from his writing was one that could be used to justify any absolute *de facto* government. It was used, in fact, to justify both the Protectorate and the Restoration governments. So Hobbes was accused of atheism and subservience to Cromwell by Royalists; but he was also suspected by Parliamentarians for his advocacy of monarchy and for his Royalist connexions, in spite of his claim that his work 'framed the minds of a thousand gentlemen to a conscientious obedience to present government' (i.e. the Protectorate).[1]

On the second issue, the subject's right to resist, Hobbes, in spite of his general condemnation of anarchy and the exercise of the individual conscience, put forward a doctrine which provided a loophole for both parties when they were not in power. The subject, he maintained, was bound to obey the government only so long as it fulfilled its sole function, which was to govern. At a time of civil strife, therefore, it became a nice question for the subject to decide when he was justified in rebelling because of the government's failure to preserve the peace.

1. E.W. VII, 336.

The third issue was, perhaps, one of the most interesting of the time – the status of law. The traditional view, defended so ably by Sir Edward Coke in his controversy with James I, was that there was a fundamental law binding on King and subjects alike, which was there to be discovered. Parliament had been regarded as a kind of court, and its statutes, like the decisions of judges, were deemed to be declarations of what the law was. With the advent of James I, Charles I, and especially the Long Parliament, it became increasingly evident that laws were being made which bore little relation to the immemorial customs of the realm. *Laws* were being *made*; the fiction could no longer be maintained that *the law* was being *declared*. Hobbes, therefore, like many other reflective people, maintained that the laws were the commands of the sovereign. They issued from his will; they were not, as Coke maintained, 'the artificial perfection of reason'. But as John Milton, the redoubtable Puritan, held also that laws were the commands of the sovereign, there was nothing very partisan in Hobbes' view; he only differed from Milton about who the sovereign should be.

On the fourth burning issue, the position of the Church, Hobbes' views were decided but not unusual. He feared and hated any religion which afforded the individual an authority other than the sovereign. The Church should be subordinated to the state and the sovereign should be finally responsible for ecclesiastical affairs both in relation to organization and ritual and in relation to the proper interpretation of divine law and the Scriptures. The Puritan who appealed to the newly translated Bible or to his own leadings from God was just as much a danger to peace as the Catholic who appealed to papal authority.

In brief, Hobbes believed that the only hope for the permanent preservation of peace was an absolute sovereign, whose commands were laws enforced by judges, bishops, and the military, all of whom should be responsible to him and appointed by him alone. Obedience to such a sovereign was always obligatory unless he should prove an ineffective autocrat. This was a geometer's panacea for peace, the clear-cut, rational construction of a ruthless theoretician who thought that definitions and demonstrations could reveal solutions to problems which had blunted the wits and the swords of practical men. And because it ignored many of the age-long traditions of Englishmen and ridiculed many of their newly-found convictions, because it smacked of a Continental *salon* rather than of an English council chamber, there was much in it to offend as well as to fascinate any of his countrymen who read it.

The French, too, because of Hobbes' withering attack on the Papacy, were incensed that they had given asylum to such a scorpion. One of the first tangible results, therefore, of the *Leviathan* was Hobbes' banishment from the Court soon after Charles' return in 1651 from his humiliation at Worcester which ended the ill-fated Scottish expedition. Hobbes, it is true, had presented the young Prince with a manuscript copy which is now in the British Museum. Nevertheless he soon had to leave France as he had left England – with fear; for he fancied that the French clergy had designs on his life. Indeed it was Hobbes' unashamed desire to return to England that later got him into trouble. For Clarendon, Charles II's unfailing counsellor and censor, reported that when discussing Hobbes' masterpiece with him he asked him how he could voice such heterodox and disloyal opinions. After a 'discourse between jest and earnest' Hobbes replied, 'The truth is I have a mind to go home.'[1] And certainly he did want to go home because as early as 1649 he had written to Gassendi, 'For my age I am well enough, and take good care, reserving myself for my return to England, if it may be.'[2] We have also seen from his letter to Sorbière about the second edition of the *De Cive* that he did not want his chance of returning to England spoilt by the suggestion that he was a member of the royal household. But although there is abundant evidence that Hobbes wanted to go home, it is absurd to take his reply to Clarendon too seriously and suggest, as his opponents did later, that Hobbes hoped to work his passage home by writing the *Leviathan*. It seems probable that Hobbes wrote the *Leviathan* much more in order to instruct his countrymen how best to reconstruct English civil society so that it was a

1. Clarendon, *Survey of Leviathan*, p. 7.
2. L.W. V, 307.

fit place for sensible people like himself, than to provide a mere passport for himself. For ever since 1640, when Hobbes issued his *Elements of Law* to his friends, he had believed that he had drawn up a ground-plan for peace. The *De Cive* was merely an expansion and the *Leviathan* a fuller and popularized English edition of the views he had always held. The execution of Charles I made his views particularly relevant; for the ruler by Divine Right having failed to preserve peace, the time was now ripe for an even more autocratic leader to emerge by popular consent. The *Leviathan* was published in 1651 before Cromwell became Protector and when he was already at loggerheads with the Rump. His doctrine, as Hobbes himself pointed out, provided advice for Royalists to stay and make their peace with Cromwell; for was not allegiance due only so long as the sovereign afforded protection? The implication was that Cromwell should become King by common consent and dispense with incompetent parliaments. And if Cromwell should fail and Charles be asked to return from Paris, the message of the *Leviathan* was just as cogent: no legitimacy without power, and if the people wanted Charles back, let them give him the power necessary to keep the peace, whatever they thought of his claim to Divine Right. Hobbes was a dogmatist who believed that most of his countrymen were either stupid or riddled with various brands of anarchic individualism or both. Surely the *Leviathan* is the over-confident appeal of an insecure, angry, and intellectually arrogant theoretician; it is not a querulous hint to an autocrat for his fare home. Indeed the importance of the *Leviathan* did not lie at all in the conclusions reached, but in the way in which they were reached. This is what made the *Leviathan* uninfluential as a political tract but of great importance as political philosophy.

Hobbes crept home at the end of 1651 after another severe illness. He gave a vivid picture of his homecoming in his Latin verse autobiography: 'I return to my country unsure of my safety, but nowhere else could I count on being any safer: it was cold, the snow was deep, I was old, and the winter was bitter; I was cursed with a horse that threw me and by the uneven road.'[1] He made his submission to the Council of State and was allowed to subside

1. L.W. I, xciii.

into private life. He settled down in Fetter Lane. His patron, the Earl of Devonshire, had submitted to Parliament in order to save his family estates which were sequestered in 1645. Hobbes, however, preferred to spend most of his remaining years in the intellectual atmosphere of London, where he built up a circle of friends which included Harvey, Davenant, Cowley, and John Selden, rather than to stay at the Earl's country house where he feared that his wits might get mouldy for the want of learned conversation. Very soon, however, he became embroiled in learned, though acrimonious controversies. In 1645 Hobbes had discussed the problem of free-will with a certain Bishop Bramhall, who had fled with Newcastle from Marston Moor. At Newcastle's request they both wrote down their views in 1646. But a young disciple of Hobbes had managed to obtain a copy of the discussion and published Hobbes' contribution in 1654 without Hobbes' consent. Bramhall was understandably indignant and in 1655 published the whole controversy under the title *A Defence of the True Liberty of Human Actions from Antecedent or Extrinsic Necessity*. In 1656 Hobbes replied, printing Bramhall's book together with some new and entertaining observations on it – his *Questions Concerning Liberty, Necessity, and Chance*. Bramhall replied in 1658 with *Castigation of Hobbes' Animadversions* and a bulky appendix entitled *The Catching of Leviathan the Great Whale*. Hobbes replied to the latter about ten years later, Bramhall having died in 1663.

The controversy with Bramhall was important in that it provided scope for Hobbes to make some interesting points on a topic of perennial philosophical interest. Hobbes' views are worth studying in some detail, along with those of Spinoza, because they represent the climate of opinion out of which so many of the misunderstandings about determinism were born. The same, however, cannot be said for the other major controversy in which Hobbes was embroiled for most of the twenty years that still remained to him. Hobbes had always been an outspoken critic of the Universities. He thought that they were hotbeds of civil disobedience because of their Puritan and Catholic connexions. He thought, too, that much of their old curriculum, inherited from the scholastic tradition, should be abandoned in favour of the study of the new sciences. But he had been out of England a long time and had not kept abreast of developments at the Universities. In 1619 Sir Henry Savile had founded at Oxford professorships in geometry and astronomy, and mathematical studies had already become advanced and respectable, although only amongst a small and brilliant circle at Wadham and Merton. Oxford was now one of the centres of the 'invisible college' which was to become the Royal Society. John Wallis was professor of geometry, famous for his development of the differential calculus. Seth Ward, later Bishop of Salisbury, another able mathematician, was professor of astronomy. John Wilkins, who was interested in mechanical inventions and astronomy, was warden of Wadham College. Robert Boyle, Sir William Petty, and Christopher Wren were also members of this brilliant group of men. They were disciples of Bacon both in their eagerness to explore Nature and in their desire to use their findings for the improvement of life. United in the Puritan religion they believed that the end of scientific learning was the 'glory of the Creator and the relief of man's estate'. John Wilkins, for instance, who later became Bishop of Chester, believed that the study of Nature was the best way of promoting reverence for its Author. It is probable that nine out of ten of the original founders of the 'invisible college' in 1645 were Puritans, and of the original list of members of the Royal Society in 1663, 42 out of 68, about whom information is available, were clearly Puritan.[1] It was only to be expected, therefore, that Hobbes' hostility to Puritanism and the Universities, together with his exalted opinion of his own contributions to knowledge, would provoke some reaction from this formidable combination of Puritanism and scientific illumination.

The first intimation that Hobbes had of the enmity of these able men was an appendix to Seth Ward's *Vindiciae Academiarum*, a book directed against an attack on the Universities by a certain John Webster. Ward claimed that Hobbes too was out of date in his attack on the Universities as he would find out to his cost when and if he produced his alleged demonstrations of the squaring

1. See R. Merton, 'Puritanism, Pietism, and Science', in *Social Theory and Social Structure*, p. 338.

of the circle. Hobbes unheedingly produced his long expected *De Corpore* in 1655, the first part of his comprehensive work in which a proper science of body was expounded to succeed the metaphysical absurdities of the Schools. In Chapter 20, however, he inserted his attempts at squaring the circle – the final triumph of the deductive method. Ward and Wallis decided to teach the old gentleman a lesson. Ward dealt with his general philosophy in his *Exercitatio epistolica* and Wallis subjected Hobbes' geometry to a most cruel exposure in his *Elenchus Geometriae Hobbianae*. For not only did he treat the argument to a withering analysis; he also traced through Hobbes' original manuscript on squaring the circle the three abortive attempts at the problem which preceded his final and futile solution. Wallis specialized in this kind of detective work; he had deciphered the King's papers taken at Naseby. Hobbes, grossly underestimating the quality of his opponent and sublimely unaware of his own limitations as a mathematician, replied with an emended English edition of the *De Corpore* with *Six Lessons* appended for Wallis. He had the temerity to attack Wallis' own work on conic sections treated algebraically, although he knew no algebra himself. Wallis answered understandably with *Due Corrections for Mr Hobbes or School-discipline for not saying his lessons right*. And so the controversy went on, becoming, as the years passed, more acrimonious, personal, and undignified. Wallis, for instance, commented on Hobbes' West country accent and social standing and charged him with writing the *Leviathan* to please Cromwell. Hobbes raked up Wallis' deciphering activities after Naseby – 'There, doctor, you deciphered ill.' But no triumphs in personal invective could atone for his discomfiture at the hands of a Puritan divine. Even when allowance has been made for the fact that squaring the circle did not then seem quite such a preposterous project as it does now, it remains evident that Hobbes' sublime confidence in his own ability led him to make rather a pathetic exhibition of himself. Wallis had probably forgotten more mathematics than Hobbes ever knew. Descartes, before Wallis, had commented on Hobbes' awkwardness with the love of his middle age. Nevertheless Wallis was not an attractive man and his brilliant demolition of Hobbes' argument was interspersed with pontifical and boorish invective. A greater man could have afforded to be kinder to the old gentleman in spite of such pretentious provocation.

Hobbes, however, did not spend all his remaining years on this unfortunate controversy. In 1657 he published the second part of his triology, the *De Homine*. This was received without much comment, being concerned mainly with optics and with human nature, on both of which Hobbes' views were already well known. At the Restoration in 1660 Hobbes was rather apprehensive about how he would be treated in view of the circumstances in which he returned to England. But his uneasiness was soon removed; for, as Aubrey relates: 'It happened, about two or three days after his Majestie's happy returne, that, as He was passing in his coach through the Strand, Mr Hobbes was standing at Little Salisbury-house gate (where his Lord then lived). The King espied him, putt of his hatt very kindly to him, and asked him how he did.'[1] The King was well disposed towards his former tutor thenceforward to whom he granted a pension of £100 per year and 'free accesse to his Majesty, who was always much delighted in his witt and smart repartees. The witts at Court were wont to bayte him. But he feared none of them, and would make his part good. The King would call him the Beare. . . .'[2] Hobbes had, in fact, become an institution. Only once again did he fancy himself in mortal danger. And on this occasion he had good cause for his apprehension. For, after the Plague and the Fire of London in 1665–6, some reason was sought for God's displeasure. What more likely than that a people should suffer who gave shelter to a notorious atheist like Thomas Hobbes? A bill was brought before Parliament for the suppression of atheism and a committee was set up to look into the *Leviathan*. The bill passed Parliament but was eventually dropped, probably through Charles' influence. Hobbes breathed again, but he was forbidden to publish his opinions.

Perhaps one of the greatest disappointments of Hobbes' declining years was the attitude of the Royal Society towards him.

1. J. Aubrey, op. cit., p. 152.
2. ibid., pp. 152–3.

At the Restoration Robert Boyle had gone to Gresham College and had acquired recognition for the 'invisible college' as the Royal Society in 1662. Hobbes thought that, in view of his Continental reputation and the royal favour that had been shown him, he should be made a fellow. He submitted papers and demonstrations, but was never elected. This hurt him. But it was hardly surprising in view of the fact that Ward, Wallis, and Wilkins from Oxford were the leading spirits of the Society, which had a predominantly Puritan membership. Hobbes showed his resentment by attacking Boyle's theory of the air. His general criticism of the Society was that they spent too much time on new-fangled devices and experiments and too little on working out the fundamental theory of motion as Galileo and Harvey had done. This was a shrewd criticism; but it would have come better from one whose mathematical ability was less suspect and who had himself done some experiments.

Hobbes made few more contributions to knowledge though he never desisted from writing. He completed his *Behemoth* in 1668 – a history of the period 1640–60 interpreted in the light of Hobbes' main tenets about society. He submitted it to Charles who advised against its publication. It was published posthumously in 1682. Hobbes was never averse to turning his hand to a new subject and was encouraged by Aubrey to write about law. Hobbes, who was then seventy-six, replied that he was too old. Nevertheless, when Aubrey sent him Bacon's *Elements of Common Law* he managed to produce his unfinished *Dialogue between a Philosopher and a Student of the Common Laws of England* in 1666. It was published in 1681. The dialogue was an attack on the defenders of the Common Law like Sir Edward Coke, who had tried to limit the royal prerogative. Hobbes, even at this age, managed to say some interesting things about law and in many respects he anticipated the analytic positivism of the Austinian school of jurisprudence in the nineteenth century. At eighty-four he wrote his own autobiography in Latin verse, after completing one in prose. At the age of eighty-six he published a verse translation of the Iliad and the Odyssey because, as he said, he had nothing better to do; there was, too, a hope that he might deflect the attention of his adversaries from his religious and political opinions to his renderings of Homer. In 1675 he left London for Chatsworth and Hardwick, and in 1679 he was still in the throes of scientific composition. He learnt, however, that he had an incurable disease and remarked: 'I shall be glad to find a hole to creep out of the world at.' It is said that he amused himself by allowing his friends to prepare epitaphs for him. He was most attracted to 'This is the true philosopher's stone'. He died on 4 December 1679.

So much, then, for the development of Thomas Hobbes in the setting of the problems which he tried to solve. But no life of Hobbes would be complete without the delightful picture given by Aubrey of the idiosyncrasies of this remarkable man who was as noted for his habits as he was notorious for his opinions.

Face not very great; ample forehead; whiskers yellowish-reddish, which naturally turned up – which is a signe of a brisque wit. Belowe was shaved close, except a little tip under his lip. Not but that nature could have afforded a venerable Beard; but being naturally of a cheerfull and pleasant humour, he affected not at all austerity and gravity to looke severe. He desired not the reputation of his wisdome to be taken from the cutt of his beard, but from his reason.

He had a good eie, and that of a hazell colour, which was full of Life and Spirit, even to the last. When he was earnest in discourse, there shone (as it were) a bright live-coale within it. He had two kinds of lookys: when he laugh't, was witty, and in a merry humour, one could scarce see his Eies; by and by, when he was serious and positive, he open'd his eies round (i.e. his eyelids). . . .

'Tis not consistent with an harmonious soule to be a woman-hater, neither had he an Abhorrence to good wine but he was, even in his youth (generally) temperate, both as to wine and women. I have heard him say that he did beleeve he had been in excesse in his life, a hundred times; which, considering his great age, did not amount to above once a yeare. When he did drinke, he would drinke to excesse to have the benefitt of Vomiting, which he did easily; by which benefit neither his wit was disturbt longer than he was spuing nor his stomach oppressed; but he never was, nor could not endure to be, habitually a good fellow, i.e. to drink every day wine with company, which, though not to drunkennesse, spoiles the Braine.

For his last 30 yeares, his Dyet, etc, was very moderate and regular.

He rose about seaven, had his breakfast of Bread and Butter; and tooke his walke, meditating till ten; then he did putt downe the minutes of his thoughts, which he penned in the afternoon. He thought much and with excellent method and stedinesse, which made him seldom make a False step.

He had an inch thick board about 16 inches square, whereon paper was pasted. On this board he drew his lines (schemes). When a line came into his head, he would, as he was walking, take a rude Memorandum of it, to preserve it in his memory till he came to his chamber. He was never idle; his thoughts were always working.

His dinner was provided for him exactly by eleaven, for he could not now stay till his Lord's howre – *scil* about two: that his stomach could not beare.

After dinner he took a pipe of tobacco, and then threw himselfe immediately on his bed, with his band off, and slept (tooke a nap of about half an howre).

Besides his dayly Walking he did twice or thrice a yeare play at Tennis (at about 75 he did it) then went to bed there and was well rubbed. This he did believe would make him live two or three yeares the longer.

In the countrey, for want of a tennis-court, he would walke up-hill and downe-hill in the parke, till he was in a great sweat, and then give the servant some money to rubbe him.

He had always bookes of prick-song lyeing on his table; which at night, when he was abed, and the dores made fast, and was sure nobody heard him, he sang aloud (not that he had a very good voice) but for his health's Sake: he did beleeve it did his Lunges good, and conduced much to prolong his life.[1]

It was recorded on Hobbes' tombstone that he was a just man well known for his learning at home and abroad. This was true; for though his work aroused more controversy than that of most academic figures, there was never any suggestion that he was anything but a man of integrity, honest and kindly in all his dealings.

1. J. Aubrey, op. cit., pp. 154–5.

CHAPTER 2

METHOD MAKETH MAN

1. Hobbes' Approach to Philosophy

MOST of the important books in philosophy have been written by men who were either worried or excited. Plato was worried by the profound social changes of his time and excited by mathematics; Kant was both worried and excited by Newtonian physics and the French Revolution; Leibniz was excited by the discovery of the microscope and worried by the mechanistic implications of Cartesian physics. These thinkers were perplexed by problems arising from new discoveries and social change just as many modern thinkers are perplexed by the implications of Freud, Marx, and Einstein, or appalled by the social problems created by rapid industrialization. Hobbes' *Leviathan* ranks as one of the great books in philosophy because it attempted a systematic answer to the problems posed by the profound social changes of the seventeenth century and by the rise of the mathematical sciences. Hobbes was desperately worried by the upheavals of the seventeenth century and excited by mathematics and mechanics. The marriage of his worry with his excitement may have pro-duced a monster – *Leviathan* – which shocked his contemporaries and successors. But at least it had the rare philosophical distinc-tion of being so lucid that on many issues it was obviously wrong, and so readable that even minor clergymen occupied themselves with trying to refute it.

Hobbes had good reason to be worried in spite of his jesting reference to the pre-natal determinants of his timorous disposition. He asked little of life – only the peace and security necessary to pursue his scholarly interests. Yet he found himself in a country where peace and security were constantly in jeopardy because of the demands for liberty and for a greater share in government by the growing class of traders, professional men, and yeomen farmers, who rated the authority of the Bible and of their own consciences above that of the magistrates, bishops, and counsellors of the King. Hobbes had little sympathy for their religion and less for their politics. Like so many others at this time, too, he lived in daily dread of the Church of Rome which he regarded as an organized conspiracy against the temporal power supported by superstition and sharp practice. The overriding need of every sensible man, he thought, was for peace and security. Yet few seemed to discern how best this need could be satisfied or even to be aware of its existence. Indeed most men seemed to be pursuing policies diametrically opposed to their real interests. How could this disastrous drift be halted? For Hobbes, the intellectual who trusted in rational understanding rather than in tradition and experience, the answer was obvious. There must be a rational reconstruction of civil society which got down to first principles. This was the only way to avoid war – especially civil war – which is the worst calamity that can befall a society. From war proceed 'slaughter, solitude and the want of all things'.[1] All men know war to be evil but they do not know how to avert it; for few men have learnt the 'duties which unite and keep men in peace'.[2] Hobbes' science of natural justice would bring them down to first principles and supply the knowledge they so sorely lacked. 'The end of knowledge is power.' The *Leviathan* contained the knowledge; Cromwell or Charles could use it to reconstruct society and perpetuate their power.

2. *The Belief in Method*

This belief in the efficacy of the book was symptomatic of the new outlook. With the gradual breakdown of the Feudal system there emerged not only challenges to traditional methods of social and political organization but also challenges to traditional ways of thought. Wisdom was not now something that lay in the past to be gained by laboriously thumbing the pages of Aristotle or by

1. E.W. I, 8.   2. ibid.

listening to the priests. Men were exhorted to find out things for themselves, to consult their own consciences, to communicate with God directly instead of through the intermediary of the priest. The discovery of America, the improvement of communications through the spread of trade, the invention of printing, the development of the new heliocentric theory of the heavens – all these influences combined to produce the conviction that there were new secrets to wrest from Nature and new possibilities for human life on earth. There were certain exceptional men who struck out on their own and who thought that the success which they achieved was due to the method of inquiry which they had adopted. They therefore wrote up accounts of their techniques to guide others on the road, and assured others that any rational man could acquire by himself the knowledge which had previously been passed on in a tradition. The age of the manual, guide, and correspondence course was beginning to dawn. There thus emerged Bacon's *Novum Organum* and Descartes' *Discourse on Method* and *Regulae*, books which assured their readers that all men were equal in the possession of reason and that if they used the proper method they could not fail to read the secrets of Nature. Of course Bacon and Descartes disagreed about what the proper method was, but they agreed on the fundamental point that there was such a method. Spinoza's *Ethics* was another such book explicitly written to guide any rational being along the path of human blessedness. The parallel in politics had been Machiavelli's *Prince* – a book of political maxims written explicitly for usurpers who were to found new states or restore existing ones to health.

Hobbes' *Leviathan* was therefore not an unusual book in so far as it exhibited the belief that knowledge meant power and that knowledge could only be obtained by adopting a certain kind of method. Its originality consisted in applying this belief to society, man, and nature all at once. Hobbes dreamed up a picture of a man in society which was a systematic delusion, the creature of a rigorous method, rather than a calm after-image of experience. Perhaps his basic delusion, which he shared with so many others, was just this belief in the efficacy of method. Generally speaking our understanding of nature and man has not been advanced by people who have applied a method which could be mastered or a technique which could be conned. Making discoveries is not like making sausages. There seems to be no recipe for making discoveries; only certain rules of procedure for communicating and testing them. Hobbes' method did not in fact provide him with new truths; it only helped him to systematize and set out in a stimulating and startling way opinions which were, in essentials, as old as Thucydides, Protagoras, and the Greek atomists, but which burst forth with new vigour in the sixteenth and seventeenth centuries with the rise of individualism, rationalism, and the mathematical sciences.

3. Philosophy and the Method of Geometry

Philosophy, said Hobbes at the start of the *De Corpore*, is now amongst men as corn and wine were in the world in ancient times. As these were not cared for, men had to live on acorns. So every man had natural reason, but, for want of improving it, most men had to be content with the acorns of daily experience. Hobbes proposed to lay open a few of the elements of philosophy which would serve as seeds from which pure and true philosophy would spring up. By showing how to cultivate wine and corn he might win some of his contemporaries away from their acorns. There was no mystery about the method. At the age of forty Hobbes had discovered and fallen in love with geometry; and it was the *method* of geometry that had captivated him. Hobbes' revolt against the Aristotelian tradition was in fact a return to that of Plato and the Pythagoreans; for Plato had insisted on knowledge of geometry as a necessary qualification for discussions in his Academy. What was it about geometry that so fascinated Plato, Copernicus, Descartes, Hobbes, Spinoza, and other eminent thinkers? It was partly the belief coming down from the Pythagoreans that the world had a geometrical ground-plan, and partly its method, which permitted certainty in its conclusions provided no slips were made in demonstration. The quest for certainty has been almost the occupational neurosis of philosophers, especially at times of rapid social change.

It was the possibility of attaining certainty which so attracted Hobbes whose deep-seated feeling of insecurity was aggravated by the objective facts of the political situation.

It requires considerable intellectual imagination for us to realize what an exciting and remarkable activity mathematical reasoning seemed to the Greeks and to the post-Renaissance physical scientists who re-discovered its importance. Plato and the Pythagoreans were so impressed by it that they regarded reason as the divine element in man. Plato was perhaps the first to see the great importance of geometry, the method of which he tried to generalize for dealing with other than mathematical problems. Instead of grubbing about with hands and eye to find out things, or laboriously sorting out the conflicting tales told by credulous informants, the geometer could just sit down and work rigorously on the creations of his own mind. The amazing thing was that if he started from definitions – e.g. of 'straight line' or 'equal' – and combined these defined terms in axioms, conclusions followed which were certain, far from trivial, and of which he was not aware when he started. The ideas, too, with which the geometer dealt, seemed to have a peculiar status. The idea of 'straight line' or 'equal' seemed to be clear and distinct in that he seemed to know intuitively what the terms meant; yet there seemed to be no concrete imagery of 'equality' or of lines that were perfectly straight. Indeed the understanding of these terms was in no way affected by the idiosyncrasies of images formed as a result of seeing various geometrical figures. This led Plato to distinguish the world of non-deceptive, perfect objects like the geometer's triangle about whose properties mathematical reasoning could provide certain knowledge, from the ordinary world of changing, deceptive objects about which the senses provide uncertain opinions. Mathematics thus came to be taken as the paradigm of all knowledge because of the requirement of certainty. Nature's ground-plan could only be revealed to reason; the senses were useful for dealing with the mundane problems of daily life but useless for the development of scientific understanding.

Descartes, another great geometer, did for mechanics, astronomy, and the other developing sciences what Plato had done for earlier developments in mathematics – he extrapolated the method by means of which he thought the results had been obtained, and developed a very similar theory of knowledge. He thought that knowledge could only be obtained by isolating intuitively certain 'simple natures' or essential properties of the physical world like 'extension' and 'motion'; a clear and distinct understanding of these would provide a certain foundation from which a deductive science of nature could be developed. The senses were biologically useful but, in relation to the development of scientific knowledge, their function was only to provide problems for rational solution by the mathematical method and to decide between mathematically equivalent postulates. Scientists had no other use for their senses.

As Hobbes' philosophical inspiration dated from his discovery of geometry, it is not surprising that he adopted fundamentally the same position as Plato and Descartes. He distinguished between experience, on the one hand, which gives rise to historical knowledge and prudence, and reason which gives rise to scientific (or philosophical[1]) knowledge and wisdom. 'The remembrance of succession of one thing to another, that is, of what was antecedent, and what consequent, and what concomitant, is called an experiment; whether the same be made by us voluntarily, as when a man putteth any thing into the fire, to see what effect the fire will produce upon it: or not made by us, as when we remember a fair morning after a red evening. To have had many experiments, is what we call experience, which is nothing else but remembrance of what antecedents have been followed by what consequents.'[2] We see a cloud and, because of past associations, we conjecture that it will rain. The prudent man is the one who has noted well these regularities of sequence and who can therefore make reliable forecasts about what is likely to happen in a given situation or who can give a shrewd opinion about what has probably led up to a given state of affairs. But this

1. Hobbes uses the terms 'science' and 'philosophy' interchangeably, whereas there has now been a separation between science and philosophy leading to a more specialized meaning for both terms.
2. E.W. IV, 16.

prudence, which is the product of experience, should not be mistaken for wisdom, '. . . for though a man have always seen the day and night to follow one another hitherto; yet can he not thence conclude they still do so, or that they have done so eternally: experience concludeth nothing universally.'[1] Wisdom is the product of reason which alone gives us knowledge of 'general, eternal, and immutable truths' as in geometry.

Prudence is much helped by the branch of knowledge which is called history, about which Hobbes makes some interesting points. History is the 'register of knowledge of fact'. It differs from scientific knowledge firstly in that it is categorical knowledge whereas science is hypothetical. The historian records what actually happened at particular times and places, whereas the scientist postulates that, e.g. 'if the figure shown be a circle, then any straight line through the centre shall divide it into two equal parts'.[2] Secondly, the historian gives only a register of 'effects'. Facts are selected and ordered which provide a storehouse for prudence. 'For he that hath seen by what courses and degrees a flourishing state hath first come into civil war, and then to ruin; upon the sight of the ruins of any other state, will guess, the like war, and the like courses have been there also.'[3] But this register of 'effects', which provides a storehouse for prudence, is quite different from the knowledge of 'causes' made possible by science. Machiavelli's maxims for his prince were only counsels of prudence culled from a study of Livy. They were as different from a *true science* of statecraft as Hobbes' early translation of Thucydides was from his *Leviathan*. Hobbes considered that he had, in his own thinking, progressed from shrewd, fallible, common sense about his country's plight to the certain knowledge of the scientist.

From a brief survey of Hobbes' account of what science or philosophy was not – experience, prudence, history – something has been gleaned of his conception of scientific knowledge. It was the product of reason rather than of sense; it yielded universal truths that were hypothetical in character; it permitted knowledge of 'causes', not simply of 'effects'. These characterizations are very

1. E.W. IV, 16, 18.   2. E.W. III, 71.   3. E.W. III, 16.

suitable signposts for a more detailed account of Hobbes' positive conception of scientific knowledge.

4. Reason and Scientific Knowledge

'When a man reasoneth,' said Hobbes, 'he does nothing else but conceive a sum total, from addition of parcels: or conceive a remainder, from subtraction of one sum from another; which, if it be done by words, is conceiving of the consequence of the names of all the parts, to the name of the whole; or from the names of the whole and one part, to the name of the other part. . . . For REASON, in this sense, is nothing but reckoning, that is adding and subtracting, of the consequences of general names agreed upon for the marking and signifying of our thoughts.'[1] Reasoning is not born with us like sense or memory; nor, like prudence, is it the product of experience. It is rather an art which we acquire by industry. We must learn, first of all, to impose names, or to define; we must learn, secondly, to devise an orderly method of proceeding from the names from which we start to statements, which are the result of connecting names together, and to syllogisms which are ways of connecting statements logically with each other. Science is 'a knowledge of all the consequences of names appertaining to the subject in hand'.[2] It gives us certain knowledge not of the nature of things but of the *names* of things. 'The only way to know is by definition.'[3]

This account of reasoning is manifestly a generalization of the method of mathematics. We start with certain terms or names about whose definition we agree. We connect these terms together into statements like 'A man is a rational, animated body' just as we add together items in an account. We then find that if we follow certain methods of combining the statements so created, conclusions follow which were contained in our premises but of which we were ignorant before we started our reckoning. We might for instance start with the definition of 'man' as 'living creature' and of 'creature' as 'animated body'. We could then argue: Every man is a living creature; every living creature is a

1. E.W. III, 29–30.   2. E.W. III, 35.   3. E.W. II, 305.

body; therefore every man is a body. Hobbes thought that science was mainly a matter of exploring 'the consequences of names appertaining to the subject in hand' or, in other words, seeing what followed from combining the various definitions with which we might start.

The procedure of deducing consequences from definitions Hobbes called the synthetical method, which is very useful for teaching or for expounding the consequences of principles already known. In the analytical method, which is employed when we wish to understand some given phenomenon, we must work backwards from a description of it until we come to what Hobbes called 'primary propositions' from which our description can be logically deduced. A primary proposition is 'that wherein the subject is explicated by a predicate of many names, as man is a body, animated, rational; for that which is comprehended in the name man, is more largely expressed in the names body, animated, and rational, joined together; and it is called primary, because it is first in ratiocination; for nothing can be proved, without understanding first the name of the thing in question. Now *primary* propositions are nothing but definitions, or parts of definitions, and these only are the principles of demonstration, being truths constituted arbitrarily by the inventors of speech, and therefore not to be demonstrated.'[1] This is Hobbes' rendering of the Aristotelian method of explanation in which to explain a thing was to refer to the essential properties of the natural kind or class of things to which it belonged. Why do men make laws? Because making laws is a way in which rationality is exercised and rationality is one of the essential properties of man. Hobbes differs from Aristotle, however, in stressing that some of these definitions which comprise 'primary propositions' are arbitrary conventions decided upon by the inventors of speech. He also says that there are certain basic terms like 'motion', 'straight line', and 'extension', which cannot be defined like 'man' by breaking them down into their component parts; they are 'well enough defined, when, by speech as short as may be, we raise in the mind of the hearer perfect and clear ideas or conceptions of the things named,

1. E.W. I, 36-7.

as when we define motion to be the leaving of one place, and the acquiring of another continually'.[1] Here we see nothing move nor is any cause of motion laid down in the definition; but nevertheless a clear idea of motion comes into our minds when we hear the circumlocution. The terms for which we can only give circumlocutions rather than definitions are those describing a genus which is not itself a species under a higher level genus. 'Man' is a species under the genus 'animal' which is a species under the genus 'body'; but there is no further genus in relation to which terms like 'body', 'motion', and 'extension' can be regarded as species.

Reasoning, therefore, whether synthetically or analytically, involves definitions. Definitions remove ambiguity, give a universal notion of the thing defined, and obviate occasions for controversy. Hobbes saw in definitions and in geometrical demonstrations the main hope for reasonable men to rid their country of those controversies which he thought to be the basis of civil disputes. 'And therefore in geometry, which is the only science that it hath pleased God hitherto to bestow on mankind, men begin at settling the significations of their words; which settling of significations they call definitions . . .'[2] Why should not men do the same in political disputes? Leibniz later had the same vision. Men might develop a universal language which would enable them, when confronted with a moral problem, to sit down with paper and pencil saying to each other 'Let us calculate'. Hobbes put his hopes succinctly: 'To conclude, the light of human minds is perspicuous words, but by exact definitions first snuffed, and purged from ambiguity; reason is the pace; increase of science, the way; and the benefit of mankind, the end.'[3] The point of philosophy or science was not just to understand society but to change it. But are we to conclude that Hobbes thought that this could be achieved by simply starting from and sticking to definitions? We are hesitant in ascribing this view to Hobbes both on general grounds and because there are strands in Hobbes' teaching which make such a simple interpretation suspect.

To take the general grounds first. Since the time of Hume and Kant it has been customary to distinguish between analytic and

1. E.W. I, 81.   2. E.W. III, 23, 4.   3. E.W. III, 36, 7.

synthetic truths. The distinction is not an absolute one but can be roughly formulated as follows. The grounds for the truth of an analytic judgement lie solely in the definitions of the terms involved. 'Centaurs are four-legged animals' is analytic if four-leggedness is one of the defining properties of centaurs, or if one would not call an animal a centaur if it did not have four legs. The grounds for the truth of a synthetic judgement, on the other hand, are observations, memories, or testimonies which confirm what is stated. Thus 'sons hate their fathers' is a synthetic truth if hatred of a father is not taken as one of the defining properties of a son (i.e. if we did not stop calling a person a son if there was no sign of his hating his father), and if sons actually do hate their fathers, our belief that they do being grounded on observations, memories, and testimonies. Hobbes himself makes a similar distinction when he differentiates necessary from contingent propositions.[1] In a necessary proposition like 'man is a living creature' we cannot conceive of anything which we would call by the subject ('man') without also calling it by the predicate ('living creature'); also the predicate is either equivalent to the subject as in 'man is a rational living creature' or a part of an equivalent name as 'man is a living creature'. A contingent proposition, on the other hand, like 'every crow is black' may be true now but false hereafter; and, as in 'every man is a liar', the predicate ('liar') is no part of a compounded name equivalent to the name 'man' which forms the subject. Hobbes, however, does not develop this distinction and does not think it important in his account of scientific knowledge; for science is concerned only with what he calls necessary truths. This is where we encounter the crucial difficulty; for though geometry, whose method Hobbes generalized, is usually considered to be composed of only what we have called analytic truths, the natural and social sciences are not. If the natural and social sciences were just like geometry, then what Hobbes says about the importance of definitions in obtaining true knowledge would be reasonable enough. But the model of analytic truths is misleading for the natural and social sciences; for, as Hume saw, geometrical propositions may be necessarily

1. E.W. I, 38.

true but need have no application in the world in which we live. Definitions may be constructed and propositions generated which are indubitable; but what is the use of them in Hobbes' ambitious project for 'the benefit of mankind' if they tell us nothing about the world? The problem which haunted Kant was how it comes about that mathematical propositions – e.g. Newton's laws – are sometimes true explanations of events in the world. Hobbes, however, assumed like Descartes that nature had an underlying mathematical structure which was not apparent to sense but which could be unfolded by the definitions and demonstrations of the geometrical method. But how were the appearances to be saved? How could what was rationally revealed be related to what could be seen with the eyes? For in the natural and social sciences it is not sufficient to define terms precisely; we must also choose those 'primary propositions' whose deduced consequences agree with what can be observed. Certainly definitions are important in that verbal misunderstandings are minimized; certainly the deductive method is employed in exploring the consequences of the postulates with which we start. But *observation* is decisive in deciding between such postulates. In this respect science is quite unlike geometry.

So much, then, for the general grounds for hesitating to ascribe to Hobbes the view that the model of geometric truth was quite adequate for the sciences of nature, man, and society. We must now pass to what he actually said on the crucial topic of scientific truth. It must be said, to start with, that he was not at all clear about the distinction between geometry and the non-formal sciences and that his theory of truth is unclear in consequence. But it is possible to defend the view that when he is speaking in a predominantly political context he stresses always the importance of definitions and usually puts forward a conventionist theory of truth; whereas when he is thinking about the natural sciences his theory is less conventionist and more like a self-evidence theory such as Descartes'.

It is Hobbes' remarks in *Leviathan* and *De Cive* which give the reader the strong impression that he held some kind of conventionist theory of truth. He starts with the important insight that 'true' and 'false' are attributes of speech, not of things. They are words about words. He then goes on: 'Seeing then that truth consisteth in the right ordering of names in our affirmations, a man that seeketh precise truth had need to remember what every name he uses stands for, and to place it accordingly, or else he will find himself entangled in words, as a bird in lime twigs, the more he struggles the more belimed.'[1] And at the end of his English translation of *De Cive* he says that truth about questions of human science is 'sought out by natural reason and syllogisms, drawn from the covenants of men, and definitions, that is to say, significations received by use and common consent of words; such as are all questions of right and philosophy . . . truth therefore depends upon the compacts and consents of men. In like manner, when it is demanded in philosophy, whether the same thing may entirely be in divers places at once; the determination of the question depends on the knowledge of the common consent of men, about the signification of the word *entire*. For if men, when they say a thing entirely somewhere, so signify by common consent that they understand nothing of the same to be elsewhere; it is false that the same thing is in divers places at once. That truth therefore depends on the consents of men, and by the same reason, in all other questions concerning right and philosophy.'[2] In such passages one could interpret Hobbes as meaning that agreement about definitions is a necessary condition for arriving at true knowledge; for otherwise men would be constantly involved in verbal misunderstandings. One could also hold that he meant that some disputes, where there is agreement about the facts, can be settled by agreement about how to use a word like 'entirely'. But it is difficult to avoid the conclusion that he saw agreement about definitions as more than just a necessary condition for arriving at true knowledge. It looks as if he failed to see the importance of the crucial difference between analytic and synthetic truths and, through the influence of geometry, extended the model of analytic truth to the natural and social sciences.

Hobbes saw that there is a certain arbitrariness about definitions in science, but he did not see that this matters very little

1. E.W. III, 23.   2. E.W. II, 295–6.

because in science *so little* depends on definitions. Terms have to be defined with sufficient precision to avoid verbal misunderstandings and to guide the researches of other scientists. But that is about all. 'In science, we take care that the statements we make should never depend upon the meaning of our terms. Even where the terms are defined, we never try to derive any information from the definition, or to base any argument upon it. That is why our terms make so little trouble. We do not overburden them. We try to attach to them as little weight as possible. We do not take their "meaning" too seriously. We are always conscious that our terms are a little vague (since we have learned to use them only in practical applications) and we reach precision not by reducing their penumbra of vagueness, but rather by keeping well within it, by carefully phrasing our sentences in such a way that the possible shades of meaning of our terms do not matter. This is how we avoid quarrelling about words.'[1] . . . 'Clear speaking is speaking in such a way that words do not matter.'[2] In the empirical sciences the main function of clear definitions is to enable us to look through the words at the facts described by them. But if the procedure of empirical science is modelled on geometry where there need be no facts described by the words, it is understandable that undue prominence should be given to the role of definition. For geometry is simply exploring the logical consequences of definitions.

If Hobbes' view that scientific knowledge depends on exact definitions was over-optimistic, his belief in the efficacy of definitions for eliminating civil discord was incredibly naïve. For suppose agreement were to be reached about how terms like 'sovereign' and 'justice' were to be used, the decision would still remain whether such a sovereign should be tolerated or whether justice, however defined, should be done. Hobbes' political arguments were, as we shall see, more than this; but *prima facie* the belief in the efficacy of definitions in promoting civil concord seems preposterous. For knowing precisely what a Communist means by 'democracy' or 'class-solidarity' may make a Liberal

1. K. R. Popper, *The Open Society and Its Enemies*, Vol. II, p. 18.
2. op. cit., p. 282.

quite clear that he is completely opposed to the convictions put forward by the use of such words. Only if agreement were reached about the definitions of such terms by getting the other person to share the convictions for which the terms were shorthand, would Hobbes' optimism be justified. But this, again, would show the relative unimportance of definitions. For agreement about definitions would then be the symptom rather than the cause of civil concord.

The stress on the need for definitions is even linked by Hobbes with the contract theory of the origins of civil society. In setting up a commonwealth men agree to use words in a certain way as well as to accept the arbitration of a sovereign on matters relating to the preservation of peace. There are passages, however, where Hobbes pushes this theory of truth by convention to its logical conclusion. For men may disagree about definitions. 'It is needful therefore, as oft as any controversy ariseth in these matters contrary to public good and common peace, that there be somebody to judge of the reasoning, that is to say, whether that which is inferred, be rightly inferred or not; that so the controversy may be ended. But there are no rules given by Christ to this purpose, neither came he into the world to teach logic. It remains therefore that the judges of such controversies, be the same as those whom God by nature had instituted before, namely, those who in each city are constituted by the sovereign. Moreover, if a controversy be raised of the accurate and proper signification, that is the definition of those names or appellations which are commonly used; insomuch as it is needful for the peace of the city, or the distribution of right, to be determined; the determination will belong to the city. . . . But the decision of the question whether a man do reason rightly, belongs to the city.'[1] Scientific disputes, which bear upon matters of public importance, must, so it seems, be submitted to the magistrate. It must be said, however, that this bizarre and authoritarian theory of truth is usually put forward when Hobbes is concerned to delimit the respective spheres of secular and ecclesiastical jurisdiction or when he is troubled about the kinds of disputes that provoke civil unrest. Indeed it may be

1. E.W. II, 268–9.

said in general that Hobbes is more enthralled by the prospect of modelling political reconstruction on geometry than troubled by doubts about the lack of parallel between geometry and natural science.

There are, however, certain strands in Hobbes' teaching which indicate a self-evidence rather than a conventionist theory of truth both in geometry and in the non-formal sciences. We have already encountered certain terms in primary propositions like 'motion' and 'straight line' which cannot be further analysed but which are 'well enough defined, when, by speech as short as may be, we raise in the mind of the hearer perfect and clear ideas of the things named'. These terms, which occur in the basic postulates of geometry and of the physical sciences, are suspiciously similar to Descartes' clear and distinct ideas of simple natures. It seems as though we do not arbitrarily decide on *all* our definitions. Rather our postulates contain terms which symbolize clear and simple conceptions of all-pervading properties of the physical world like motion and extension. It is not the decision of the magistrates which generates the truth of these postulates but the self-evidence of the conceptions which their terms symbolize.

This interpretation is supported by taking into account Hobbes' odd subjective account of evidence. At the start of his early work entitled *Human Nature* he says that knowledge necessarily implies two things – truth and evidence. Truth he has already exemplified by an analytic truth. 'Charity is a virtue' is true if the name of virtue includes that of charity. Evidence he defines as 'the con-comitance of a man's *conception* with the *words* that signify such conception in the act of ratiocination'.[1] A parrot could *speak* truth but it could not *know* it; for it would lack the conceptions which accompany the speaking of truth by a man who knows truth. 'Evidence is to truth, as the sap to the tree, which, so far as it creepeth along with the body and branches, keepeth them alive; where it forsaketh them, they die: for this evidence, which is meaning with our words, is the life of truth. Knowledge thereof, which we call science, I define to be *evidence of truth*, from some beginning or principle of sense: for the truth of a proposition is

1. E.W. IV, 28.

never evident, until we conceive the meaning of the words or terms whereof it consisteth, which are always conceptions of the mind: nor can we remember those conceptions, without the thing that produced the same by our senses.'[1]

Now there are several points of interest in this key passage. In the first place Hobbes makes the interesting and important distinction between *speaking* truth and *knowing* truth. A man with scientific understanding must know truth and not just speak it. This involves not only speaking in accordance with agreed definitions but also having conceptions of 'evidence' or of the 'meaning' of terms. By 'meaning' he does not refer to the definition of terms by introducing other terms but to mental conceptions of which words are supposed to be signs. Whatever the merits of the theory of meaning here suggested, it is surely significant that Hobbes sees the necessity for introducing the notions of evidence and meaning. In the second place it is important that Hobbes links this very subjective account of meaning with the doctrine that our conceptions *originate* in sense experience. His doctrine of evidence thus preserves a connexion, albeit a very tenuous one, between observation and knowledge of truth. For we cannot have true knowledge without 'conceptions' and these are produced in us from without by our sense experience of things. Names are then given to the things of which we have conceptions and are joined together to make true propositions. These in their turn are joined together into the syllogisms of scientific demonstration. This working on the material provided by sense with the help of the tools of definition and deduction differentiates science from prudence. For the latter is merely the experience of the effects of things working on us from without. This may lead to *error* if we are mistaken in our perceptions, memories, or expectations. But we are only guilty of *falsehood* if we speak. For instance, if we see the image of the sun in water and imagine it to be there, and act as if it were there, we are in error. But we only commit a falsehood if we go on to call both the heavenly sun and the sun in the water 'sun', and say that there are two suns.

It seems, then, as if Hobbes thought that true knowledge or

1. E.W. IV, 28.

science involved correct speech in accordance with definitions but that this had meaning because it was in some way related to conceptions derived from sense experience.[1] There are two processes – talking and thinking – which go on concomitantly and which culminate in the enunciation of the basic postulates of science which symbolize our simple and clear conceptions of motion, extension, and so on, which we have originally seen with our eyes. The definitions of the scientist are thus connected with his sensory experience of the world which he tries to explain. But in thus trying to save the appearances Hobbes committed himself, surely, to a strangely private theory of scientific meaning that both underestimated and misconceived the role of sensory observation in science. For his suggestion that scientific postulates have meaning, and therefore, in contrast to those of the theologian, have impeccable credentials, because they are signs of conceptions which originate in sense, is surely irrelevant. For it does not matter much how scientific postulates *originate*; what matters is that their deduced consequences should be testable by observation. The role of sensory observation is at the end, in deciding between postulates, however they originate or however clear and distinct the conceptions may be of which they are alleged to be signs. Galileo saw this; for he insisted that even the most rational and mathematically satisfactory theories should be tested by comparing their deduced consequences with observations. This, of course, raises the problem of the empirical meaning or interpretation of scientific postulates which Hobbes touched on in his theory of evidence; but at least it raises the problem in the right place. Hobbes nowhere assigned a decisive role to sensory observation in *deciding between* postulates. He was in love with geometry and, absorbed in the enjoyment of his own conceptions, he averted his eyes from the face of Nature.

5. *Scientific Knowledge and History*

We have so far attempted to disentangle what Hobbes meant when he characterized scientific knowledge as the product of

1. For difficulties in this theory see *infra*, Ch., 5, sect. 3.

reason rather than of sense. We must now turn to his second characterization of it as universal and hypothetical knowledge. He has in mind that when we talk, for instance, of a circle in geometry we are not talking of any particular circle drawn in a particular colour on a particular piece of paper. Rather we are enunciating universal truths about any circle, about any figure that conforms to the initial definitions. These statements are hypothetical because we say that if a figure is a circle, then any straight line through its centre will divide it into two equal parts. We do not say that there is or was or will be a circle at any particular place at any particular time which conforms to these specifications. We only say that if a figure has certain properties then certain propositions will be true about it. Science provides us with truths that are universal, hypothetical, and eternal.

This analysis seems to be substantially correct both for natural science and for geometry. The main business of scientists is to establish laws which are universal and hypothetical statements like 'Everywhere and always if iron is heated, then it expands'. But Hobbes does not sufficiently inform us of his views about the relationship between these truths and the register of facts which he calls history. In his *Behemoth* Hobbes used his science of human nature to explain the causes and course of the Civil War. But he was only able to do so because he did not make an impassable gulf between his rational understanding on the one hand and the particular events which he witnessed, remembered, or heard about on the other. Observation, memory, and testimony provided him with categorical statements about particular events at particular times which served as minor premisses for the major premisses provided by his rational science of human nature. Self-interest, taught Hobbes, is the only operative motive. Men go to war only because of their desire for power. The Presbyterians waged war on Charles. They did so, therefore, in order to get power for themselves. Whatever their alleged reason might be for making war on a King – the injustice of ship-money, the orders of God, the influence of a Catholic Queen – the reality behind the appearances was their desire for power for themselves. In cases like these Hobbes *uses* his universal truths about human nature in

61

order to explain particular events. At other times he even uses such categorical statements to *confirm* his universal statements as any scientist would who believes in the importance of observation. For instance Hobbes quotes as evidence for his principle 'by experience known to all men and denied by none, to wit, that the dispositions of men are naturally such, that except they be restrained through fear of some coercive power, every man will distrust and dread each other', the fact that people shut their doors against their neighbours even in well-governed states and lock up their trunks and coffers for fear of domestics.[1] These statements, it is true, are lower order universal statements; but the sole evidence for them could only be that Hobbes had seen, remembered, or heard about these examples of neighbourly conduct at particular times and places. There thus seems to be an obvious connexion between Hobbes' rational science of human nature and his record of historical events, which is an interpretation guided by his assumptions about human beings. His rational science which is quite different from experience seems rather a fraud. When he makes use of his science, however mistaken his postulates, what he in fact does seems much more intelligible than what he claims to be doing. This is often the case with philosophers of science.

6. Science as Knowledge of Cause and Effect

The first two characterizations of scientific knowledge as the product of reason and as hypothetical knowledge were manifestly a generalization of the method of geometry. Although much has been said about Hobbes' mistake in equating the method of geometry with that of physical science, it was quite understandable in view of the great contribution of the geometric method to the development of the new science of motion from which Hobbes obtained his third characterization of scientific knowledge – that it yields knowledge of causes.

There is a sense in which it is misleading to stress too much the role of observation in science; for most great advances in scientific

1. E.W. II, xv.

theory have come about through the postulation of *unobservables* to explain the observable. Galileo worked out his theory by imagining perfect spheres moving on frictionless planes in perfectly straight lines. He was able to conduct such imaginary experiments because his mind had been set free from the earth-bound Aristotelian system by the method of geometry which accustoms its students to conduct such experiments with parallel lines that are perfectly straight and stretch out to infinity, with angles that are really equal, and with perfect circles. Aristotelianism, on the other hand, was an earth-bound system with a premium on rapes of the senses. The sun revolved round the earth because it was actually observed to do so. The elements of earth, water, air, and fire had their natural places, in that order, with the water on the earth separated by the region of air from the fiery region occupied by heavenly bodies. This too was based on crude observation. And so was the all-important assumption that rest is the natural state of bodies which move only so long as a mover imparts motion to them. It was only because Galileo and his contemporaries at Padua were versed in geometrical modes of thought that they were able to make the momentous advance of imagining motion as the norm; for it is not through *observation* that we become convinced that bodies continue their motion unless something impedes them. It was through imagining the perfect case of a body moving without impediment as the norm that Galileo was set free to work out a new system of mechanics. These ideal experiments were very important in Galilean method. We shall find Hobbes having recourse to them. Indeed this is the most convincing way of interpreting his account of the state of nature and the social contract.

We tend to think of Galileo as a lone pioneer at war with the Inquisition; but a little research reveals him as the inheritor of a long tradition of the Averroistic branch of Aristotelianism that had flourished at Padua for centuries.[1] His famous resoluto-compositive method, which Hobbes adopted, was taken over from Zabarella and fused with a new mathematical tradition that had

1. The details of this tradition can be found in J. H. Randall's article, 'Scientific Method in the School of Padua', in the *Journal of the History of Ideas*, 1940.

gathered support at Padua after the translation of Archimedes' works into Latin in 1543. Hobbes adopted the terms 'analysis' and 'synthesis' for his method which were the terms used by Euclid and Archimedes rather than the 'resolution' and 'composition' of the Paduan school. But it was more or less equivalent to the mathematicized version of the resolution and composition of the Paduan tradition.

What, in brief, was this method which worked such magic in the hands of Galileo? Suppose we want to explain something like the fall of a body towards the earth. We take a *typical* phenomenon like the rolling of a ball down an inclined slope. We think away characteristics like the colour and smell of the ball, which are presumed to be irrelevant to the problem, and resolve the situation by analysis into components which can be *qualified* – the length and angle of the slope, the weight of the ball, and the time taken to cover the distance to the ground. We then think about the mathematical relations disclosed until we find some formula in which one variable is a function of another. In this case we find that the velocity of the body, or the units of space travelled in a unit of time, is a function of the time it has been falling from rest, the distance being proportional to the square of the time taken. The 'composition' or 'synthesis' of the situation is the reconstruction of the situation in mathematical terms by deducing consequences from the laws discovered. The situation has been transformed into a rational structure of mathematical relations. In view of the great deductive power of this method, is it surprising that Galileo and his followers thought of shape, size, quantity, and motion as the reality behind the appearance of colours, tastes, smells, and other properties unamenable to mathematical expression?

When, therefore, Hobbes spoke of the search for causes we must bear in mind that his paradigm for causal explanation was the resolution and composition of the Paduan school. One of his most famous definitions of philosophy or scientific knowledge occurs at the beginning of *De Corpore*: 'PHILOSOPHY is such knowledge of effects or appearances, as we acquire by true ratiocination from the knowledge we have first of their causes or generation: And

again, of such causes or generations as may be from knowing first
their effects.'[1] By 'effects or appearances' he meant properties in
virtue of which, at a common sense level, we distinguish things
from each other. The example of a circle reveals how knowledge
of effects can be obtained from knowledge of its generation. For if
we are presented with a plane figure, we cannot possibly tell by
looking at it whether or not it is a true circle; but if we know how
the figure was constructed by the circumduction of a body, one of
whose ends remained fixed, we can reason that this must be a
circle, because the body, as it is pivoted round on one end, must
provide a succession of radii for the figure which are all equal
to one another. The motion of the body is the cause of the
appearance or generates it. Hobbes in fact equated 'cause' with
antecedent motion. 'I say then, that in the first place you are to
inquire diligently into the nature of motion. For the variations of
fancies, or (which is the same thing) of the phenomena of nature,
have all of them one universal efficient cause, namely the variety
of motion. For if all things in the world were absolutely at rest,
there could be no variety of fancy; but living creatures would be
without sense of all objects, which is little less than to be dead.'[2]
Similarly, in the section 'Of cause and effect' in *De Corpore*,
Hobbes equates cause with 'the aggregate of all the accidents both
of the agents how many soever they be, and of the patient, put
together; which when they are all supposed to be present, it
cannot be understood but that the effect is produced at the same
instant; and if any one of them be wanting, it cannot be understood but that the effect is not produced'.[3] Causation and the production of effects consist in a continual mutation in agents by the
working on them of other agents. For instance, as the heat of a
fire increases, so bodies in proximity gradually get hot as well. All
such mutations consist in motions and there can be no cause of
motion except in a body contiguous and moved.

For Hobbes, then, a cause of an event amounted to the antecedent motions in contiguous bodies necessary and sufficient to
produce it. The inquiry into causes can be conducted in two ways.
Either, as in the case of deducing that a figure must be a circle

1. E.W. I, 3.   2. E.W. VII, 83.   3. E.W. I, 121-2.

from our knowledge of the motions by means of which it was produced, we are not sure of an effect and deduce what it must be
from our knowledge of its causes. Or we may know an effect and
may wish to know what are its causes. This is what Hobbes calls
the analytical method. To discover, for instance, the cause of
light, we must conduct an imagined experiment to discover those
motions which invariably precede light and which are absent
when light also is absent. We discover that there must be some
principal object which is, as it were, the fountain of light, together
with a transparent medium and a body with a fitting disposition
of organs to receive impressions from without. There must also be
some kind of motion in the object which is continued through the
medium to the eye and thence to the 'last organ of sense, the
heart'. Light is 'nothing but the alteration of vital motion, made
by the impression upon it of motion continued from the object'.[1]
The effect has been broken down by analysis into the various
circumstances necessary and sufficient to produce it. Such a
mental experiment can only be carried out if we make use of
names to register our conceptions; and names are definitions or,
as in the case of 'motion', terms which conjure before our minds
'perfect and clear ideas or conceptions of the things named'. And
so we are back where we started in the account of scientific knowledge – with the indispensability of definitions or of clear ideas
symbolized by terms which permit only circumlocutions.

There is, however, a distinction which Hobbes makes between
these two scientific inquiries of discovering effects when we know
causes and discovering causes when we know effects, which he
does not develop at length, but which is of paramount importance in any attempt to assess his account.[2] At the beginning
of Part IV of *De Corpore*, when Hobbes embarks on physics with
the chapter 'Of Sense and Animal Motion', he distinguishes his
two types of scientific inquiry and says: '. . . one, from the generation of things to their possible effects; and the other, from their
effects or appearances to some possible generation of the same. In

1. E.W. I, 79.

2. This contrast can also be found in Zabarella. See Randall article referred
to on p. 63.

the former of these the truth of the first principles of our ratiocination, namely definitions, is made and constituted by ourselves, whilst we consent and agree about the appellations of things.'[1] This method Hobbes had already used in the preceding sections of the *De Corpore* on parallel lines, refraction and reflection, circular and other forms of motion, angles, and so on. However, 'I now enter upon another part; which is the finding out by the appearances or effects of nature, which we know by sense, some ways and means by which they may be, I do not say they are, generated. The principles, therefore, upon which the following discourse depends, are *not such as we ourselves make and pronounce in general terms, as definitions: but such, as being placed in the things themselves by the Author of Nature, are by us observed in them*; and we make use of them in single and particular, not universal propositions.'[2] He then embarks on the attempt to explain 'apparition itself', the fact that some 'natural bodies have in themselves the patterns almost of all things, and others of none at all', which had puzzled him on his third journey to the Continent when he witnessed the inability of certain learned men to explain the nature of sense. Explanations of the phenomena of the physical world, starting with sensation itself and animal motion, and including the world, the stars, light, heat, colours, cold, wind, hardness, ice, lightning, thunder, the heads of rivers, sound, odours, savour, touch, and gravity, all these depend upon hypotheses, 'which unless we know them to be true, it is impossible for us to demonstrate that those causes which I have here explicated, are the true causes of the things whose productions I have derived from them'.[3] They may be the true explanations but we cannot demonstrate that they must be. Physics seems to differ from geometry in that we do not create the phenomena in the way in which we create triangles. Therefore there is always the chance that the effects of nature have been generated in accordance with a formula other than the one which we suggest in our hypotheses. This is a most important admission of whose far-reaching implications Hobbes did not seem properly aware.

With the state, however, the case is different. For the state is an

1. E.W. I, 388.   2. E.W. I, 388 (my italics).   3. E.W. I, 531.

artificial, not a natural, body. We can therefore come to know with certainty the formula of its construction. To use his own words; 'Geometry, therefore is demonstrable, for the lines and figures from which we reason are drawn and described by ourselves; and civil philosophy is demonstrable because we make the commonwealth ourselves. But because of natural bodies we know not the construction, but seek it from effects, there lies no demonstration of what the causes be we seek for, but only of what they may be.'[1] This explains the link in Hobbes' thought between geometry and social reconstruction. But it leaves the science of animate bodies in an awkward predicament between the two; for Hobbes' intention was to explain the behaviour of men in society as a particular case of the motion of bodies having sense organs and animal spirits.

In general, there is little mystery about Hobbes' theory of causation; for it was the usual theory adopted by the new natural philosophers. In his *Epistle Dedicatory* to the *De Corpore* Hobbes announced his indebtedness to Copernicus who revived the opinion of Aristarchus, and Philolaos in his heliocentric theory of the heavens; to Galileo, 'the first that opened to us the gate of natural philosophy universal, which is the knowledge of the nature of motion';[2] and to Harvey for his *Motion of the Blood* and *Generation of Living Creatures*. Before these, says Hobbes, there was nothing certain in natural philosophy. Copernicus had regarded astronomy as a branch of mathematics – the geometry of the heavens. He believed, like most people before Hobbes and Leibniz, that the space of geometry was the space of the universe; his heliocentric theory provided a geometrical ground-plan of the universe that was much simpler than the Ptolemaic one used by the Aristotelians. Kepler, whom Hobbes praised along with Mersenne and Gassendi, for advancing natural philosophy, thought of the 'underlying harmony discoverable in the observed facts as the *cause* of the latter, the reason, as he actually puts it, why they are as they are'.[3] Mathematics was the key to the universe's structure since mathematical harmonies in the mind of the Creator

1. E.W. VII, 184. 2. E.W. I, viii.
3. E. W. Burtt, *The Metaphysical Foundations of Modern Physical Science*, p. 53.

furnish the cause 'why the number, the size, and the motions of the orbits are as they are and not otherwise'.[1] It was, however, in the natural philosophy of Galileo that this Pythagorean-Platonic tradition was applied in detail to terrestrial phenomena and linked with the doctrine that all causes are antecedent motions. Galileo allowed a place for God, the great geometer, who constructed the atoms and then set them in motion. But in mechanics we deal with what he called 'secondary causes' which are specific motions. 'That and no other is in the proper sense to be called cause, at whose presence the effect always follows, and at whose removal the effect disappears.'[2] To all intents and purposes a scientific explanation of an event amounts to finding the antecedent motions co-present and co-absent with the event to be explained.

7. Body, Man and Citizen

This, then, was Hobbes' conception of philosophy or scientific knowledge. It was by means of laying down definitions in the search for causes that the universal truths of science were to be proclaimed. Hobbes' imaginative idea was to use this method in order to expound a complete philosophy of body, man, and civil society. The method of analysis or resolution was to be used to arrive at the most universal notions necessary for a knowledge of the causes of all things. We might start, for instance, with 'gold' and resolve this into the ideas of 'solid', 'visible', 'heavy', and so on. These terms could be resolved into more universal ones like 'extended', but in our search for causes we must always arrive in the end at 'motion', which could have no cause save motion. There were also other terms which would permit no further resolution like 'place' – definitions 'which are nothing but the explication of our simple conceptions'.[3] Geometry was the first science in which we could see how different types of figures were generated by varieties of motion. This was the science of simple motions. Secondly came the philosophy of motion (presumably

1. E. A. Burtt, op. cit., p. 54. 2. E. A. Burtt, op. cit., p. 92.
3. E.W. I, 70.

Galileo's) in which the effects of the manifest motions of one body on another were to be considered. Thirdly we were to pass to physics, the investigation of the *internal and invisible* motions which explain why 'things when they are the same, yet seem not to be the same, but changed'.[1] Sensible qualities like light, colour, sound, heat, odour, were to be explained together with the nature of sensation itself, by which is meant seeing, hearing, smelling, tasting, and touching, whose causes have to be determined. After physics we could proceed to moral philosophy or a study of the motions of the mind – appetite, aversion, love – whose causes should be investigated. This science, which we would now call psychology, would follow physics because the motions of the mind had their causes in sense and imagination which were the subject of physical contemplation. 'And, therefore, they that study natural philosophy, study in vain, except they begin at geometry; and such writers or disputers thereof, as are ignorant of geometry, do but make their readers and hearers lose their time.'[2]

Geometry, however, was not quite so indispensable in the case of civil philosophy, whose status seems a trifle ambiguous. As Hobbes claimed that his originality consisted in trying to do for civil philosophy what Galileo had done for natural philosophy and Harvey had done for the science of the human body, the case of civil philosophy needs careful consideration. In the Preface to the Reader of the English translation of *De Cive*, Hobbes stated explicitly the method he had followed. The philosopher must proceed from 'the very matter of civil government' to its generation and form. 'For everything is best understood by its constituent causes. For as in a watch, or some such small engine, the matter, figure, and motion of the wheels cannot well be known, except it be taken insunder and viewed in parts; so to make a more curious search into the rights of states and duties of subjects, it is necessary, I say not to take them insunder, but yet that they may be so considered as if they were dissolved; that is, that we rightly understand what the quality of human nature is, in what matters it is, in what not, fit to make up a civil government, and how men must be agreed amongst themselves that intend to grow up into a well-grounded

1. E.W. I, 72.   2. E.W. I, 73.

state.'[1] This is a project fraught from the start with an ambiguity which is crucial to our estimate of Hobbes' whole civil philosophy. For was he really proposing to explain the causes of a state at all? When he says that he will inquire about the matters in which human nature is *fit* to make up a civil government and 'how men *must* be agreed amongst themselves that intend to grow up into a *well-grounded* state', he obviously is proposing to show how a rational state *ought* to be constructed; he surely is not attempting an explanation of actual states. However, he proceeds as if he were conducting a Galilean experiment rather than enunciating a rational plan for reconstruction. The resolution of the state into its constituents, men, is followed by the analysis of the causes of their entry into a commonwealth – man's dread and distrust of his fellows, and his fear of death which, together with his self-interest, lead him to devise a compact guaranteeing the conditions of peace which is enforced by an absolute sovereign power.

How did Hobbes arrive at these axioms about human nature to which he appealed in his analysis of a well-grounded state? In his chapter 'Of Method' in *De Corpore*, after sketching his plan for geometry, the science of motion, physics, and moral philosophy, as already indicated, he says that men might attain knowledge of the passions and perturbations of the mind by reasoning syntheti-cally from the first principles of philosophy and deduce from these the causes and necessity of constituting commonwealths, the knowledge of what is natural right and what are civil duties; for the principles of politics consisted in the knowledge of the motions of the mind which comes from knowledge of sense and imagina-tion. But he also says that even those who were ignorant of geo-metry and physics might attain the principles of civil philosophy by the analytical method. For they could start, for instance, with the question whether an action be just or unjust; 'unjust' could be resolved into 'fact against law', and 'law' into 'command of him or them that have coercive power'; 'power' could in its turn be derived from the wills of men that constituted such power to the end that they might live in peace. In the end the axiom would be reached that the appetites of men and the passions of

1. E.W. II, xiv.

their minds were such that, unless they were restrained by some power, they would always be making war on each other. Any man would admit that his experience confirmed this if he were to examine his own mind. This admission seems to indicate the possibility of an almost self-contained civil philosophy depending only on certain axioms of moral philosophy, vouched for by self-evident conceptions. In *Leviathan*, too, Hobbes not only followed this method but advocated it to his readers in his introduction. After speaking of the danger of inferences about people's designs from the evidence of their overt behaviour he concludes: 'He that is to govern a whole nation, must read in himself, not this or that particular man; but mankind: which though it be hard to do, harder than to learn any language or science; yet when I shall have set down my own reading, orderly and perspicuously, the pains left another, will be only to consider, if he also find not the same in himself. For this kind of doctrine admitteth no other demonstration.'[1]

Hobbes was not modest in the claims he advanced for his civil philosophy. At the end of Part II of *Leviathan* he compared his work with Plato's *Republic*, whose main theme was that society could not be saved till philosophers became kings or kings philosophers. Hobbes did not go quite so far as this. He claimed only that a sovereign who understood his science of natural justice, which neither Plato nor any other philosopher hitherto had worked out, could learn to govern. Perhaps some sovereign would gain possession of his writing and 'convert this truth of speculation, into the utility of practice'.[2] The principles of his science of natural justice were rules like 'Every man ought to endeavour peace, as far as he has hope of attaining it', 'That men perform their covenants made', and 'That every man strive to accommodate himself to the rest'. Hobbes regarded these rules as self-evident axioms that any rational man could not help accepting. For, he argued, man's desire to increase his own power is balanced by his fear of death; and that, in so far as man is afraid of death, he must accept rules like these, which are the necessary conditions of peace.

1. E.W. III, xii.   2. E.W. III, 358.

What can have led Hobbes to think that mankind can be moved only by such motives? For his whole civil philosophy really depends upon the acceptance of this assumption. The evidence Hobbes gives is mainly introspective. He asks us to look into ourselves and to agree with him that these considerations alone move us to act. Hobbes, like Descartes, seems to have thought that if postulates are self-evident, they are true. Men cannot doubt that they are moved solely by such motives; this seems to them to be self-evident when they look into themselves; therefore it must be true. This is surely a mistake; for although some statements that are true may *also* seem self-evident, they are not true *because* they are self-evident, and many statements that are not true may seem to be self-evident. The history of thought is littered with self-evident assumptions that were later discarded. Newton, for example, tried several other formulations of his laws of motion before coming back to the one for which he is famous because this formulation did not seem to him to be self-evident. It soon became self-evident to scientists once they became accustomed to it. Indeed the self-evidence of assumptions is largely a product of habituation. Many Freudian assumptions, which surprised and shocked our grandfathers, seem almost self-evident to us. But what makes assumptions true or false in science has nothing to do with self-evidence. It depends on whether or not conclusions deduced from them are confirmed or falsified by observation, not on whether they seem clear and distinct to those who think about them.

Many would say that Hobbes used the attractiveness and persuasiveness of geometrical demonstration to enunciate as self-evident the generalizations about man reached by a timid academic who had, during his formative years, been swept away by the rhetoric of Thucydides. They might further maintain that he pretended that a generalization of his own timid egoism could be deduced from the laws of motion in order that men would be disposed to accept a despotism that would permit him enough peace and security to pursue his intellectual interests without danger and distraction. Such an interpretation is possible, but it is irrelevant and lacks historical perspective. It is irrelevant

73

because, as in the case of all theories of the psychological, economic, or social causes of people's beliefs, the causes which prompt a man to put them forward have no bearing on the evidence which makes them true or false. Marx may have put forward his theory of economic change because he had a certain kind of upbringing in a middle-class Jewish home; but such considerations have no bearing on the question whether or not his theory of economic change was true or false. The causes or origins of a theory are different from the grounds or evidence for it.

The suggestion lacks a sense of historical perspective because it omits to dwell on the historical importance of Hobbes as a methodologist. He was right in making claims for the originality of his civil philosophy; for he attempted to establish political science and psychology as objective studies, untrammelled by theological assumptions or moral convictions, preserving a detached and uninvolved attitude towards man and society as well as towards nature. He tried to explain the behaviour of men in the *same sort of way* as he explained the motion of bodies. This was a comparatively novel undertaking at that time. Perhaps it was mistaken. Perhaps man's ability to alter the course of events through his knowledge of causal laws introduces a quite novel factor in nature which makes Hobbes' dream of a complete deductive science of man unrealizable. Perhaps the long line of psychologists and social scientists who, like Hobbes, have been fired by the imaginative idea of an all-inclusive deductive science of body, man, and citizen, have been the victims of a gigantic mistake. This may be so. But the objective attitude necessary for such an undertaking was a great step forward. Hobbes was wrong in thinking that the method of geometry was adequate for the development of physical theories; he was wrong in thinking that psychological explanations are entirely similar to physical and hence to geometrical explanations; but his supreme importance was to have been wrong about psychology and political science *in the same sort of way* as he was about physics. This was a great achievement.

CHAPTER 3

NATURE AND MIND

1. Hobbes the Metaphysician

THE ground-plan of Hobbes' deductive system of body, man and citizen was set out in his *De Corpore*, published in 1655, after thirteen years' intermittent work. This was Hobbes' last word on the philosophy of nature. Yet it is a strange book. When compared with Galileo's great works on nature it seems abstract and lacking in observational confirmation; yet when viewed as a philosophical treatise it is remarkable for its lack of interest in and detailed treatment of problems that are now regarded as 'philosophical'. The explanation of the peculiar scope of the book is not simply that Hobbes was a rationalist who decried the importance of observation in obtaining certain knowledge, nor that philosophy and science were almost indistinguishable in the seventeenth century. It is probably to be found in the nature of the problem which fascinated Hobbes and in his speculative solution which provided the motif of *De Corpore*.

The problem which haunted Hobbes is stated in a celebrated and striking passage of *De Corpore*: 'Of all the phenomena or appearances which are near us, the most admirable is apparition itself, τὸ φαίνεσθαι; namely, that some natural bodies have in themselves the patterns almost of all things, and others of none at all.'[1] We are familiar with Hobbes' perplexity about the cause of sense, of which the learned doctors were ignorant,[2] and of his imaginative idea that the cause of everything, including sensation itself, was in variations of motion. His *Little Treatise* and his early optical treatises were his first attempts at working out this speculative suggestion. The *De Corpore* was a more ambitious attempt to

1. E.W. I, 389.   2. See *supra*, p. 22.

solve this problem by constructing a system of principles which would also be adequate as a foundation for a science of man and citizen. Motion, which obsessed Hobbes on his third journey to the Continent, permeated his treatment of geometry, physics, and animal psychology. Sensation occupied a shadowy central position between the motions of the external world and the endeavours or minute motions of the bodily organs.

The *De Corpore*, then, represented a greatly expanded version of a picture the elements of which were sketched in the *Little Treatise*. But in spite of this expansion the details of the deductive system were not elaborated with too close a watch on the appearances. No engineer, after reading Hobbes, would return to his daily tasks with a clearer grasp of heat, velocity, or the paths of projectiles. But he might derive a certain intellectual excitement from Hobbes' mechanical vision. For Hobbes is to be regarded as the metaphysician of the new scientific movement rather than as one of its field-workers. Whitehead has described metaphysics as 'the science which seeks to discover the general ideas which are indispensably relevant to the analysis of everything that happens'.[1] It involves 'the utilization of specific notions, applying to a restricted group of facts, for the divination of the generic notions which apply to all facts'.[2] Hobbes used the specific notions of the new physical sciences and generalized them to cover man, who was viewed as part of the mechanical system of nature. In this extrapolation of the concepts of body, motion and efficient cause to the sphere of human affairs Hobbes justly prided himself on his originality. Bacon ridiculed the Aristotelian notion of final causes as adequate to explain the processes of nature but retained them for the explanation of human affairs. For human beings, after all, do have purposes and move towards appropriate goals. Similarly Descartes held that only *involuntary* actions could be mechanically explained in terms of antecedent push. But Hobbes ruthlessly, if perhaps inappropriately, pushed the mechanical model into the innermost sanctuaries of human intimacy, endeavour and decision. Most of the details of this

1. A. N. Whitehead, *Religion in the Making*, p. 84 (footnote).
2. A. N. Whitehead, *Process and Reality*, p. 6.

ambitious project were left to the imagination of the reader; and many have been sufficiently fascinated by its audacity to attempt to supply them.

2. *The Cause of Sense*

Many philosophers have been worried about imagery, which Hobbes called τὸ φαίνεσθαι, or apparition, because of the problematic status of images. When a man sees a tiger in his dreams, a ghost in a churchyard or a vivid picture of his drowning son, does it make sense to say that these appearances exist? Certainly they do not exist in the same way as do the tiger in the jungle, the tombstone in the churchyard or the solid son squatting on the floor playing soldiers. Have they existence, then, only as 'mental contents'? Yet perhaps, it is argued, sensation as well as imagery is a kind of mental picturing. Our private screen of appearances intervenes between us and the things we see. When we say we have perceived rather than imagined a tiger, we mean that in the one case something really exists independently of us which is represented on our private screen, whereas in the other case there are only the private pictures. Or the physical thing itself may be only an organization of or a construction out of our private pictures. And so the problem of perception and the related mind–body problem begin to develop.

Now the strange and tantalizing thing about Hobbes is that though he was troubled about sensation and imagery, he does not seem to have been at all troubled about the sort of philosophical problems which came to be traditionally associated with them. He seems to have assumed in a hard-headed way that things exist independently of our perceptions of them and to have been convinced that 'conceptions and apparitions are nothing really but motions in some internal substance of the head'.[1] He distinguished the faculties of the body from those of the mind, imagery being one of our mental powers.[2] But he never supposed that our minds contained a sort of stuff which was different in kind from that of our bodies. Phantasms or apparitions were simply one class of material

1. E.W. IV, 31.   2. E.W. IV, 2.

movements. At least that is what he explicitly said, though it may well be that he in fact regarded them as concomitants of movements in the brain rather than as the actual movements. For there is something rather incredible about a rigid materialist who maintains that our thoughts and feelings *are* simply motions of the body; epiphenomenalism, which holds that thoughts and feelings are appearances or products of bodily motions, sounds prima facie less incredible. Experienced heat or pain may well be an appearance or product of motions in our body in contact with other bodies; but it is odd to *equate* the experiences with the motions. But Hobbes does not seem to have been sufficiently interested in this problem to define carefully what his position was. He was able, too, to sustain this ambiguity in his thought because he used terms like 'agitation', 'disturbance', 'celerity', 'tranquillity', and so on, to describe mental occurrences, terms which have both a mentalistic and a physical interpretation. His key concept of 'endeavour', too, has also this double interpretation. This twilight kind of language enabled Hobbes to talk like a physiologist and yet preserve the common touch of everyday experience.

Why, then, was Hobbes so preoccupied with sensation and imagery and why did he think it so wonderful? To take the first question: Hobbes seems suddenly to have hit upon the idea that a correct causal analysis of sensation was the key both to nature and to man. His prose biography, after recording the interview with the learned doctors who did not know the cause of sense, says: 'From that time onwards he often pondered upon the cause of sense and by chance and good fortune it occurred to him that if bodies and all their parts were to be at rest, or were always to be moved by the same motion, our discrimination of all things would be removed, and (consequently) all sensation with it; and therefore the cause of all things must be sought in the variety of motion. And this was the first principle which he employed. Then he was led to geometry to learn the varieties and modes of motion. . . .'[1] Hobbes regarded apparition as a kind of meeting place of motions. Our sense-organs are agitated by external movements.

1. L.W. I, XXI.

Without such movements there would be no sensation. To give the entire cause of sensation must therefore require an analysis of movements in bodies external to us which are passed on to us via a medium. The problem of the learned doctors is only soluble in terms of a general mechanical theory. And sensation is important, too, not just as a receptor of external motions but also as the means by which actions are initiated. Hobbes held an ideo-motor theory of action. By this is meant that actions are reactions to external stimuli passed on by means of the sense-organs. In Hobbes' language phantasms are the efficient causes of action. Hobbes therefore regarded a correct causal analysis of sensation as the key both to physics and psychology.

Why, then, did he describe apparition as a wonderful thing? There is a sophisticated and a simple explanation of this. The sophisticated theory is briefly as follows: Hobbes' conviction was that a causal analysis of sensation is the kernel of any physical inquiry; for sensations are caused by external movements transmitted to us via a medium. Yet this means that all we can know of nature *depends upon* our sense organs; for how else could we know that there were different classes of external movements? But according to Hobbes, the rationalist, we could only acquire prudence by the use of our senses, not scientific understanding. However, the conclusion must be drawn with regard to apparition 'that if the appearances be the principles by which we know all other things, we must needs acknowledge sense to be the principle by which we know those principles, and that all the knowledge we have is derived from it. And as for the causes of sense, we cannot begin our search of them from any other phenomenon than that of sense itself. But you will say, by what sense shall we take notice of sense? I answer, by sense itself, namely, by the memory which for some time remains in us of things sensible, though they themselves pass away.'[1] Hence the great wonder of apparition; for without it there could be no science, yet science itself is a matter of reason, not of sense.

The simple explanation is that he was struck by the marvel of imagery '... the most admirable is apparition itself, τὸ φαίνεσθαι;

1. E.W. I, 389.

namely that some natural bodies have in themselves the patterns almost of all things, and others of none at all.'[1] The fact that men can measure the heavens and range over continents in their imagination, that they can run over their past lives and anticipate their future death 'sitting still in our closets or in the dark'[2] impressed Hobbes enormously – especially as he thought of imaginings as motions of part of a natural body. Yet certain natural bodies 'have in themselves the patterns almost of all things. . . .' There is a strong streak of rustic wonder in Hobbes' thought just as there is a strong element of the vernacular in his forceful, homespun style and in the vigour and homeliness of his metaphors and similes. Hobbes' verse autobiography gives the impression of a man almost bemused by the wonder of motion. The sophistication of the court and of continental circles was grafted on the shrewd, almost mystical wonderment of a man who was brought up in the country and spent long hours in adolescence pondering and poring over the seas charted by Drake and Magellan. Hobbes was above all a man who could become intellectually excited. Even modern professors of psychology can be filled with wonder when they ponder over the peculiarities of imagery. How much more so could Hobbes, who lived at a time when thinkers sailed on comparatively uncharted seas?

Sensation and imagery, then, are the central problems round which Hobbes' philosophy of nature revolves. The first part of *De Corpore* deals with the method necessary for the attainment of scientific understanding. The second part analyses the main concepts necessary for a mechanical explanation of nature in general and sensation in particular. Amongst these the most important are motion, body and accident, space and time, cause and effect. The third part is concerned with the details of the various modes of magnitude and motion. The fourth part is addressed specifically to the problem of sensation and animal motion and then proceeds to physics. This opens with a chapter on the world as a whole – whether it is a plenum or whether it contains empty space, which is followed by an analysis of the various parts of the world, grouped together, significantly enough, on the basis of their

1. E.W. I, 389.　　　　　2. E.W. I, 92.

appearance to the different senses. It is interesting to notice that Hobbes' first venture into the philosophy of nature in his *Little Treatise*, concerned explicitly with the cause of sense, had a similar structure on a greatly reduced scale. It began with an analysis of agent and patient, substance and accident, and cause; it then proceeded to deal with the problem whether motion is transmitted by a medium or by species (effluxes from agents); it ended with the explanation of sense and animal motion. This similarity of structure reinforces the suggestion that Hobbes' philosophy of nature was like a snowball which gathered more and more accretions round the central core of the explanation of sensation. We must now turn to his imaginative solution of the problem – that the explanation of sensation and of everything else in nature lay in variations of motion.

3. Motion

Hobbes believed, like many of his contemporaries, that Euclidean geometry really represented the ground-plan of the physical world, and that it was the foundation and paradigm of all other sciences. He also believed that he could outline a deductive system encompassing body, man and citizen. But this imposed a certain logical requirement on him. 'The end of science is the demonstration of the causes and generations of things; which if they be not in the definitions, they cannot be found in the conclusion of the first syllogism, that is made from those definitions; and if they be not in the first conclusion, they will not be found in any further conclusion deduced from that. . . .'[1] Thus Hobbes saw quite correctly not only that his psychology and politics must describe human action in terms of bodies in motion in order to be deducible from his science of mechanics and physics, but also that, if his mechanics and physics were to be deducible from his basic science of geometry, then his geometry too must contain statements about motion in its initial definitions. Hobbes' speculative feat was the two-way extension of motion into geometry on the one hand and into psychology and politics on the other.

1. E.W. I, 82.

Little need be said about the details of Hobbes' geometry except to indicate how he introduced motion into it, so making geometry a particular branch of kinematics. 'Lines, superficies and solids, are exposed, first, by motion . . . but so as that the marks of such motion be permanent; as when they are designed upon some matter, as a line upon paper; or graven in some durable matter. Secondly, by apposition; as when one line or length is applied to another line or length, one breadth to another breadth, and one thickness to another thickness. . . . Thirdly, lines and superficies may be exposed by section, namely, a line may be made by cutting an exposed superficies; and a superficies by the cutting of an exposed solid.'[1] A line is made by the motion of a point, superficies by the motion of a line, and so on. Similarly, circles are generated 'by the motion of a compass or other equivalent means'.[2] No one can understand what the definitions of geometry mean unless he has performed such actual or imaginary experiments with motion. 'To imagine motions with their lines and ways is a new business, and requires a steady brain, and a man that can constantly read in his own thoughts, without being diverted by the noise of words.'[3] Hobbes claimed that Euclid's definitions of circle and sphere supported his contention, but that he himself was 'the first that hath made the grounds of geometry firm and coherent'.[4] The mathematical merits of this introduction of motion into the definitions of a formal science like geometry are very questionable.[5] Wallis, amongst others, took strong exception to it. But it was certainly an imaginative conception. His mature fascination for motion enabled him to reconcile his abiding concern for social security with his middle-aged passion for geometry. It is seldom that such harmonious relations can be established between the loves of the different stages of a man's development.

Geometry, then, was the science which dealt with those *simple* motions involved in the construction of lines, circles and the other geometrical properties of bodies. It paved the way for mechanics which dealt with the effects of the motions of one body on another, and for physics which explained the generation of

1. E.W. I, 140.   3. E.W. VII, 272.   5. See Laird, pp. 102–9.
2. E.W. VII, 205.   4. E.W. VII, 242.

sensible qualities out of the insensible parts of a body in contact with other moving bodies. Geometry, as has been seen,[1] was a *demonstrable* science; for we ourselves make the motions which generate lines and figures just as we ourselves construct commonwealths; but we are not responsible in the same way for the generation of natural bodies, so we have to proceed by analysis to discover what their causes may be rather than must be.

Causation, or the production of effects in nature, consisted, according to Hobbes, in a continuous process. There is continuous mutation in substances which affects other substances. The fire gets hotter and the bodies close to it are affected as the heat spreads outwards. It was a cardinal principle of Hobbes' philosophy that all such mutations consisted in motion and that 'There can be no cause of motion, except in a body contiguous and moved'.[2] He assumed this principle more or less as self-evident throughout the *De Corpore*, though he did make some rather half-hearted attempts to prove it. Action at a distance was to philosophers of this period an intuitively repugnant idea. If bodies were not contiguous and yet influenced each other, contact must be brought about either by means of emanations or through a medium. In his *Little Treatise* Hobbes stoutly defended a theory of species, according to which small particles are emitted from the agent which move across space to the patient. In his later *Tractatus Opticus* he changed his mind on this point and maintained a mediumistic theory. Contiguous movement could thus be carried over from agent to patient as if people went about with invisible antennae projecting from their sense organs. Air, water, glass, or crystal were examples of media of different degrees of density. Hobbes continued to hold this mediumistic theory in *De Corpore*. All his attempts to demonstrate the impossibility of action at a distance *presupposed* that bodies with empty space between them could not influence each other.

Hobbes, however, assumed not only contact between bodies but also the transmission of *motion* in order for causal interaction to take place. 'Whatsoever is at rest, will always be at rest, unless there be some other body besides it, which, by endeavouring to

1. See *supra*, pp. 67-8.   2. E.W. I, 124.

get into its place by motion, suffers it no longer to remain at rest.'[1] Hobbes sought to establish this by assuming the very point at issue – that there can be no reason within a body at rest for its movement. If a body at rest in empty space initiated its own movements it 'would be moved alike all ways at once; which is impossible'.[2] Similarly, 'whatsoever is moved, will always be moved, except there be some other body beside it, which causeth it to rest',[3] and 'whatsoever is moved, will always be moved on in the same way and with the same velocity, except it be hindered by some other contiguous and moved body'.[4] Hobbes was here merely stating part of the principle of inertia first formulated by Galileo with regard to horizontal motion, that a body once in motion continues to move with the same velocity and in the same direction unless some force acts upon it. Galileo abandoned the traditional dichotomy between motion and rest and, by distinguishing instead between accelerated and uniform motion, he had been able to treat rest as a limiting case of uniform motion. This advance made by Galileo was unquestionably the source of Hobbes' inspiration that all change was a change in motion; but it is questionable whether Hobbes really understood the details of Galileo's treatment of inertia.[5] His attempt to prove that all mutation is motion was singularly unconvincing.

The importance of Hobbes' principle that 'there can be no cause of motion, except in a body contiguous and moved', in its application to man as well as to nature, cannot be over-emphasized. The traditional Aristotelian view was that everything moved towards its natural end or final cause in its natural place and in accordance with its formal cause or law of development. The earth was the centre of rather an intimate world in which everything had its due place in a hierarchical system existing for the glory of God and to provide a theatre for man's endeavours. Hobbes remarked briefly and baldly: 'A final cause has no place but in such things as have sense and will; and this also I shall prove hereafter to be an efficient cause.'[6] This was the death-knell of the Aristotelian world-view. As Brandt puts it: 'It is

1. E.W. I, 115.   3. E.W. I, 115.   5. See Brandt, op. cit., pp. 282–5.
2. E.W. I, 115.   4. E.W. I, 125.   6. E.W. I, 132.

curious to read these few lines about final causes; on his Aristotelian contemporaries they must have had the effect of the blow of a bludgeon. A whole world perished with the giving up of the final causes.'[1] In its place Hobbes conceived a world of bodies composed of particles, moved by other bodies and other particles. The appearances of nature which stimulated the artist and haunted the poet were phantasms in bodies whose peculiarity consisted in having in themselves the patterns of almost all things. But phantasms themselves were but motions produced by other motions and producing the motions of animal bodies. . . .

In the transition from mechanics to what Hobbes called physics and moral philosophy the concept of 'conatus' or 'endeavour' was most important. He defined 'endeavour' as 'motion made in less space and time than can be given; . . . that is, motion made through the length of a point, and in an instant or point of time'.[2] The quantity or velocity of endeavour Hobbes called 'impetus' – 'the swiftness or velocity of the body moved, but considered in the several points of that time in which it is moved'.[3] In brief, the term 'endeavour' was used to designate *infinitely small* motions. Hobbes took over the term from the physical scientists and generalized its application to bridge the gaps between physics, physiology and psychology. As Brandt has so painstakingly shown,[4] the term was used for the internal beginnings of animal motions in Hobbes' early *Elements of Law* in order to bring out the analogy between appetite and impulse to motion. In the *Tractatus Opticus* he expanded the concept to denote the beginnings of motion in the mediumistic process from the object of sense to the brain, which transmitted pressure. In both these cases minute motions were postulated. In a later optical treatise in criticism of Descartes, the term appeared again to denote the property of a body in virtue of which it falls to the earth or would fall to the earth if it ceased to be suspended. In *De Corpore* weight and equiponderation were defined by conatus – weight, for instance, being 'the aggregate of all the endeavours, by which all the points of

1. Brandt, op. cit., p. 290.   2. E.W. I, 206.   3. E.W. I, 207.

4. Brandt, op. cit., pp. 300–15, to which this account of 'endeavour' is greatly indebted.

that body, which presses the beam, tend downwards in lines parallel to one another'.[1] Bodies seemingly at rest really have motion, albeit an infinitely small or conatus motion. Pressure and resistance were similarly defined by conatus.[2] All distance effects like light and sound were explained by the propagation of conatus motions in a medium. Hobbes also used the conatus concept to give an account of appetite and aversion. Thus, to quote Brandt: 'The conatus concept enters freely into Hobbes' collective endeavour to understand everything by motion. What is common to the different uses of the conatus concept is merely this that it refers to very small motions; it is therefore used in apparently widely different domains. . . . Endeavour attributed to heavy bodies by the ancients, as their "appetitus", "explaining" gravitation, is by Hobbes conceived as motion itself. . . . In the kinetic endeavour we have Hobbes' purpose with the conatus concept. By means of this he succeeds in understanding a multiplicity of phenomena kinetically, phenomena which either seem quite withdrawn from motion, such as the static phenomena, or which might perhaps be understood as motions, but as infinitely small motions such as the act of illuminating, perception, the nerve processes, appetite, etc., –'.[3]

'Endeavour' was the bridging concept which enabled Hobbes to describe human behaviour in terms of his general theory of motion. External objects working on the organs of sense produce not only phantasms, but also what Hobbes called 'animal motions'. 'For seeing in all sense of external things there is mutual action and reaction, that is, two endeavours opposing one another, it is manifest that the motion of both of them together will be continued every way, especially to the confines of both the bodies.'[4] This motion from the sense organs proceeds to the heart and makes some alteration or diversion of vital motion, the motion of the blood. When it helps the vital motion we experience pleasure; when it hinders it, we experience pain. If vital motion is helped by the motion made by sense, the body will be guided in such a way as to preserve that motion. 'And in animal motion this is the very

1. E.W. I, 351. 3. Brandt, op. cit., pp. 313–14.
2. E.W. I, 211. 4. E.W. I, 405.

first endeavour, and found even in the embryo; which while it is in the womb, moveth its limbs with voluntary motion, for the avoiding of whatsoever troubleth it and for pursuing of what pleaseth it. And this first endeavour, when it tends towards such things as are known by experience to be pleasant, is called appetite, that is, an approaching; and when it shuns what is troublesome, aversion, or flying from it.'[1] Appetite and aversion are thus the first endeavours of animal motion. The postulation of these minute movements in the bodies of animals and men made the suggestion plausible that human action as well as the movement of projectiles can be explained mechanically. After all men move towards and away from objects and each other. And just as there are minute incipient movements involved in resistance, weight, and pressure even though no gross movements of the body are visible, so also a human body, though seemingly immobile, is the vehicle of myriads of minute movements. 'These small beginnings of motion, within the body of man, before they appear in walking, speaking, striking, and other visible actions, are commonly called ENDEAVOUR.'[2] Even its habits are nothing but motions made more easy and ready by perpetual and repeated endeavours in a way that is different from the motion that was natural to it originally; they are comparable to the bend of a cross-bow.

Hobbes left the details of human psychology to the second work in his trilogy, the *De Homine*. In *De Corpore* he outlined only the general principles of animal psychology, men only differing from animals in their ability to impose names and, in their disinterested curiosity, their desire to know the causes of things. For animals deliberate like men and have will or the appetite that emerges after a process of deliberation. Their motions towards or away from objects are not started just by contact via sense organs but also by images or conceptions which are 'nothing but motion in the head'. These give rise to passions which are pleasures or pains which 'arise from the expectation, that proceeds from foresight of the end or consequence of things; whether those things in the sense please or displease'.[3] Passions are pleasure or displeasure that men have from opinion of their power. 'So that in the first

1. E.W. I, 407.　　2. E.W. III, 39.　　3. E.W. III, 43.

place, I put for a general inclination of all mankind, a perpetual and restless desire of power after power, that ceaseth only in death.'[1] The prospect of the cessation of vital motions in death arouses the most violent aversion of all and leads men to construct the state. Motions of the mind are thus the causes of the artificial human association called the state just as motions of points and lines are the causes of geometrical figures. Motion, too, permeates Hobbes' description of social life. Life is a race with no other goal but being foremost. There can be 'no contentment but in proceeding'.[2] Liberty is 'an absence of the lets and hindrances of motion'.[3] Individual differences in wits are due to differences in quickness or 'swift succession of one thought to another'.[4] Life itself is 'but a motion of limbs';[5] there can be 'no such thing as perpetual tranquillity of mind, while we live here; because life itself is but motion, and can never be without desire, nor without fear, no more than without sense'.[6] Hobbes has often been called a materialist; but he is more aptly described as the great metaphysician of motion.

4. Body and Accident

'Every thing is eyther Substance or Accident,'[7] said Hobbes at the beginning of his *Little Treatise*. 'Substance' he defined in the traditional manner as 'a ground, a base, anything that hath existence or subsistence in itself'.[8] 'Body . . . is that substance which hath magnitude indeterminate and is the same with corporeal substance; but a body is that which hath magnitude determinate, and consequently is understood to be totum or integrum aliquid.'[9] The definition of 'body' in *De Corpore* is 'that which having no dependence upon our thought, is coincident and coextended with some part of space'.[10] Bodies need not be visible; indeed bodies which were understood by reason rather than actually observed played a very important part in his explanations. For 'endeavours' were movements of such minute un-

1. E.W. III, 85-6. 4. E.W. III, 56. 7. El. of L., p. 153. 9. E.W. IV, 309.
2. E.W. IV, 33. 5. E.W. III, ix. 8. E.W. IV, 308. 10. E.W. I, 102.
3. E.W. II, 120. 6. E.W. III, 51.

observable bodies. Of course the ordinary man calls something a body which he can touch or see; but he had not achieved scientific understanding.

Hobbes maintained that there was nothing else in the world but bodies. How, then, did he deal with the claims of theologians that there are spirits or incorporeal substances also? In *Leviathan* Hobbes boldly equated 'substance' with 'body' and did not flinch at the logical consequence of this – that 'substance incorporeal' is a contradiction in terms.[1] God may be a spirit. But that does not entail that he is an *incorporeal* substance. Indeed he must have a subtle, fluid, and invisible body. For was it not recorded that the Spirit of God moved upon the face of the waters, which attributes motion and place to God – characterizations intelligible only when applied to bodies? To Bishop Bramhall's question what he took God to be, Hobbes replied categorically: 'I answer, I leave him to be a most pure, simple, invisible, spirit corporeal.'[2]

By 'accident' Hobbes meant a property or characteristic. It is misleading, he says, to call properties *parts* of things; rather 'they answer best that define an accident to be the manner by which any body is conceived'.[3] To view an accident as part of a thing would be to assimilate the relation between redness and blood to that between blood and a bloody cloth, which would be to make the accident another body. Everyone, including Aristotle, has an intuitive understanding of how magnitude and motion can be in that which is great or moved without being part of it. Most accidents can be absent without the body also perishing. The exceptions are extension and figure. For if these were to be taken away, the body also would perish. All other accidents are appearances either of motions of the mind of the perceiver or of the bodies themselves which are perceived.

This account of accident was a weak point in Hobbes' philosophy; for his definition of accident as 'the manner by which any body is conceived' overlooked the status of extension and figure which was quite different from that of all other accidents. For these are defining attributes of 'body'; whereas motion and rest

1. E.W. III, 381.   2. E.W. IV, 313.   3. E.W. I, 103.

seem to have the same status as accidents like colour and hardness. Presumably Hobbes meant that extension and figure are alone 'necessary accidents' of body because a body could be conceived without motion and colour, but not without extension and figure. But if the criterion is one of *conceivability* what is the status of colour? For, as Berkeley remarked later, it is no more possible to conceive of something with shape and no colour than it is possible to conceive of something with colour and no shape. Hobbes did not even seem to be consistent in his opinion. For he says in the same passage: 'And as for the opinion that some may have, that all other accidents are not in their bodies in the same manner that extension, motion, rest or figure, are in the same; for example, that colour, heat, odour, virtue, vice, and the like, are otherwise in them, and, as they say, inherent: I desire they would suspend their judgement for the present, and expect a little, till it be found out by ratiocination, whether these very accidents are not also certain motions either of the mind of the perceiver, or of the bodies themselves which are perceived; for in search of this a great part of natural philosophy consists.'[1] Here extension, motion, rest and figure are classed together and contrasted with secondary qualities like colour, heat and odour. This was the usual distinction made by Galileo, Descartes and others, between the primary qualities which were thought to be real characterizations of objects and secondary qualities which were thought of as being subjective appearances due to the interaction of the object with the percipient. We have seen[2] how Hobbes and Descartes came independently to believe in the subjectivity of secondary qualities like colour, heat and odour. In Part IV of *De Corpore* a whole chapter (XXVII) is devoted to light, heat and colour, and an attempt is made to give a mechanical explanation of them in terms of bodies characterized by primary qualities.

The explanation of this lack of consistency in Hobbes' treatment is probably that he never seriously questioned the underlying assumptions of the new science of motion. He accepted without question the underlying presupposition that the real world was characterized only by those qualities, called the primary ones,

1. E.W. I, 104–5.   2. See *supra*, pp. 27–8.

which were susceptible to *mathematical* treatment in the sciences of geometry and mechanics. They are also qualities which are accessible through more than one sense modality. This methodological convenience, which was his underlying criterion of distinction, was exalted by all members of the new movement into a metaphysical postulate about the reality behind the appearances. But he, like Descartes and Locke, got into difficulties when he tried to rationalize this criterion in terms of the *conceivability* of bodies with some qualities rather than with others. For his underlying concept of 'body' was that *defined* by the postulates of the mathematical sciences. As soon as he started bringing in questions of conceivability the common-sense notion of body insinuated itself with ensuing havoc to the unassailable status of the scientist's 'body'. Berkeley was later to take his stand on common-sense criteria and to attack the assumptions of the physical scientists which were really definitions and methodological conveniences masquerading as metaphysics. Modern philosophy stemming from Berkeley has shown the muddles that arise if a concept of common sense is not distinguished from a concept of an exact science.

5. Space and Time

Hobbes had defined body as 'that, which having no dependence upon our thought, is coincident or co-extended with some part of space'.[1] From this we would expect him to hold that space, like body, existed independently of our conceptions. Yet he speaks constantly of space as a 'phantasm'. He defines space as 'the phantasm of a thing existing without the mind simply'.[2] By this he meant that what we call space is the appearance of externality. He maintained that it was a phantasm because if the world of physical things were to be destroyed and a man were to be left alone with his imaginations and memories, some of these would appear external to him, or located in space, which must therefore be a subjective frame of reference. This conviction is reinforced by the consideration that 'when we calculate the magnitude and motions of heaven or earth, we do not ascend into heaven that we may divide it into parts, or measure the motions thereof, but we do it sitting still in our closets, or in the dark'.[1] In other words though bodies exist independently of us and are external to us or located in space, the system of co-ordinates we use to describe their relative positions is a subjective framework. 'Place is nothing out of the mind nor magnitude anything within it.'[2] A body always keeps the same magnitude, whether moved or at rest, but when it is moved it does not keep the same place. Place cannot therefore be an accident of body. Place is feigned or imagined extension – an order of position constructed out of our experience of real extended things to provide a framework of externality for them. Our concept of space is thus an abstraction from our experience of bodies which have real rather than feigned extension.

Time is treated in a similar manner. It is 'the phantasm of before and after in motion'.[3] Bodies leave ideas of their motion as well as of their extension in consciousness. Out of our experience of succession or 'before and after in motion' we construct time systems, in which we make use of the movement of the sun or of hands round a clock. Hobbes' treatment of time was even more sketchy than his treatment of space, and suffered from a similar defect. For Hobbes never made clear the relationship between the subjective frames of spatio-temporal reference within which any particular individual orders what he experiences (psychological space) and the co-ordinate systems constructed by physical scientists. It may well be the case that what we call space and time are abstractions from our experience of extended bodies in motion. But what is the relationship between such private frames of reference which are notoriously unreliable and the dependable inter-subjective constructs of the scientist? Hobbes typically failed to see the philosophical problem suggested by his treatment. His view of space and time was subsidiary to and a way of restating his dominant conviction that the real world was composed only of extended bodies in motion.

This somewhat cursory and cryptic treatment of space and time illustrates well the problems which Hobbes' philosophy of

1. E.W. I, 92.   2. E.W. I, 105.   3. E.W. I, 95.

nature and mind present to a philosopher. He was fascinated by sensation and imagery – especially because some bodies 'have in themselves the patterns almost of all things'; yet he never bothered to make clear whether such mental apparitions were themselves motions of the brain or merely accompaniments of such motions. Still less did he ask himself what kind of relationship held between such appearances and the external things of which they were appearances. He held that all thoughts were images and yet he assumed that the images of bodies in motion really represented bodies in motion whereas images of colours, sounds and other secondary qualities were only subjective appearances. Both types of images were causally explicable in terms of antecedent motions transmitted from the external world to the brain. Some of these, when names were fixed to them, led to science as opposed to prudence. Yet scientific truth depended upon the correct use of names almost cut adrift from its origin in sense experience. In his science of nature he presupposed that all mutation was motion and that there was no action at a distance, the causal relation holding only between bodies contiguous and moved; yet all his attempts to prove these assumptions presupposed them. The transition from mechanics to physiology was accomplished by a generalized use of the notion of 'endeavour' – a good illustration of Hobbes' tendency to tear terms out of technical contexts and to use them to bridge gaps in his speculative scheme. This tendency was further exemplified in his dubious transition from physiology to psychology by use of a terminology of motion which, because of its twofold interpretation, obscured the jumps which he was in fact making. His account of accident was slipshod and suffered from a confusion of the concepts of science with those of common sense. His account of space and time suffered from a similar failure to relate the subjective frameworks of private experience to the complicated constructs of physical science, and from his more general failure to bridge the gap between what appears to sense and what is rationally reconstructed.

These defects in his treatment justify and illustrate the suggestion that Hobbes was the great metaphysician of the new science

of motion in that his *De Corpore* admirably illustrates 'the utilization of specific notions, applying to a restricted group of facts, for
the divination of the generic notions which apply to all facts'.
Fired by his imaginative idea of extending the science of motion
into geometry and civil philosophy he could not help taking for
granted the basic assumptions of the new science of motion whose
details he probably understood but imperfectly. He thus presupposed that the real world was a world of bodies in motion; that
the secondary qualities, because mathematically intractable, were
subjective appearances of the underlying primary ones; that all
causal relations held between bodies contiguous and moved; that
extension and figure were the only defining properties of body.
This unquestioning acceptance of the presuppositions of Galilean
mechanics accounts for many of Hobbes' philosophical defects.
Most of his other defects derive from his extrapolation of the
concepts of the new science to spheres where their applicability
is dubious or trivial. There is of course a sense in which life is
motion of the limbs; but there is also a sense in which work is
moving bodies about and love is motion of the heart, lips, and
sexual organs. But are such descriptions particularly illuminating?
They only become so if they lead to a detailed theory which has
important and novel deductive consequences. Hobbes never produced such a theory. Instead he produced a redescription of what
we already know in rather a bizarre terminology or descriptions
which seem absurd because of the inapplicability of mechanical
concepts. Certainly his enthusiastic diffusion of the concepts of
mechanics involved him in the dubious extension of the term
'endeavour' to bridge the gap between minute motions and
animal strivings; it also occasioned a cavalier disregard for
whether thoughts and feelings were motions of the brain and
corporeal organs or just accompaniments of them, a disregard
that was fostered by his terminology of movement. In general
such an extension of the concepts of a science, without developing
another science for the new sphere covered by the extrapolation,
will lead to constant perplexities created by the clash between the
technical meaning of terms and their common-sense usage. This
is particularly in evidence in Hobbes' treatment of 'body' and

its 'accidents' and in his tantalizing treatment of space and time which even won the admiration of Leibniz, who remarked of Hobbes, 'What a man!'

And Leibniz's reaction is perhaps the appropriate one to Hobbes' achievement. Many are disappointed, on reading him, that he did not develop some of his insights in more detail and that he did not see some of the philosophical problems they suggested. But Hobbes lived at a time when a new world-view was dawning and when it was exciting as well as dangerous to be abreast of novel speculations. Men did not then know enough to be specialists and discussions in philosophy were not cut short by the plea that a scientific and not a philosophical problem was being raised. Hobbes applied himself with a robust versatility to problems in logic and epistemology, optics, mechanics, physics, physiology, psychology, ethics, politics and jurisprudence, and speculated about the connecting links between them. This is what makes his very failure to see what later generations have called 'philosophical problems' in some ways so refreshing.

95

CHAPTER 4

SENSE AND IMAGINATION

Introductory

H o b b e s' treatment of sensation and imagery reflected his major interests. He never attempted an exhaustive psychological examination of the different sensory mechanisms or types of imagery. He disregarded cheerfully the philosophical perplexities connected with sensation which were later to fascinate Locke, Berkeley and Hume. His disjointed and often rather cryptic remarks on the subject were designed mainly to show that both sensation and imagery could be explained in terms of the theory of motion and to exhibit in more detail the wonder of apparition – 'that some natural bodies have in themselves the patterns almost of all things'. Having indicated the representative function of sensation and imagery he usually passed to his theory of speech to show that there is a form of representation peculiar to man and to indicate how it is related to that which we share with animals.

The search for the causes of sensation, imagery, and speech unified his treatment. But it led him to neglect the crucial logical problems of how 'apparition' can be said to *represent* bodies and how words *refer* to that which is not verbal. In other words Hobbes gave a *causal* theory of sensation and meaning and often spoke as if he was solving the *logical* problems involved. The result is stimulating to psychologists; indeed many of his speculations have a distinctly modern ring about them. But philosophers find his suggestions tantalizingly undeveloped and often conclude, to quote a modern critic,[1] that Hobbes, 'as well as a great political thinker, was an interesting minor philosopher'. This verdict on

1. A. Flew in a broadcast talk printed in the *Listener*, 15 November 1951.

Hobbes is also a comment on the modern philosophical attitude to politics.

1. Sense

To explain sense in terms of the new theory of motion, Hobbes had both to describe sensory processes in mechanical terms and to show that smells, colours, sounds and other secondary qualities were really appearances of the movements of bodies. He therefore proclaimed boldly that 'we have discovered the nature of sense, namely, that it is some internal motion in the sentient'.[1] The external body presses the organ proper to each sense, either immediately as in taste or touch, or through a medium as in seeing, hearing, and smelling, '. . . which pressure, by the mediation of the nerves, and other strings and membranes of the body, continued inwards to the brain and heart, causeth there a resistance, or counter-pressure, or endeavour of the heart to deliver itself, which endeavour, because outward, seemeth to be some matter without'.[2] All sense qualities 'are in the object, that causeth them, but so many several motions of the matter, by which it presseth our organs diversely. Neither in us that are pressed, are they anything else, but divers motions; for motion produceth nothing but motion'.[3] These motions appear to us as fancy 'the same waking, that dreaming'. Although they are nothing but motions in some internal substance of the head, they have the character of externality because of the outward endeavour of the heart. The definition of sense is therefore 'a phantasm, made by the reaction and endeavour outwards in the organ of sense, caused by an endeavour inwards from the object, remaining for some time more or less'.[4]

These descriptions provided only a general framework for a mechanical theory, but they limited the sort of explanation which it was possible for Hobbes to give of some of the more obvious characteristics of perception as we experience it. And some of these are bound to prove troublesome for any such mechanical theory; for when we perceive something, it is not just an atomic

1. E.W. I, 390.   2. E.W. III, 2.   3. E.W. III, 2.   4. E.W. I, 391.

event initiated by an external stimulus. There is always an element of recognition in perception; we select and group what is before us in the light of our past experience and present interests. Hobbes tried to account for recognition and selectivity in mechanical terms. Perception, he said, is not a simple reaction of bodies. If it were so, all bodies that react would have sense, a theory that some philosophers have actually suggested. But a simple reaction requires the constant presence of the object to which the reaction is made. The phantasm, if it could be produced by the reaction of an inanimate body, would cease as soon as the object was removed. Sense organs relieve us from the necessity of constant contact; for they act as retainers for the movements of external bodies which bump into us and pass on their way. Without such retention of motions what we call sense would be impossible; for 'by sense we commonly understand the judgement we make of objects by their phantasms; namely, by comparing and distinguishing those phantasms; which we could never do, if that motion in the organ, by which the phantasm is made, did not remain there for some time, and make the same phantasm return'.[1] Sense has therefore always 'some memory adhering to it' which permits comparison and discrimination.

Selectivity, too, is shown in perception; for, though sensory discrimination would be impossible without a constant variety of phantasms, the nature of sense is such that it does not permit a man to discern many things at once. 'For seeing the nature of sense consists in motion; as long as the organs are employed about one object, they cannot be so moved by another at the same time, as to make by both their motions one sincere phantasm of each of them at once.'[2] Two objects working together will produce one compounded phantasm rather than two separate ones. But why is one object rather than another selected from amongst the many possible objects that could be perceived on any occasion? Hobbes said nothing of the interests and attitudes which predispose us to see some things rather than others. Indeed his ideo-motor theory made it very difficult for him to do so; for according to this theory all reactions of organisms are initiated by external stimuli, and

1. E.W. I, 393.　　　　2. E.W. I, 394.

the theory had not, in the seventeenth century, developed the degree of sophistication necessary to speak of stimuli from the 'internal environment' of an organism. If reactivity is made subordinate to sensitivity, it is very difficult to do justice to the selecting and grouping of stimuli. Sensation is made to look like an automatic registering of stimuli on a photographic plate instead of like the active ranging of a search-light.

Hobbes also attempted a mechanical explanation of the phenomena of attention or concentration. Once a strong action from an external object stirs the sense-organ, the motion from the root of the nerves of the sense-organ to the heart persists contumaciously, and makes the sense-organ impervious to the registering of other motions. 'For study is nothing but a possession of the mind, that is to say, a vehement motion made by some one object in the organs of sense, which are stupid to all other motions as long as this lasteth.'[1] Hobbes illustrated this speculation about the cause of the focus of attention by the dubious example of reading. He claimed that when we read we see the letters successively one by one and not all together, even though the whole page be presented to the eye. When we look at the whole page we read nothing. 'From hence it is manifest, that every endeavour of the organ outwards, is not to be called sense, but that only, which at several times is by vehemence made stronger and more predominant than the rest; which deprives us of the sense of other phantasms, no otherwise than the sun deprives the rest of the stars of light, not by hindering their action, but by obscuring and hiding them with his excess of brightness.'[2]

These rather sketchy remarks about sensation exhibit Hobbes' interest in it as limited to a phenomenon that can be mechanically explained. Like the British Empiricists who followed him, he was a martyr to the current physiological account of sensation according to which objects imprinted themselves on us by isolated, disconnected sorties on our sense-organs. Hobbes ingeniously combined this sort of account with deductions from the theory of motion. It is true that he tried to explain phenomena like attention, selectivity, and the ineradicable intrusion of past experience

1. E.W. I, 395.   2. E.W. I, 396.

into present perceptions. But the limitations of his mechanical hypothesis precluded him from giving these aspects of perception the attention they deserve.

We must now pass to the other facet of Hobbes' limited interest in sensation – his view that secondary qualities were subjective appearances of the movements of bodies having only primary qualities. In his early *Elements of Law* Hobbes stated succinctly, using the example of colour, the main points of his contention:

(1) That the subject wherein colour and image are inherent, is not the object or thing seen.

(2) That that is nothing without us really which we call an image or colour.

(3) That the said image or colour is but an apparition unto us of that motion, agitation or alteration, which the object worketh in the brain or spirits, or some internal substance of the head.

(4) That as in conception by vision, so also in the conceptions that arise from other senses, the subject of their inherence is not the object, but the sentient.[1]

Hobbes produced a string of reasons in the *Elements of Law* to support these contentions and briefly recapitulated them at the start of *Leviathan*. They were singularly unconvincing because Hobbes never quite made clear precisely what they were designed to prove; the result was that they proved too much and too little. The kernel of his claim about secondary qualities was that what seemed to be qualities of objects external to us were in fact only phantasms in our heads *caused* by the primary properties of external objects interacting with our sense-organs but *representing* nothing outside us. He adduced in support of this claim facts like double images, reflections of the sun in water, echoes and light produced by a blow on the optic nerve, which brought out that images may seem to be located where things cannot be; for in some cases there is no thing and in other cases things appear to be in two places at once, which is impossible. Therefore he argued that images and colours were 'inherent in the sentient'. But this proved too much; for our images of reflected suns, stars caused by stimulation of the optic nerve and double images, all have exten-

1. El. of L., p. 3.

sion and motion. In this respect primary qualities are on a par with secondary. If Hobbes' arguments were valid they would support only his thesis that *all* perception was by way of phantasms, that a private picture always intervenes between us and the qualities of the object perceived. In this sense of 'subjective' all qualities are subjective because we are confronted not with them but with their phantasmal representations. As Hobbes himself put it: 'And though at some certain distance, the real and very object seem invested with the fancy it begets in us; yet still the object is one thing, the image or fancy is another.'[1]

Hobbes, however, wished to establish that secondary qualities were subjective in a further sense – the sense in which the distinction between a quality and our representation of a quality cannot be made. For he maintained that in the case of secondary qualities what we call qualities of objects were *only* phantasms in the sentient *caused* by external objects reacting on our sense-organs, but *representing* no qualities of external objects, whereas in the case of primary qualities our phantasms were both caused by and represented qualities external to us. But here his argument proved too little. Tastes, smells and sounds, said Hobbes, appear differently to different sentients. They cannot therefore be properties of the object. But this argument neither proves what it purports to prove nor does it establish any difference between primary and secondary qualities. For it is absurd to make such generalizations about the relativity of perception to the individual percipient without taking into account the conditions of perception and the state of the percipient. All cows look grey in the twilight and there are objective tests for establishing that a man is colour-blind. Also, as Berkeley later insisted, primary qualities are in precisely the same boat. Golf-greens change their shape as we approach them and the movements of a train appear quicker to a man travelling in the opposite direction than to a man on the station. Things appear to pass by more quickly in the dark than in the light and all movement appears slower to a tired man than to a man dosed with benzedrine. The arguments which stress the relativity of secondary as opposed to primary qualities also ignore

1. E.W. III, 2, 3.

the fact that standard conditions can be established for reaching agreement about secondary as well as about primary qualities, in spite of the fact that the primary qualities can be perceived each through more than one modality of sense, thus permitting correlation, for instance between touching and seeing a moving object. How else could there be standard methods of colour matching or how could people make a living by tasting wine and tea or by tuning pianos? It would indeed be very odd if both primary and secondary qualities did *not* in fact appear different to different percipients under different conditions.

Hobbes in fact gave but halting philosophical excuses for a distinction which was embedded in the practice of the physical scientists. He never questioned their basic assumption that bodies in motion exist independently of our perception of them, and that mathematical thinking about them represented their real properties. 'The things that really are in the world without us, are those motions by which these seemings are caused.'[1] The real was what was amenable to mathematical treatment; the convenience of physical science was exalted into a metaphysical dogma. Hobbes produced a kind of philosophical patter while the rabbits of the new science of motion popped out of the hat. He was the arch-metaphysician of motion.

The basic trouble with Hobbes' philosophical arguments was that he never examined the relationship of 'representing' which he presupposed in his wonder that some natural bodies had in themselves the *patterns* of all things. Presumably he thought that there was nothing mysterious about a phantasm, which is a motion in some internal substance of the head, being a pattern of motions in external bodies. He never asked himself, as Berkeley was later to ask Locke, how we could ever know that such a pattern was a correct pattern of an external body if we could never know anything of an external body except by means of our private patterns of it. Hobbes may have thought that as a motion can only produce another motion, so a motion (in this case a phantasm) could never *represent* anything like a colour unless it was also a motion. But it does not seem that he was ever much troubled by

1. El. of L., p. 6.

this kind of problem. He simply developed a *causal theory* of sensation and saw no need for a theory of representation.

Hobbes, therefore, in his theory of phantasms, took the first step down the path that was to be trodden later by so many of his countrymen; but he neither saw nor pursued the implications of his position, and he was led to it by rather different preoccupations. For the conviction of Locke, Berkeley and Hume, that even in sensation we are confronted with our own mental states, derived from epistemological worries about the reliability of *thinking*, which they inherited from Descartes. Descartes was absorbed by the quest for certainty and came to the conclusion that he could be certain only that he was thinking; for it would be self-contradictory to doubt that he was thinking as doubting was *thinking* that he did not think. The implications and influence of his first certainty were enormous. The British Empiricists were constrained by it to believe that they had some kind of certainty about their own mental states and that, provided that they did not pass beyond isolated ideas and make inference about their connexions with other ideas, they had a sure foundation for reliable knowledge. Their interest in sensation was therefore, as Locke put it, to inquire into the 'original, extent, and certainty of human knowledge'. By tracing ideas back to their *origin* in simple sensory impressions they could establish their epistemological credentials. Indeed, Locke defined an idea as 'the object of the understanding when a man *thinks*', and referred to sensations as simple ideas. And, after all, the view is plausible in relation to *thinking* that we are confronted with our own ideas and not with things; for when we think we do seem sometimes to conjure up images or phantasms. If, therefore, the interest is in explaining thinking, the next step is plausible – that images are *copies* or relics of sensations which are *also* shadowy entities intervening between us and objects.

In Hobbes' case, however, it is not clear why he passed so easily into the belief that in sensation a phantasm intervenes between us and objects. For he was unimpressed by Descartes' first certainty and was as much interested in the causes of ideas as in their epistemological credentials. Indeed, he said that the task of physics was to investigate these phantasms which we experience as a result of the outer world impinging on our sense-organs. It seems probable that his main interest in explaining sense lay in giving an account of the conditions in the external world and in the sentient which gave rise to *secondary qualities* which he believed to be subjective. But he could not avoid the conclusion that in the case of primary qualities as well 'the object is one thing, the image or fancy is another'. As is evident from the opening of the *Elements of Law*, and from the passages on heat and light and so on in the fourth part of *De Corpore*, Hobbes was greatly intrigued by current explanations of secondary qualities; it looks as if his interest in physics led him to hold a philosophical position whose difficulties and implications he did not grasp. His was not an unusual predicament.

2. Imagination

The theory of motion was very much in evidence in Hobbes' account of imagination. His explanations of some of its characteristics were deductions from the Law of Inertia, which was stated in general terms at the start of the chapter 'Of Imagination' in *Leviathan*. Unwillingness to accept it was attributed to the projection into nature of man's weariness after a lot of movement – 'little considering, whether it be not some other motion, wherein that desire of rest they find in themselves, consisteth.'[1] The application of the law to the phenomenon of imagination was then made. 'When a body is once in motion, it moveth, unless something else hinder it, eternally; and whatsoever hindreth it, cannot in an instant, but in time, and by degrees, quite extinguish it; and as we see in the water, though the wind cease, the waves give not over rolling for a long time after: so also it happeneth in that motion, which is made in the internal parts of a man, then, when he sees, dreams, etc. For after the object is removed, or the eye shut, we still retain an image of the thing seen, though more obscure than when we see it. . . . IMAGINATION therefore is nothing but decaying sense . . .'[2] This decay in sense is not a decay

1. E.W. III, 4.   2. E.W. III, 4.

in motion; for that would be contrary to the Law of Inertia. Rather it comes about because the sense-organs are moved by other objects 'in such manner as the light of the sun obscureth the light of the stars; which stars do no less exercise their virtue, by which they are visible, in the day than in the night'.[1] Evidence which supports this deduction is that phantasms in dreams are no less clear than in sense itself, the passages of sense being shut up and external actions thus being excluded. When, however, sense impressions are constantly crowding in upon us, the imagination of the past is obscured and 'made weak, as the voice of a man is in the noise of the day'. Thus the longer the time that elapses after sensing an object, the weaker our imagination of it.

The suggestion is made, also, that a mechanical explanation can be given for the more impressive feats of the imagination. Hobbes distinguished simple imagination 'as when one imagineth a man or horse, which he hath seen before' from compounding imagination 'as when, from the sight of a man at one time, and of a horse at another, we conceive in our mind a Centaur'.[2] This he explained as a phenomenon similar to water moved in one motion which is a product of compounding diverse movements.[3] When, too, there has been long and vehement action of sense, as when we gaze steadfastly at the sun or pore over geometrical figures,[4] a peculiarly clear and striking image is formed which stands out clearly even when we lie awake in the dark.

The distinction made by Hobbes between imagination and memory is not altogether satisfactory. When sense is fading, old, and past, he called it memory. 'So that imagination and memory are but one thing.' Memory is an image together with an awareness that we have had the same image before. He compared it to a sixth sense and said explicitly in *De Corpore*: 'But you will say, by what sense shall we take notice of sense? I answer, by sense itself, namely by the memory which for some time remains in us of things sensible, though they themselves pass away. For he that perceives that he hath perceived remembers.'[5] Memory differs from imagination only in that it 'supposeth the time past'.[6]

1. E.W. III, 5. 3. El. of L., p. 8. 5. E.W. I, 389.
2. E.W. III, 6. 4. E.W. III, 6. 6. E.W. I, 398.

Presumably he meant that when we remember as opposed to perceive or imagine something, we have a fading image together with the conviction that we have had this picture before. But how then could a case of memory be distinguished from a case of perceiving for a second time? Suppose that a person walked past a pillar box for the second or third time and had rather a weak impression of it. Could it not be said that he was remembering and not perceiving it? For the weak sensation would be accompanied by the conviction that he had experienced this before. Also if conviction of pastness distinguishes memory from imagination, would we be said to remember a street in a certain town when we were convinced that we had seen it before while all the evidence from our previous travels indicated that we could never have been there?

Many have attempted to give subjective criteria like feelings of pastness, vividness, and order for distinguishing memories from sensations and images. Hume notoriously came to grief in the quicksands of these elusive subjective criteria. All such attempts have proved inadequate to do justice to a distinction which common-sense people handle perfectly well. The reason is, surely, that the distinction is not a psychological one at all. Very probably there are no cut and dried differences in personal experience between perceiving and remembering or between remembering and imagining. The distinction is primarily an epistemological one – between what is asserted when a person claims that he remembers something rather than imagines it or perceives something rather than remembers it. The test of whether a person remembers or imagines is not the subjective conviction of pastness accompanying the imagery, but the evidence which confirms or refutes what is asserted about the relationship between the situation thought about and the thinker's participation in actual events. And to establish whether or not such a relationship holds – whether it *is* a case of remembering rather than of imagining – a person's private conviction is a good guide but an unreliable test.

Perhaps the most interesting aspect of Hobbes' treatment of the imagination was his account of trains of thought. Why is it that one thought is succeeded by another? Hume was later to apply a mechanical model to this process. Ideas, he suggested, were mental atoms bound together by the principles of association in a similar fashion to Newtonian atoms attracted to each other by gravitation. Hobbes, however, for all his devotion to the new sciences, was more influenced in his account by Aristotle than by mechanics. Nevertheless he introduced it in such a way that he made it sound as if it had something to do with the theory of motion. 'In the motion of any continued body,' he said, 'one part follows another cohesion.'[1] Motions which appear as images become predominant in the same order as they were formerly generated by sense '. . . and those motions that immediately succeeded one another in the sense, continue also together after sense: insomuch as the former coming again to take place, and be predominant, the latter followeth, by coherence of the matter moved, in such manner, as water upon a plane table is drawn which way any one part of it is guided by the finger.'[2] But we so often perceive things in different contexts that it is understandable that our thoughts appear to succeed each other in rather a haphazard way. For the other thoughts that succeed them may belong to another context. For instance, if I see a horse and then a plough, I will tend to think of a plough when next the picture of a horse presents itself. But supposing I then see a horse with a cart, it is difficult to predict whether I will think of a plough or of a cart next time I have the picture of a horse.

We should thus not make the mistake of thinking that there is no rhyme or reason in even our most wild ranging of the mind, to use Hobbes' expression. 'For in a discourse of our present civil war, what could seem more impertinent, than to ask, as one did, what was the value of a Roman penny? Yet the coherence to me was manifest enough. For the thought of the war, introduced the thought of the delivering up the King to his enemies; the thought of that, brought in the thought of the delivering up of Christ; and that again the thought of the thirty pence, which was the price of that treason; and thence easily followed that malicious question, and all this in a moment of time; for thought is quick.'[3] This kind of sequence of thoughts Hobbes called 'unguided' because it lacked a passionate thought to govern and direct those that

1. E.W. I, 398.   2. E.W. III, 11, 12.   3. E.W. III, 12, 13.

followed. He did not use the phrase 'association of ideas' to describe the dependence of one thought on another; neither did he attempt to state principles like those of similarity, and spatio-temporal contiguity which many have thought to be implicit in it. He had the insight to see that such trains of thought are un-important in comparison with those regulated by some desire or design. For a seventeenth-century thinker it would have required something akin to clairvoyance or pre-cognition to suggest that even apparently wild rangings of the mind were controlled by desire. For at this period it was unthinkable that a desire could be unconscious. Too many people criticize Aristotle and Aquinas for not having read Darwin, and Hobbes and Hume for ignoring Freud.

Hobbes' account of regulated thinking owed a lot to and was an improvement on Aristotle's analysis of deliberation. Desire for an end holds the train of thought together and determines the relevance of its content. Hobbs suggested that the strength of the attraction of the end is so great that it not only prevents our thoughts from wandering but sometimes even prevents or hinders our sleep. There are two main types of regulated thinking. One is the classic Aristotelian type where desire provides us with an end and we work backwards with the planning of means until we come to an action which it is in our power to perform here and now. Hobbes instanced searching the mind for a place to begin looking for something that has been lost, 'or as a spaniel ranges the field, till he finds a scent; or as a man should run over the alphabet, to start a rhyme'.[1] This search for the means of produc-ing an end or faculty of invention is shared by the animals. Man, however, is alone capable of the other kind of regulated thinking which Hobbes called prudence. For animals have no curiosity – only sensual passions like hunger, thirst, lust, and anger. In prudence we do not work from an end but start from an action within our power and use our store of past experience to speculate about its probable effects. 'As he that foresees what will become of a criminal, reasons what he hath seen follow on the like crime before; having this order of thoughts, the crime, the officer, the

1. E.W. III, 14.

prison, the judge, and the gallows.'[1] Deliberation in this case leads on to an end which is either desired or feared.

This is a very valuable addition to Aristotle's analysis; for he pictured people going about their lives with premeditated ends to lure them and to guide their deliberation. This is only half the story; for too often we cannot act like chess-players planning means to independently premeditated ends. Rather we are confronted by situations in which, regrettably, we have to act; our deliberation consists in gloomily working out which of the actions possible in the circumstances is likely to have the least disastrous consequences. Hobbes seemed to think that people will be more prudent in proportion to the amount of past experience which they are able to use. This sounds improbable; for though few children are prudent, many old people miss the relevance of their past experience. Perhaps this suggestion is a recrudescence of the quantitative symptoms of his mechanical theory; or possibly he meant that much past experience was a necessary though not a sufficient condition of prudence – a plausible suggestion in the light of Hobbes' statement in *The Elements of Law* that 'PRU-DENCE is nothing else but conjecture from experience, or taking signs of experience *warily*. . . .'[2]

Dreams were the other phenomena of the imagination which interested Hobbes. He was intrigued by the characteristics which distinguished them from the thoughts of waking life and stimulated to give an explanation of them – if possible a mechanical one. He thought, firstly, that dreams lacked coherence and order, the explanation of this being that we lack thought of an end in sleep which might hold them together. Secondly, we dream of nothing but what is compounded and made up of the phantasms of sense past. The explanation of this was 'that in the silence of sense there is no new motion from the objects, and therefore no new phantasm, unless we call that new, which is compounded of old ones, as a chimera, a golden mountain, and the like'.[3] Thirdly, dreams are clearer than the imaginations of waking men, 'except such as are made by sense itself'. There are two causes of this phenomenon: the predominance of the internal motion which

1. E.W. III, 14, 15.   2. El. of L., p. 12 (my italics).   3. E.W. I, 400.

makes the phantasm in the absence of external stimulation, and the making up with 'other fictitious parts' of the parts of our phantasms which are decayed and worn out by time. Fourthly, when we dream we 'admire neither the places nor the looks of the things that appear to us'.[1] Neither is our wonder aroused at finding ourselves in a strange place without consciousness of how we came there. This is because wonder presupposes comparison with the past whereas in sleep all things appear as if they were present. Fifthly, we never remark on the absurdity of waking life in dreams as we remark on the absurdity of dreams in waking life. When we are awake we seldom think that we are dreaming, but when we are dreaming we always think that we are awake.

Hobbes maintained that there was an intimate connexion between dreams and bodily states. Lying cold produces dreams of fear and raises up the image of a fearful object. The motion from the brain to the inner parts and from the inner parts to the brain is reciprocal. So just as anger causes heat in some parts of the body, so when we sleep the overheating of the same parts causes anger, and produces the picture of an enemy in the brain. Our dreams are thus the reverse of our waking imaginations. Motion begins at one end when we are awake and at the other end when we are asleep.

This tendency to project images which are produced by bodily states gives rise to belief in apparitions and visions. If we always undressed and went to sleep in our beds all would be well; for we would not be so likely under these conditions to believe that when we had dreamed we had been doing anything other than dream. But people tend to drop off while sitting fully clothed in chairs and other cold places. They then have fearsome dreams and mistake their dream for an apparition. Marcus Brutus' vision on the night before Philippi is a good example. 'For sitting in his tent, pensive and troubled with the horror of his rash act, it was not hard for him, slumbering in the cold, to dream of that which most affrighted him; which fear, as by degrees it made him wake, so also it must needs make the apparition by degrees to vanish; and having no assurance that he slept, he could have no cause to think

1. E.W. I, 400.

it a dream, or any thing but a vision.'[1] Other tales of ghosts are similarly explicable; stories spread and our strong imagery in the dark is enhanced by fear.

Hobbes' treatment of dreams and apparitions typified his restless curiosity and tough-mindedness. The philosophical tradition stemming from Descartes became preoccupied with the epistemological status of dreaming in so far as it cast doubts on the trustworthiness of everyday experience. Hobbes took dreams for what every man knows them to be and concentrated on explaining their peculiarities.

1. E.W. III, 9.

CHAPTER 5

SPEECH

Introductory

HOBBES' interest in and attitude to speech was epitomized in his famous epigram: 'For words are wise men's counters, they do but reckon by them; but they are the money of fools, that value them by the authority of an Aristotle, a Cicero, or a Thomas, or any other doctor whatsoever, if but a man.'[1] This occurs in a passage whose theme is that the extremes of wisdom and folly are only open to the literate. 'Natural sense and imagination are not subject to absurdity.' Speech is a dangerous gift. For if it is properly used with due regard to definitions, it is the gateway to certain knowledge and even to civil peace. But if it is improperly used, as by the philosophers of the Schools, it generates absurdities and a type of danger to peace of which no unlettered man would be capable.

We have already had occasion to explain and comment on Hobbes' positive claim that definition is the gateway to wisdom and civil peace.[2] In this chapter we shall be concerned mainly with Hobbes' interest in speech as a source of absurdity. For the questions he raised about speech were limited by his interests. And these were mainly polemical. He wished to fashion a theory of speech which was consistent with the practice of the physical scientists and which could be used as a weapon to expose the absurdities of the Aristotelian metaphysicians of the Schools. In this he was a precursor of the empiricist school of philosophy in this country whose theory of meaning has tended to be modelled on the logical behaviour of low-level scientific terms and for whom

1. E.W. III, 25.
2. See *supra*, pp. 52–8.

the theories of metaphysicians have provided generations of ghosts to be exorcized by linguistic analysis.

Most prominent amongst the cherished doctrines of the Schools was the theory of universals which, according to Hobbes, encouraged belief in mysterious entities and so perpetuated the superstitious hold of the Catholic Church on the minds of men. 'It is to this purpose, that men may no longer suffer themselves to be abused, by them, that by this doctrine of *separated essences*, built on the vain philosophy of Aristotle, would fright them from obeying the laws of their country with empty names; as men fright birds from the corn with an empty doublet, a hat, and a crooked stick. For it is upon this ground, that when a man is dead and buried, they say his soul, that is his life, can walk separated from his body, and is seen by night amongst the graves. Upon the same ground they say, that the figure, and colour, and taste of a piece of bread, has a being, there, where they say there is no bread. And upon the same ground they say, that faith, and wisdom, and other virtues, are sometimes *poured* into a man, sometimes *blown* into him from Heaven, as if the virtuous and their virtues could be asunder; and a great many other things that serve to lessen the dependence of subjects on the sovereign power of their country.'[1]

1. The Theory of Universals

Hobbes contrived to make the doctrine of essences sound so ridiculous that it is difficult to see how its numerous supporters thought that anything was explained by means of it. To understand why it exerted so much influence we must see how it arose in the context of Greek thought and how people came to think that to find the essence of something was the only method of explaining its behaviour.

The Greeks had a passionate desire to understand the world in which they lived and a conviction that things were not as complicated and complex as they seemed. In their drama they suggested that the vagaries of human destiny were governed by rules laid down by the gods – e.g. that men who get too prosperous tend to

1. E.W. III, 674, 5.

commit some arrogant act which is a turning point, ushering in the doom which inevitably overtakes them. Their speculations about the world were also characterized by this search for the One in the Many. Thales, for instance, suggested that everything in the world was a manifestation of water; Heraclitus put the case for fire. A more fruitful suggestion was that the differences in nature as it appeared to the senses were due to different mathematical combinations of the underlying homogeneous atoms or units. This speculation was later to prove the guiding inspiration of the post-Renaissance physical scientists, including Hobbes himself.

There was, however, another manifestation of this preoccupation with generality, for which Socrates achieved fame. When we describe things and situations we use terms like 'courage', 'justice', and 'love' which seem applicable to different situations. Often we misunderstand each other because we use these terms in slightly different ways. Socrates tried to discover the rationale underlying the use of the same word to describe different situations. Now Plato seems to have combined the Socratic search for definitions with the insight of the early Greek scientists. For he thought that the search for definitions would reveal the 'Forms' or 'essences' to the intellect and that these were also the One in the Many. In other words, not only do we know the true meaning of a term like 'bed', 'man', 'state', or 'courage' when we grasp intellectually certain essential characteristics which permit the general terms to apply to all the instances; but also these 'Forms' or 'essences' are the One in the Many, the explanatory principles of particular things. They 'participate' in the world of appearances which is also a copy of and a degeneration from them.

Aristotle modified this model of explanation in so far as he maintained the essences were not separable, except in thought, from the particulars. But he developed in much more detail what was implicit in Plato's theory, that to give a definition in terms of essence of a thing is to explain why things are as they are and behave as they do. Hence the great importance of essences in Aristotelian thought. The mathematical road of the atomists to the One in the Many was rejected; instead, science must aim at a vast catalogue consisting in definitions of all essences – i.e. names of *infinae species* like 'man' or 'horse' plus their defining formulae. Explanation of the behaviour of a thing consisted in looking up the essential properties of the natural kind or class of things to which it belonged. Why do bodies fall or smoke rise? Because it is part of their essence to seek their natural places on the earth or in the heavens. To quote Hobbes on Aristotelian physics: 'If you desire to know why some kind of bodies sink naturally downwards towards the earth, and others go naturally from it; the Schools will tell you out of Aristotle, that the bodies that sink downwards are heavy; and that this heaviness is it that causes them to descend. But if you ask what they mean by heaviness, they will define it to be an endeavour to go to the centre of the earth. So that the cause why things sink downward, is an endeavour to be below: for which is as much as to say, that bodies descend or ascend, because they do.'[1] Particular men like Socrates exist, and so does the essence of man. Nouns like 'man' designate the essence which is the object of thought in the same kind of way as 'Socrates' designates Socrates who is an object of perception. So, to adopt Hobbes' standpoint, the world became full of occult qualities which, being revealed only to the intellects of the learned doctors of the Schools, perpetuated the superstitious hold of the Catholic Church on the minds of men.

To free men from these dangerous absurdities it was not enough to develop the new science of motion as applied to men in society. It was also necessary to expose the Aristotelian doctrine of the universal in re or essence, which was an integral part of his theory of explanation. This could not be done without a proper theory of speech, which would exhibit how general terms could have meaning without it being necessary to postulate a realm of occult essences which they were alleged to designate.

2. *The Nature and Uses of Speech*

Hobbes defined speech as 'the joining together of words determined by the decision of men, to stand for the train of conceptions

1. E.W. III, 678.

of those things which are objects of our thoughts'.[1] He also said in *De Corpore* that 'Names are signs not of things, but of our cogitations'.[2] He wanted to stress both that there was a close connexion between thought and language in that the latter in some way was a sign of the former and that human speech differed from animal signs because of its arbitrariness. On the one hand he attempted a causal theory of language; yet on the other hand he insisted on its arbitrariness, on 'the decision of men'. It is hard to see how these two approaches can be made consistent with each other. But it is worth exploring briefly what he actually said.

In Hobbes' view every man has his own private world of phantasms, and words are signs of these phantasms of things. We start with our own private marks by means of which our conceptions become associated with noises that are uttered – a kind of private system of mnemonics – 'as men that have passed by a rock at sea set up some mark, thereby to remember their former danger, and avoid it'.[3] Thus, words are *caused by* external things through the intermediary motions of the phantasms. They become connected together as a result of experience and come to act as *signs* to others of what we think and feel. Hobbes seemed to have thought that our private system of marks or 'notes of remembrance' antedate and are independent of a public language. This sounds a most improbable suggestion. Perhaps it was linked in Hobbes' mind with the anarchic state of nature when every man was solitary; the social contract put an end to anarchy both of conduct and of communication.

Now a causal theory of *signs* is quite plausible, provided that they are what are often called natural signs. And Hobbes distinguished natural signs from arbitrary ones. A thick cloud is a natural sign of rain. Similarly animals use natural signs when they give warnings of danger or summonses to food. These noises burst forth from the animals in certain typical predicaments. There is very little variety in them because their predicaments and nature are similar the world over. But human language comes about through *decision* and the signs employed are *arbitrary*, 'namely, those we make choice of at our own pleasure, as a bush hung up,

1. L.W. II, 88.   2. E.W. I, 17.   3. E.W. IV, 20.

signifies that wine is to be sold there'.[1] Animals may understand some of our words but 'they do this not in so far as words are words, but in so far as they are signs; for they do not understand the meanings which men have decided on for words'.[2] Their noises come about by necessity, not by decision as does human speech. That is why animals, though capable of imagery, cannot reason; for reasoning presupposes words with meanings fixed by decision. Animals do not do geometry; therefore they do not reason.

Whether or not this is a useful way of defining 'reasoning' is disputable; but Hobbes certainly hit upon one of the crucial distinctions between men and animals. Men had traditionally been distinguished from animals by their possession of reason. Yet as 'reason' was often used in rather an omnibus way so as to include the planning of means to ends and the use of past experience to solve present problems, it was very plausible to hold that men are not really very different from animals. For animals obviously plan means to ends and make primitive inferences. Hume, for instance, could even say that reasoning is nothing but a wonderful and unintelligible instinct in our souls. . . . 'Nature, by an absolute and uncontrollable necessity, has determined us to judge as well as to breathe and feel.'[3] But we do not do geometry by instinct; and Hobbes, by confining 'reason' to the construction of symbolic systems, brought out a very important distinction between men and animals, even if he did violence to the ordinary use of the term 'reason'. How such an *intentional* activity can be encompassed within a causal theory is, of course, a further question.

The arbitrariness of speech, which distinguishes it from animal signs, is one of Hobbes' favourite themes. Speech, like civil society, is an artificial construction, not a natural growth. That is why it does not come about by 'natural necessity' like the signs of animals. Indeed, he even spoke as if the social contract included also a linguistic contract. '. . . the order of numeral words is so appointed by the common consent of them who are of the same language with us (as it were by a certain contract necessary for

1. E.W. I, 14.   2. L.W. II, 88.
3. D. Hume, *Treatise on Human Nature*, Bk I, Part IV, Sec. 1.

human society) . . .'[1] This is to be taken like the social contract itself, as an attempt at rational analysis rather than historical speculation. So, too, are his sly accounts of the origins of speech taken over from Genesis, which also emphasize its arbitrariness. God, he said, instructed Adam how to name such creatures as he presented to his sight. 'But this was sufficient to direct him to add more names, as the experience and use of the creatures should give him occasion; and to join them in such manner by degrees, as to make himself understood. . . .'[2] Hobbes, characteristically, went on to point out that God gave Adam no instructions for naming figures, numbers, measures, colours, and other items of scientific curiosity; neither did he lay down names of words and of speech like 'general', 'affirmative', 'negative', and so on; least of all did he teach Adam names like 'entity', 'intentionality', 'quiddity' and 'other insignificant words of the school'.[3] However, this promising, if limited, progress in naming was all lost at the Tower of Babel, and those who were dispersed had to make a fresh start! Hobbes' stress on the artificiality of language was thus part of his polemic against the doctrine of essences. How it squared with his attempt to give a causal explanation of marks and his theory that decisions were *determined* is difficult to see; for if decisions are 'determined' they must *at least* be causally explicable.[4] Yet Hobbes was anxious to contrast the arbitrariness of human speech with the 'natural necessity' of that of animals.

Hobbes saw that speech has many specific uses as well as the general one of transferring 'the train of our thoughts into a train of words'. It is used to register what we find to be the cause of any thing and its effects, to share this knowledge with others, to make known our wills and purposes so as to ensure mutual help, and to please and delight ourselves and others by playing with words. Hobbes' main interest, however, was in the descriptive use of language covered by the first two uses which he assigned to it; for this use is best exemplified in science and mathematics. But the imperative use of language was also important to him, though he did not examine its peculiarities. It featured in his doctrine that

1. E.W. II, 303.   3. E.W. III, 19.
2. E.W. III, 18.   4. See pp. 116–17 and pp. 167–77.

law is the command of the sovereign, and in the light of the contemporary controversy about the status of law, it was crucial for him to emphasize the arbitrary character of legal rules and definitions.

3. Hobbes' Theory of Names

Hobbes' theory of the meaning of words is co-extensive with his theory of names. This is one of the major defects of his treatment. For a name is typically a noun expression used to designate things, people, places, and so on. His quarrel with the Aristotelians was that they thought that nouns like 'man' designated abstract entities in the same sort of way as 'Socrates' designates Socrates. But both Hobbes and his adversaries were primarily concerned with the meaning of noun expressions. It was not therefore surprising that Hobbes got into difficulties with his treatment of the accidents of bodies. For here he was raising the problem of how *predicates* have meaning. And the model of how names have meaning tends to creak when it is used in this context.

'A NAME is a word taken at pleasure to serve for a mark, which may raise in our mind a thought like to some thought we had before, and which being pronounced to others, may be to them a sign of what thought the speaker had, or had not before in his mind.'[1] Names, then, are signs of our conceptions of things, not of things themselves, for 'that the sign of this word stone should be the sign of a stone cannot be understood in any sense but this, that he that hears it collects that he that pronounces it thinks of a stone.'[2] Hobbes was writing here as a mechanical theorist and was developing a causal theory of names as signs. When a person uses a word, others are led to expect that he has a certain type of 'conception' in his mind which, in its turn, has been 'caused' by some external stimulus. Unfortunately, however, Hobbes also used words such as 'meaning' and 'denote' as well to speak of this sort of relationship between 'conceptions' and words. This has led most commentators to assume that he thought that names 'refer to' or 'stand for' conceptions, where the term 'refer to' is

1. E.W. I, 16.　　　　　2. E.W. I, 17.

used to characterize the relationship between a name and that of which it is a name, when used as such by a language user who uses words intentionally to refer to things.[1] Hobbes, however, held that, though some words 'name' or 'refer to' conceptions in the mind in this sense, not all words do so. Indeed most words 'name' things external to us such as trees, and some words are names of names. Hobbes gave no proper account of this intentional relationship of 'naming' or 'referring to'. This is not surprising; for it is a relationship which is impossible to characterize in terms of the causal theory which absorbed him.

Names may be either concrete or abstract. Concrete names can denote bodies or their accidents or names. Abstract names only come into being with propositions and denote 'the causes of concrete names'. There are two classes of concrete names, proper names and universal names. Proper names like 'Peter' and 'this tree' are singular to one thing only; a universal name like 'man', 'horse', and 'tree', denotes *each* member of a class of things, though the pronunciation of it will arouse in the mind an image of a particular member. For a universal name, 'though but one name, is nevertheless the name of diverse particular things; in respect of all which together, it is called a universal; there being nothing in the world universal but names; for the things named are every one of them individual and singular. One universal name is imposed on many things, for their similitude in some quality, or other accident; and whereas a proper name bringeth to mind one thing only, universals recall any one of those many.'[1] The crucial sentence in his attack on the doctrine of essence was 'there being nothing in the world universal but names'. The world contains no essences for universal names to designate. 'Universal' is the name of certain names, not of a type of entity *designated* by a name.

Thus, 'universal' is a name of a name which ascribes a certain *use* to it. The error of the Aristotelians derived from treating a universal name as if it were a peculiar kind of *proper* name.

1. I am indebted to J. M. Brown's review of my original edition of *Hobbes* in *Philosophical Review*, Oct. 1957, for this and other corrections. See also Watkins, J. W. N., *Hobbes' System of Ideas* (Hutchinson, 1965), pp., 138–50.

Proper names like 'Churchill' denote a singular body with a unique combination of properties. The name is, as it were, a cap which fits over the individual named, or a ticket attached to him. The Aristotelians used the same model for universal names and thought that they could be fitted over or attached to an object of thought, the essence of man. Confronted with the term 'man' the philosopher had to look for the essence designated by it in the same kind of way as a policeman might look for Mr Brown with a picture in his hand to identify him. Hobbes, a hard-headed mechanist, held that the world is composed only of moving bodies; there are no essences behind the appearances for our universal names to fit. Names are called 'universal' purely because they are *used* to refer to different men rather than just one particular individual.

So much for Hobbes' analysis of names of bodies. His treatment of names of accidents was not nearly so clear. He said that 'One universal name is imposed on many things, for their similitude in some quality, or other accident'.[1] So obviously his account of names of properties like 'extended' is very important especially as it seems inconsistent with his nominalism. It is linked with what Hobbes said about the joining together of names into propositions, a process which gives rise to what Hobbes called '*abstract* names'. A proposition is 'a speech consisting of two names copulated, by which he that speaketh signifieth he conceives the latter name to be the name of the same thing whereof the former is the name'.[2] For instance, in 'man is a living creature' the speaker conceives 'living creature' and 'man' to be names of the same thing, the name 'man' being comprehended by the name 'living creature' – rather in the way in which a surname is more extensive in its application than a Christian name. Some languages bring out this relation of 'comprehension' by the order of words without recourse to the verb 'to be'. The copulation of the two names 'makes us think of the cause for which these names were imposed on that thing', and this search for the causes of names gives rise to abstract names like 'corporeity', 'motion', 'figure', 'quantity', 'likeness', and so on. But these denote only the *causes of concrete*

1. E.W. III, 21.   2. E.W. I, 30.

names and not the things themselves, which are designated by concrete names. For instance, we see something which is extended and fills space and we call it by the concrete name 'body'. The cause of the name is that the thing is extended, 'or the extension or corporeity of it'. These causes of names are the same as the causes of our conceptions, 'namely, some power of action, or affection of the thing conceived, which some call the manner by which any thing works upon our senses, but by most men they are called accidents'.[1] Accidents are neither the things themselves, nor parts of them, but 'do nevertheless accompany the things in such manner, that (saving extension) they may all perish, and be destroyed, but can never be abstracted'.[2]

The great advantage of abstract names is that they permit us to reason and calculate without moving about and manipulating the bodies themselves. Their abuse consists in the manipulation of names, as is done by metaphysical writers, without constant regard for the anchorage of accidents to bodies. For instance, it is possible to *think of* thought without also thinking of body, and this leads such writers to think that thinking can go on without a body that thinks. This sort of absurdity is generated by failure to understand the function of the copula. Indeed, terms like 'essence', 'reality', 'quiddity', and so on, 'could never have been heard of among such nations as do not copulate their names by the verb *is* but by adjective verbs as runneth, readeth, . . .'[3] Such terms are not the names of things but signs 'by which we make known, that we conceive the consequence of one name or attribute to another: as when we say, *a man is a living body*, we mean not that the *man* is one thing, the *living body* another, and the *is* or *being* a third; but that the *man*, and the *living body* is the same thing; because the consequence, *if he be a man, he is a living body*, is a true consequence, signified by that word *is*. Therefore, *to be a body, to walk, to be speaking, to live, to see,* and the like infinitives; also *corporeity, walking, speaking, life, sight,* and the like, that signify just the same, are the names of *nothing*.'[4]

Hobbes' treatment of the copula is interesting; for he seems to have adumbrated later attempts to remove the ambiguities of the

1. E.W. I, 32–3.   2. E.W. I, 33.   3. E W. I, 34.   4. E.W. III, 674.

word 'is'. There is a sense of 'is' or 'exists' which assigns a date and a place to something. If we say 'Here is a man' or 'Churchill exists' we are not assigning a property but are literally or figuratively pointing to an object with a date and a place. There is another sense of 'is', however, when we say 'man is a living body', where 'is' has the function of what Hobbes called 'comprehension' or class-inclusion. We are stating something like 'Everywhere and always *if* X is a man *then* X is a living body'. We are not committing ourselves to the existence of men in the first sense of 'is' or 'exists'. We could equally well say 'centaurs are four-legged animals'. Hobbes suggested that terms like 'moved' and 'extended' refer to accidents of bodies as they are caused by them through the intermediary of conceptions, just as do terms like 'stone' and 'tree' which are names of bodies. When propositions are invented the copula of class-inclusion enables us to calculate and reason about the accidents of bodies without having to move them about or have them actually in front of us. But people are misled by the copula into thinking that 'is' refers to an entity or essence. Thus, when they use abstract terms like 'motion' or 'corporeity' to reason about the class-inclusion relationships between properties, they, as it were, inject this essence into the accidents referred to by the property words and think that such abstract terms refer to essences of motion and corporeity. But in order to use the copula meaningfully we have not to intuit some essence but to think clearly and distinctly about the causes of concrete names, i.e. accidents, as was made clear in Hobbes' account of evidence.[1] Metaphysicians talk nonsense by omitting to do this as well as by mistaking the function of the copula.

This account of abstract names gives an ingenious explanation of how people come to believe in essences; it also brings out in rather a tortuous way that Hobbes thought that all statements in which abstract names occur could be translated without loss of meaning, though with considerable loss of time, into statements in which only concrete names occurred. But suppose we use terms like 'extended' and 'moved' instead of 'extension' and 'motion', is there not still a puzzle about the status of these terms? Hobbes

1. See *supra*, pp. 58–9.

certainly said some rather puzzling things about them. In *De Corpore* he made a distinction between things like men which are known to us via our senses, of which it is true that the whole is better known than any part of it, and things 'known to nature' of which we know better the parts like figure, motion, and rest, than the whole which we reconstruct by means of such scientific concepts. Such accidents he sometimes called 'universal things'[1] and remarked that the endeavour of the scientist was to understand their universal cause – motion – without knowledge of which he could not achieve this reconstruction. By 'known to nature' Hobbes explained that he meant not something which is known to no man, but our rational reconstruction of things, in which, of course, abstractions like figure, quantity, and motion would be used; for without abstraction we could have only categorical knowledge, not the hypothetical knowledge of the scientist. He had in mind here, as the preceding section made clear, the resoluto-compositive method of Galilean mechanics. But it is difficult to reconcile this importance ascribed to 'universal things' with nominalism.[2]

It may well be, however, that Hobbes' analysis of how predicates have meaning is very faulty, partly because he tried to give an account of them as if they were names or noun-expressions. Certainly the difficulties that he both encountered and slurred over in his treatment suggest that the model of nouns like 'Socrates' and 'man' breaks down when it is extended to adjectives like 'extended' and 'moving'. But a discussion of this problem would take us too far afield. So too would the discussion of the adequacy of nominalism in general. Hobbes' particular brand of nominalism, however, had one great strength and two great weaknesses. Its strength consisted in its exposure of the redundancy of abstract entities, which, in his view, rested on the fallacy of treating universal names as if they were a species of proper names, distinguished by the status of the entities which they were alleged to

1. See E.W. I, 66–9.

2. See J. Laird, *Hobbes*, p. 148. [In the previous edition I tried to defend Hobbes – I now think unsuccessfully – against this accusation of inconsistency. See Watkins, op. cit., p. 148.]

designate. No one disputes that there are bodies, that they are extended and move about. Sometimes we use a name like 'Churchill' to designate one of them; at other times we use a name like 'man' to designate *any* body conforming to the expectations we have which can be verbalized in the definition or connotation of 'man'. Dogs can be taught the difference between these two classes of names; and they have no inward eye, as far as we know, to intuit essences. For on hearing a certain kind of whistle a dog can be trained to expect his master and no one but his master, Mr Brown. Yet, on hearing a different kind of whistle, he can be trained to expect *any* object which he will be able to eat – i.e. conforming to certain criteria which could be verbalized in a connotation. Without such universal names language would be of very limited value; for it would merely be a mass of proper names reduplicating all the bodies we happened to encounter. But the fact that we can use such universal names does not necessitate the explanation which is often given of this fact – that there must be essences designated by the names in the same way as individuals are designated by proper names. Hobbes hung grimly on to this cardinal point in his distinction between proper names and universal names, and in his insistence that abstract names refer to nothing, but are only shorthand devices for enabling us to think about what is designated by concrete names. This, of course, raises the problem of how terms for properties like 'extended' have meaning and how their meaning is related to those for bodies. Obviously they are connected; for, as Hobbes remarked, we impose a universal name on many things because of their 'similitude in some quality, or other accident'. Certainly the analytic tool, which Hobbes fashioned to deal primarily with names of bodies, was too clumsy to deal with the intricacies of this problem. But it was sharp enough to do its main job – to show that, on the assumption about names shared both by himself and his opponents, the postulation of abstract entities to account for the differences between singular and universal names was superfluous.

The major weakness of his account sprang from his fascination with phantasms and with mechanical explanations. Words were for him marks which could be manipulated like a mathematician's counters; yet they are *caused* by external things through the intermediary of phantasms, the word being a sign of the private phantasm. He spoke of accidents as the *causes* of concrete names just as he spoke of them as the causes of our conceptions. But he also spoke of names as *naming* and *denoting* bodies and accidents. He never, however, examined the *logical* relations expressed by terms like 'denote', 'refer to', and 'name', any more than he examined the relation of representation in his account of phantasms. It may well be that there is little that can be said about a relation like that expressed by the term 'referring', it being a primitive relation which cannot be explained in terms of anything simpler and for which most analogies are unilluminating. But it certainly does not help to muddle it with a *causal* relation. For though perhaps a causal explanation can be given for words which, like the signs of animals and birds, have only an expressive or an evocative function, it seems fantastic to suggest that a descriptive language, with all its artificiality and arbitrariness, can be causally explained simply by the movements of bodies impinging on the sense-organs. Hobbes set his face against this suggestion when he contrasted the arbitrariness of human language with the 'natural necessity' of animal signs. But at times his obsession with mechanical explanations led him to ignore the implications of his own insight. For the possession of reason, which enables men to construct descriptive languages, makes men different from moving bodies as well as from brutes.

The second weakness in his account was the presumed intermediary of phantasms between things and names which was part and parcel of his peculiarly private theory of meaning. It derived from his general view that we are confronted with our own phantasms of things, not with things themselves, and from his mechanical theory. He thought that our conceptions are marked by names which are like signposts rearing themselves out of an unfamiliar country; these marks, when uttered as words, bring to the minds of those who hear them similar conceptions as they, too, go on their journeys. But this presupposes not only that the speaker and the hearer always have a similar conception when they hear a word, but also that they always have *some* conception. And by 'conception' Hobbes meant a concrete determinate image. Both these assumptions seem plainly false. For words evoke all sorts of different imagery in different people and, as was demonstrated with great labour by the Würzburg school of introspective psychologists,[1] talking and problem-solving can be carried on perfectly well without any determinate imagery at all. In his account of evidence[2] Hobbes suggested that meaningful talk was different from parrot-talk in that our words mirrored our conceptions. Is this always the case? Perhaps this double process of thinking and talking occurs when we are wrestling with an unfamiliar problem. We may then need the help of imagery which is probably a more primitive method of problem-solving. When, however, our talk is proceeding smoothly it can be perfectly meaningful without any accompanying shadow process in our heads. Hobbes modelled his account too much on the mental contortions of a scientist like Descartes struggling for clear and distinct ideas.

4. The Exposure of Absurdities

Whatever the defects of Hobbes' theory of names he used it in a most interesting and aggressive manner to expose and explain the absurdities of metaphysicians. We have already met with his suggestions that abstract entities are generated not by God but by our failure to understand the function of the copula. We have also seen that he thought that a great deal of mental confusion was the product of failure to start from agreed definitions. But more interesting than either of these suggestions was his view that metaphysicians are led into absurdities by being insensitive to the logical behaviour of different classes of words.

Hobbes believed, roughly speaking, that names could name bodies, accidents or names. Now if one of these classes of names were used as if it belonged to another class, all sorts of confusions were likely to be propagated. For instance, those who say that

1. For an account of their work see G. Humphreys, *Thinking* (London, 1951), Chs. II–IV.
2. See *supra*, p. 58.

faith is 'infused' or 'inspired' are treating 'faith' as if it were a name of a body. For only bodies can be poured or breathed into anything. Similarly, those who believe 'that there be things universal' confuse the name of bodies with the names of names, or misunderstand the different senses of 'in'. For an accident is not in a body in the same kind of way as a body is in a body – 'as if, for example, redness were in blood, in the same manner, as blood is in a bloody cloth'.[1] He also attacked the use of metaphors like 'the proverb says this or that', which cloud the search for truth, and fulminated against 'names that signify nothing; but are taken up, and learned by rote from the schools, as hypostatical, transubstantiate, consubstantiate, eternal-now, and the like canting of schoolmen'.[2]

This demand for plain speech and the anchoring of terms to palpable things like bodies has been one of the main characteristics of British philosophy since Bacon and Hobbes initiated it; but Hobbes anticipated modern techniques of logical analysis by supplementing the demand for clarity and concreteness of speech by a theory of absurdity. He tried to show how absurdities are generated by mistakes about the logical behaviour of different classes of terms. The instrument he forged was too crude to do the job very elegantly. But in using this kind of weapon he was a pioneer, and in this respect, as in many others, he failed to develop in detail the implication of his insight. What emerged from his theory of names was a bludgeon for pulverizing some of the more extravagant verbal structures of the schoolmen and a crude theory of meaning modelled on what he thought to be the practice of those whose thoughts were limited to the contemplation of bodies in motion. And this was more or less all that he set out to do in constructing a theory of names.

1. E.W. I, 104.　　　　2. E.W. III, 34–5.

CHAPTER 6

MOTIVATION

Introductory

HOBBES' theory of motivation linked his general theory of motion with his moral and political theory. His exposition of it therefore tended to conform to a certain pattern. He first of all introduced it by means of the bridging term 'endeavour' and tried to show how the gross motions of the body towards or away from objects in desire or aversion could be explained in terms of its endeavours or minute movements of muscles, animal spirits, and so on. This was to show how all life was but motion of the limbs and of the minute parts of the body. He then introduced his theory of the passions in which movements towards objects were classified as forms of the desire for power and movements away from objects as forms of fear, in order to explain the acceptance of moral rules and the necessity for civil society. Indeed, the use to which he put his theory of motivation very much dictated its form and content. For though it was ostensibly a deduction from the theory of motion, it was in fact constructed with an eye much more on its political relevance than on its theoretical adequacy.

1. Pleasure and Pain

There are two sorts of motion in the body. The first is *vital* motion which is begun in generation and continued without interruption through life. It is manifest in the circulation of the blood, in breathing, nutrition, excretion and other such processes, and proceeds without the help of the imagination. *Animal* motion, which is the same as voluntary motion, manifests itself in walking, speaking, moving the limbs, and so on; it is always 'first fancied in our minds'[1] the imagination being always the first beginning of voluntary motion. Motions from the external world not only move to the brain and produce phantasms; they also effect the vital motions of the heart. This gives rise to another kind of sensation – pleasure if the motion of the blood is helped and pain if it is impeded.

Hobbes distinguished between sensual and mental pleasures. The former have the main functions of helping the preservation of the individual and the continuation of the species; the latter have no obvious connexion with any part of the body. The basic difference between the two is that sensual pleasures require the presence of the object associated with pleasure whereas mental pleasures do not. Amongst sensual pleasures are 'all onerations and exonerations of the body; as also all that is pleasant, in the sight, hearing, smell, taste, or touch. Others arise from expectation, that proceeds from foresight of the end, or consequence of things; whether those things in the sense please or displease. And these are pleasures of the mind of him that draweth those consequences, and are generally called JOY.'[2] Hobbes paid little attention to sensual pleasures except to suggest quantitative explanations of harmony and of the difference between light 'the most glorious of all colours' and colour 'that is to say unequal light'.[3]

2. Appetites and Aversions

Pleasure and pain are thus our introspective awareness of vital motions. Pleasure is 'nothing really but motion about the heart, as conception is nothing but motion in the head'.[4] When the action of sensible objects hinders this motion, it may be resolved again 'by bending or setting strait the parts of the body; which is done when the spirits are carried now into these, now into other nerves, till the pain, as far as is possible, be quite taken away'.[5]

1. E.W. III, 38.   4. E.W. IV, 31.
2. E.W. III, 42–3.   5. E.W. I, 407.
3. E.W. IV, 36, 7.

Similarly, in the case of pleasure the spirits[1] are guided by the help of the nerves to preserve and augment the motion. When this endeavour tends towards things *known by experience* to be pleasant, it is called an appetite; when it shuns what is painful, it is called aversion. Appetite and aversion are the *first endeavours* of animal motion. They are succeeded by the flow of animal spirits into some receptacle near the 'original' of the nerves which brings about a swelling and relaxation of the muscles causing contraction and extension of the limbs, which is animal motion.

There are some appetites and aversions which are born with men 'as appetite of food, appetite of excretion and exoneration, which may also and more properly be called aversions, from somewhat they feel in their bodies; and some other appetites, not many'.[2] These sound very much like the 'drives' about which so much has been heard in recent psychological theorizing.[3] But even in these cases Hobbes thought that the initiation of movement was from without. Food seen causes the organism to move towards it. This sounds an insufficient account of the matter. For there is good evidence to suppose that organisms are born with innate needs which *predispose* them to seek out and pay attention to some features of their environment rather than others,[4] and to move towards or away from them in ways which need not be learnt. And, as we said in commenting on Hobbes' account of

1. The notion of 'spirits' is to be found in Galen, in whose work the tradition of the Pneumatists reached its culmination. Life is due to 'spirit' which charges the blood at the key centres of the body – the liver, the heart, and the brain, Blood, which was produced by the liver and charged with natural spirits, met air from the lung at the heart and became 'vital spirits' to be distributed by the arteries. Some of these went to the brain where they became transformed into a third type of spirits, 'animal spirits'. These were distributed by the nerves which were pictured as hollow tubes. Hobbes, like Descartes, abandoned this picture on account of Harvey's discovery of the circulation of the blood. But he still retained the notion of animal spirits coursing through the nerves as the means by which animal motion was propagated.

2. E.W. III, 40.

3. See C. Hull, *Principles of Behaviour*; E. Tolman, *Purposive Behaviour in Animals and Men*; and P. T. Young, *Emotion in Man and Animal*.

4. See, for instance, K. Lorenz, *King Solomon's Ring*.

sensation, only those external stimuli register which relate to the needs of the organism.

Hobbes' account of the increase and decrease in vital motions was also vague. Yet this was a crucial point in his transition from physiology to psychology. His suggestion was that increase in vital motions round the heart, occasioned by contact with an external object, is *felt* as pleasure or pain. He was referring to movements of 'vital spirits' in what we would now call the autonomic nervous system. But surely there is not a simple correlation between increase in such internal motions and pleasure; some pains are accompanied by a great increase in vital motion. Hobbes must have meant more than the simple increasing or impeding of motion, but it is doubtful whether his account, as it stands, amounts to more than an attempt to describe in the language of motion the *felt* difference between pleasure and pain.

Appetite and aversion referred to the *beginning* or first endeavour of motion. And Hobbes was most anxious to point out that he meant actual movement, not simply a state of readiness to move.[1] He called the end of movement its 'fruition', but did not indicate whether this referred to obtaining the object towards which movement was directed (e.g. drinking a tankard of ale) or the end-state of increase in vitality which supervenes.[2] He did, however, observe that the supreme end of felicity, about which the ancients had spoken so much, was a mirage: 'for while we live, we have desires, and desire presupposeth a further end. . . . Seeing all delight is appetite, and presupposeth a further end, there can be no contentment but in proceeding. . . . Felicity, therefore, by which we mean continual delight, consisteth not in having prospered but in prospering.'[3] Implicit in this observation is not merely Hobbes' devotion to motion; there is also the insight that the 'utmost end' of happiness cannot be an end in the sense in which having a meal or going to bed are ends. 'Continual delight' is a fitting description not for an additional end but for the way we go about and

1. E.W. III, 39.

2. See Freud's distinction between the *object* and *aim* of an instinct. S. Freud, *Instincts and Their Vicissitudes*, Collected Papers, Vol. IV, p. 65.

3. E.W. IV, 33.

succeed in attaining whatever ends we may have. To be happy is not to arrive at an additional destination; it is to be in process of calling according to some schedule at those places which we really want to visit.

The point of Hobbes' remark that all final causes are efficient causes can now be seen. The end or final cause only functions as a cause in so far as it features in the consciousness which initiates the movements. This, however, was a very intellectualistic account of goal-directed behaviour; for it assumed that all behaviour towards an end is initiated by foresight of the end. This is not the case. There is, first of all, the ambiguity already noted in the concept of 'end' which can mean the object of pursuit or the state of satisfaction which follows the capture of the quarry. Behaviour is seldom initiated by foresight of an end of the second sort. Huntsmen are lured by thoughts of killing foxes, not by thoughts of the satisfaction of having killed them. But more important are the cases where we move towards ends in the first sense which we do not consciously envisage as objectives. Many men are consistently rude to their employees although they consciously try to be nice to them; husbands protest love for their wives, yet constantly act as if they hated them. Often we are never conscious of these goals towards which our behaviour veers like a moth towards a light. It was not until Freud that their theoretical importance was seen. They render implausible Hobbes' account of the initiation of behaviour, though, perhaps, they can be fitted into a more subtle account of efficient causes.

The will is often referred to in accounts of the initiation of behaviour. Hobbes believed that there was a sense in which we can talk of willed actions without postulating a special faculty of will. It often happens that we deliberate before we act. Indeed, Hobbes thought that all human action was voluntary.[1] In this 'alternate succession of appetite and fear'[2] the last one that emerges triumphant is called will. 'Will therefore is the last appetite in deliberating.'[3] This is an inadequate analysis, but an analysis which is along the right lines. What we call 'will' is

1. See *infra*, p. 145 (footnote).
2. E.W. IV, 68.   3. E.W. III, 49.

certainly to be linked with deliberation successfully terminated; there is no need to postulate specific mental acts of something called 'the will'. But is not a special kind of deliberation involved? Are not the alternatives examined in relation to what is either in the long-term as distinct from the short-term interest of the agent or in accordance with some ideal picture of himself that he has built up, his 'ego-ideal', to use Freudian terminology? Suppose I am lying in bed in the early morning deliberating about whether to get up. My fear of the cold alternates with my desire to get the morning post. If I get up because my desire wins it would be odd to call this a willed action. But suppose I think about getting up from the point of view of the necessity of earning a living. Or suppose I compare myself hogging it in bed with a picture I have of myself as a brisk man like Sir Stafford Cripps, who was always at his desk by 9 a.m. And suppose, as a result of either of these reflections, I grit my teeth and leap out of bed. Surely we would be more inclined to call this a willed action? Will is not simply the *last* appetite in deliberating; for often we would be inclined to say of a man who eventually decided to stay in bed that he did not exert his will. Rather it is deliberation carried on under the aegis of self-regard, in which self-regard reinforces what Hobbes called an appetite and enables it to be the last one in the field.

3. The Passions

For Hobbes love and hate were more or less the same as appetite and aversion, the only difference being that love and hate require the actual presence of the object, whereas appetite and aversion presuppose its absence. These, together with joy and grief which both involve foresight of an end rather than just an immediately perceived object, are the simple passions out of which all others are compounded. Hope, for instance, is appetite with an opinion of attaining, despair is the same without such opinion. Fear is aversion with opinion of hurt from the object, courage the same with hope of avoiding that hurt by resistance. Passions are distinguished by the objects of appetites and aversions as well as by our opinion of attaining these objects. Ambition is desire for office and covetousness desire for riches. Love of persons for society is kindliness and love of persons for pleasing the sense only is natural lust. Hobbes' detailed classification of the passions scarcely repays detailed study. It looks very much like the account of the passions in Aristotle's *Rhetoric* served up in rather a piecemeal manner to provide a transition from physiology to politics.

Nevertheless it does indicate the lines along which Hobbes thought that all human actions could be explained. It is therefore worth-while pausing for a moment to summarize his assumptions and to comment on them. Hobbes postulated:

(a) The *initiation* of action by an external stimulus producing a phantasm in the brain or by a phantasm of some absent object. (We shall call this an *efficient cause* of an action.)

(b) The augmenting or impeding of vital motions as a collateral effect of the actual or imagined object. (These tensions in the body are *felt* as pleasure and pain.)

(c) Movements towards or away from an *objective*, of which we are conscious, which preserve or augment the vital motions. (We shall refer to the *objective* of an action and to its *function* in augmenting or impeding vital motion.)

Hobbes seems to have thought that all elements of this model of explanation had to be postulated when we assign a desire or a passion to a person in order to explain his behaviour. This does seem to display a certain inelasticity in approach to the problem of psychological explanation. For, in the first place, many of the explanations which we in fact give of human behaviour do not in fact commit us to such a complicated set of assumptions. Hobbes' model of explanation is plausible, perhaps, for what we might call 'drives' like fear, hunger, sex and thirst, where there are obvious external stimuli or internal organic conditions which *initiate* action and which are felt as pleasant or unpleasant, where there are palpable goals towards which actions are consciously directed, and where there are recognizable end-states of quiescence which enable us to assign a *function* to the action. But is it plausible to suggest that covetousness, ambition, liberality, impudence and countless other of Hobbes' 'passions' conform to this model? Some of these terms certainly imply that actions have typical *objectives*. Ambition, says Hobbes, is a desire for office and precedence, and covetousness is desire for riches. But can it be said that the actions of an ambitious or covetous man are *initiated* by antecedent tensions in the same sort of way as the actions of a hungry man? To explain an action in terms of ambition is surely only to suggest a typical *objective* or reason for it; it is not to ascribe an *efficient cause* to it, or even to imply one. Of course, there may be occasions on which actions performed out of covetousness or ambition are initiated by the impeding of vital motions occasioned by the absence of certain objects which could be felt as gnawings, hankerings, cravings and so on. But we would not have to assure ourselves of the occurrence of these antecedent motions before venturing the suggestion that a politician acted out of ambition or a business man out of covetousness. We would, however, have to assure ourselves that they consciously aimed at certain objectives.

There are, in the second place, certain other examples which Hobbes gives of passions which conform even less to his desire-aversion model. Courage, says Hobbes, is aversion with hope of avoiding hurt by resistance; confidence is constant hope and diffidence constant despair. But of actions done out of courage, confidence, or diffidence is it even appropriate to ask 'What was the point of the action?' let alone to believe that something has been implied about their efficient causes? Surely when we use such terms as these we are ascribing *traits* of character to a person. We are *classifying* his action as being in accordance with a certain type of *rule* or socially accepted norm. We do not necessarily ascribe a typical objective to it; still less do we suggest an efficient cause. But Hobbes had to try to fit such terms into his desire-aversion model because of an assumption about explanatory terms that permeated his physical theory as well as his psychology. He assumed that all explanatory terms referred to actual occurrences. He set his face resolutely against the Aristotelian conception of potentiality, or what we would now call the ascription of dispositional properties to bodies. In his chapter on 'Power and Act' in *De Corpore* he said: 'Wherefore the power of the agent and the efficient cause are the same thing. But they are considered with this difference, that cause is so called in respect of the effect already produced, and power in respect of the same effect to be produced hereafter; so that cause respects the past, power the future time.'[1] But surely Hobbes missed the point in his reference to future time in the analysis of 'power'. To ascribe a power to something is not to refer to anything actually occurring in the past, present or future. It is to say that *if* certain conditions are fulfilled, then certain other things happen. Solubility is a 'power' of sugar; for if it is put into water (at *any* time, past, present or future) then it dissolves. To ascribe a cause to something, on the other hand, is to indicate an event actually occurring at a *particular* time which is a necessary condition for another event to occur. But Hobbes refused to give any terms which describe bodies a dispositional interpretation; all terms refer to actual occurrences. We have seen the importance of this in his account of 'endeavour'.[2] It also had a considerable influence on his account of the passions. For Hobbes even interpreted *habits* as *actual motions* made more easy and more ready by perpetual endeavours.

Now of all terms that are used to explain human behaviour 'habit' is the most obviously dispositional. To say that a person has a habit of punctuality is not to say that he is doing anything at a particular moment. It is to say that *if* he goes to the office, he is always there at the stipulated time, that *if* he goes to catch a train, he never misses it, and so on. A great number of terms for giving an account of human actions are of this sort. But for Hobbes a 'passion' cannot be a term for making this sort of dispositional statement about a person; it must refer to actual occurrences. Thus the term 'desire', which has both a dispositional and an occurrent interpretation,[3] must refer in Hobbes' account to actual movements towards an object accompanied by actual prospective picturings of it. And this underlying assumption about the analysis

1. E.W. I, 127–8.

2. See *supra*, pp. 85–7.

3. Talking about e.g. the desire for power can suggest an actual picturing of ourselves as Prime Minister and actually taking steps to attain such a goal, or it can imply only that in certain situations we will tend to aim at dominating others.

of dispositional terms imposed a severe limit on his treatment of terms like 'ambition', 'courage', 'confidence', 'benevolence', 'covetousness' and so on, which he classed as 'passions'. Indeed, Hobbes' analysis of 'powers' reinforced the necessity of using only one model of explanation in which continuous motions from stimuli to response were postulated as invariably occurring.

The truth of the matter is that common-sense explanations of actions usually take the form of assigning an objective or classifying them as instances of traits and habits. They also postulate efficient causes where these are external stimuli which set off a train of behaviour. But seldom do ordinary people have recourse to functional explanation or to the more recondite types of intra-organic efficient causes suggested by Hobbes. And if they do it is because they have picked up a smattering of physiology or read a bit about Freud. Hobbes tried to underwrite common-sense explanations in terms of objectives and traits with a scientific theory postulating invariable causes and function. The result was rather bizarre and led to a lot of subsequent trouble, as we shall see when we discuss his alleged psychological hedonism. And he certainly gave only a very broad outline of a theory of the passions because of his predominantly political bias. Indeed, it is only when we pass on to the passions which seemed to him politically important that Hobbes' account comes to life again. One of the striking features which rejuvenates his treatment is his fascination for motion which bursts forth again when we pass from arid classification to social implications.

Social life, for Hobbes, was a race for precedence which had no final termination except death. To last in the race needed foresight and scheming. There are therefore specific pleasures and pains which encourage or deflect men on their journey. These are the mental pleasures and pains which 'arise from the expectation that proceeds from foresight of the end or consequence of things; for whether those things in the sense please or displease'.[1] Their generic name is joy and grief. These presuppose not simply anticipation of the future based on past experience but a peculiar

1. E.W. III, 43.

kind of anticipation in which the individual is conscious of his *power* to produce something. For we cannot conceive of what is in the future without also knowing of something at the present that has power to produce it. 'Wherefore all conception of future, is conception of power able to produce something. Whosoever therefore expecteth pleasure to come, must conceive withal some power in himself by which the same may be attained.'[1] This is an odd doctrine. But it was made startling by the shift which Hobbes contrived in the meaning of the word 'power'. He sometimes used it in its very general sense and spoke, like Aristotle, of nutritive, generative, motive and mental powers. He added power acquired by the exercise of these faculties – riches, place of authority, friendship or favour, and good fortune, and remarked that as 'the power of one man restricteth and hindereth the effects of the power of another, power simply is no more but the excess of the power of one above that of another; for equal powers opposed destroy one another; and such their opposition is called contention'.[2] But this is surely a more restricted sense of 'power' than the first sense which refers generally to bodily or mental faculties. Indeed, the term 'power' is another bridging term like 'endeavour'. Hobbes used it most ingeniously to fashion a psychological theory suitable for his political theory. For instance, his celebrated announcement: 'So that in the first place, I put for a general inclination of all mankind, a perpetual and restless striving of power after power, that ceaseth only in death'[3] would be comparatively innocuous, though quaint, if it referred just to his general theory that all striving for future ends involves a conception of our power to produce them. For Hobbes often did use his general theory to say rather bizarre things – for instance, that the fear of death involves the fear of our inability to produce effects. But 'power' in most of the key passages where he speaks of the desire for power means our ability to dominate or win precedence over others. He passes smoothly from the more general to the more limited sense. To fail to *compete* was to die.

It follows that in their dealings with others men are very sensitive to honour or the acknowledgement of power. They cherish

1. E.W. IV, 37.　　2. E.W. IV, 38.　　3. E.W. III, 85–6.

their power generative which shows itself in beauty 'consisting in a lively aspect of the countenance and other signs of natural heat'.[1] They are honoured, too, for their power motive whose signs appear in bodily strength, and for their faculty of knowledge which appears in their ability to teach or persuade. Riches, nobility, authority and good fortune are also honourable adjuncts since they are acquired by various powers. A man who is convinced that his own power overshadows that of his rivals is subject to what Hobbes called 'glory' or 'internal gloriation or triumph of the mind', which may be just, false, or vain, depending on whether it is based on his own experience, other people's opinions or his own imaginings unrelated to concrete action. The opposite of glory is called humility or dejection, depending on the observer's attitude to it. Pity is grief for the calamity of another arising from the imagination that a like calamity may befall ourselves. This was the sort of deduction from his theory that rankled with Hobbes' critics. For pity was transformed by it into a sophisticated sort of self-interest.

Hobbes prided himself on being the first to give a convincing explanation of laughter. It is the expression of sudden glory caused by something new and unexpected in which we discover some superiority in ourselves to others. Laughter is most common amongst those who are conscious of few abilities in themselves and are therefore forced to keep themselves in their own favour by glorying in the imperfections of others. Hobbes was also very interested in curiosity to which in the sphere of the passions he assigned a place similar to that occupied by giving names in the cognitive sphere. For in both man is quite unlike animals. 'For when a beast seeth anything new and strange to him, he considereth it so far only as to discern whether it be likely to serve his turn, or hurt him, and accordingly approacheth nearer to it, or fleeth from it: whereas man, who in most events remembereth in what manner they were caused and begun, looketh for the cause and beginning of everything that ariseth new unto him. And from this passion of admiration and curiosity, have arisen not only the invention of names, but also supposition of such causes of all

1. E.W. IV, 38.

things as they thought might produce them. And from this beginning is derived all philosophy. . . .'[1]

But all men are not equally skilled in science; nor are they equally equipped in wits on which worldly success mainly depends. Hobbes put down these differences in attainment to differences in passion. He ruled out differences in the natural temper of the brain; for if that were the cause, men would differ as much in their perceptual abilities as they do in wisdom. And this is not so. Differences in wits, therefore, originate in the different passions and the ends to which appetites lead. Some men are addicted to predominantly sensual delights – ease, food and exonerations of the body; they are little moved by the attractions of honour and glory which presuppose imagination of the future. Such dullness probably derives from 'a grossness and difficulty of the motion of the spirits about the heart'.[2] Quick ranging of the mind, which, joined with curiosity, leads to grasping the similarities and differences between things, spring from 'a tenuity and agility of spirits'.[3] Levity is a sign of excessive mobility in the spirits, which prevents people from sticking to the point. A man of judgement must have strong passions to control the relevance of his thoughts. 'For the thoughts are to the desires, as scouts and spies, to range abroad, and find the way to the things desired: all steadiness of the mind's motion, and all quickness of the same, proceeding from thence: for as to have no desire, is to be dead; so to have weak passions, is dullness; and to have passions indifferently for everything, GIDDINESS, and distraction; and to have stronger and more vehement passions for anything, than is ordinarily seen in others, is that which men call MADNESS.'[4] Indeed, in madness we are consumed by a passionate conviction of our own superiority or inferiority – an excess of vain glory or vain dejection – like the man who preached in a cart in Cheapside that he himself was Christ, or those who prophesy the world's end or emulate Don Quixote, or fancy themselves as brittle as glass. To be successful a man must have not only steadiness and strength of passion, but also a clear grasp of his own abilities. The

1. E.W. IV, 50–1.   3. E.W. IV, 56.
2. E.W. IV, 55.   4. E.W. III, 61–2.

madman is one whose conception of his own power is out of touch with the realities of his nature and situation.

There are many shrewd insights in this rather rambling account of the passions and individual differences. It is interesting to speculate on the extent to which the striving for power and precedence in fact was rampant in the society in which Hobbes wrote; for, as has been noted before, he lived at a time when the new men of the commercial classes were wresting power from the landed aristocracy. His was an age of individualism, competition and social mobility. His preoccupation with *honour* is most significant. It is difficult for his readers, who have often lived in more settled times, to realize that psychological traits like aggressiveness, acquisitiveness and the striving for power are enormously dependent on social conditions which vary. Yet we are familiar with a similar theory put forward in a less intellectualistic manner, by Alfred Adler in Vienna between the two World Wars. His doctrine of 'organ inferiority' reminds us of Hobbes' general theory of the conception of our own power; his famous 'will to power' recalls Hobbes' 'perpetual and restless desire of power after power, that ceaseth only in death'. But whereas Adler cited case histories to support his thesis, Hobbes presented a vivid picture of life as a race in which 'we must suppose to have no other goal, nor other garland, but being foremost'.[1] He gave not a new theory of motivation with concrete evidence to support it but a *re-description* of the familiar processes of living, in which the theory of motion linked social life with his physics and the striving for power prepared his readers for his political theory.

> To endeavour, is appetite.
> To be remiss, is sensuality.
> To consider them behind, is glory.
> To consider them before, is humility.
> To lose ground with looking back, vain glory.
> To be holden, hatred.
> To turn back, repentance.
> To be in breath, hope.
> To be weary, despair.

1. E.W. IV, 53.

To endeavour to overtake the next, emulation.

To supplant or overthrow, envy.

To resolve to break through a stop foreseen, courage.

To break through a sudden stop, anger.

To break through with ease, magnanimity.

To lose ground by little hindrances, pusillanimity.

To fall on the sudden, is disposition to weep.

To see another fall, is disposition to laugh.

To see one out-gone whom we would not, is pity.

To see one out-go whom we would not, is indignation.

To hold fast by another, is to love.

To carry him on that so holdeth, is charity.

To hurt one's self for haste, is shame.

Continually to be outgone, is misery.

Continually to outgo the next before, is felicity.

And to forsake the course, is to die.[1]

4. Psychological Hedonism

Hobbes summed up his theory of human nature in two principles from which he thought he could demonstrate the absolute necessity of leagues and contracts and the rudiments of moral and civil prudence – 'the one arising from the concupiscible part, which desires to appropriate to itself the use of those things in which all others have a joint interest; the other proceeding from the rational which teaches every man to fly a contra-natural dissolution, as the greatest mischief that can arrive to nature'.[2] Everything we do springs either from the desire for power or from fear. '. . . Men from their very birth, and naturally, scramble for everything they covet, and would have all the world, if they could, to fear and obey them.'[3] The fear of death, especially violent death, which encompasses all the aversions, alone can damp down the jet of appetite. The appearances, our pretensions to generosity or to disinterestedness, are but cloaks to hide the struggle between these egoistic motives; the reality beneath is the thrust and recoil of a pleasure-pain calculating machine.

This is the stark picture which Hobbes presented. Before passing

1. E.W. IV, 53.   2. E.W. II, vii.   3. E.W. VII, 73.

to the consequences that follow from this description of human nature, let us pause to remind ourselves how Hobbes came to suggest it. To understand what Hobbes was about we must disabuse our minds of the hope that Hobbes would have been much worried by the citation of cases which do not appear to conform to his account. Mothers are moved by love of their children, we might say. Surely this is not fear for themselves or the desire for power. Hobbes would reply like a Freudian analyst when a patient denies that he wants to kill his father. That is a superficial, unscientific account of the matter, he would say. The real motives must be discovered and the clothes discarded in which we dress them up. Of course the scientific account is not altogether beyond the experience of the ordinary man. For do we not prefer to travel in company? Do we not lock our doors when we are asleep and lock up our chests in our houses?[1] This shows, surely, that the ordinary man's attitude to his fellows is consistent with the scientist's account. Man to man is wolf to wolf.

But Hobbes did not attach much weight to such observations on the actual behaviour of men. His postulates of motivation were not empirical assumptions which could be refuted or confirmed by observation. Rather they were self-evident truths which any man could discern if he looked into himself.[2] Many men took his advice and, needless to say, there were many who vociferously protested that Hobbes had misrepresented human nature. His ablest and most coherent critic was Bishop Butler who explicitly attacked Hobbes' theories in his first and eleventh *Sermons on Human Nature*. These sermons, delivered in the Rolls Chapel in the more peaceful period at the beginning of the eighteenth century, raised points which are shrewd comments on Hobbes and of lasting philosophical importance. Butler's purpose was to persuade his sophisticated listeners that living virtuously was their Christian duty as well as in their interest. The love of God was quite consistent with self-love. His objection to Hobbes was that in his system everything was a manifestation of self-love. This was a shocking doctrine in which good-will and benevolence were misrepresented in order to fit into a theory that may have seemed

1. See E.W. III, 114.   2. See E.W. III, xi, xii.

clear to Hobbes when he retired into himself but which went against acknowledged facts and actions. And after all 'whether man be thus or otherwise constituted, what is the inward frame in this particular, is a mere question of fact or natural history, not provable immediately by reason.'[1] So much for Hobbes' method.

Hobbes' theory, according to Butler, rested on the failure to make two cardinal distinctions. Firstly, Hobbes treated all action as if it were calculating action in which the agent aimed at an increase of his own power. But many actions proceed without foresight of an end to be achieved. 'Though a man hated himself, he would as much feel the pain of hunger as he would that of gout. . . . One man rushes upon certain ruin for the gratification of a present desire: nobody will call the principle of this action self-love.'[2] The trouble with men, argued Butler, is not just that they have too little benevolence; it is also that they act *too little* from self-love, being at the mercy of fleeting impulses. This may well be so. But it was not really an informed objection to Hobbes. For he did distinguish between sensual and mental pleasures, the former being occasioned by the presence of an object and requiring no foresight of an end. He did also single out appetites and aversions like hunger, thirst, excretion and exoneration which are born with men, and which, unlike appetites for particular things, need no previous experience and trial of their effects which Butler laid down as a necessary condition for the operation of self-love. Finally, Hobbes was careful to distinguish real from apparent objects of desire and his whole account of prudence and natural law presupposed the distinction between short-term and long-term goods. Hobbes dealt cursorily, it is true, with impulsive action,[3] probably because of his political approach to motivation. In ethics and politics actions are only interesting in so far as they

1. J. Butler, *Sermons on Human Nature*, I, footnote to section 6 (ed. Matthews, 1914).

2. J. Butler, op. cit., I, footnote to section 7.

3. Hobbes thought that all human action was voluntary. In cases where there was no time to deliberate action followed 'the present thought he hath of the good or evil consequence thereof to himself. As for example, in sudden anger, the action shall follow the thought of revenge.' E.W. IV, 272.

are consciously directed towards goals. And this brings us to Butler's second cardinal distinction.

Hobbes, argued Butler, was able to treat benevolence as a special case of self-love because he failed to distinguish the object towards which an action is directed from the satisfaction which may attend its attainment. The cruel man aims at hurt to his neighbour. He may get satisfaction from hurting him but he does not *aim at* such satisfaction. It is the same with benevolent actions. The fact that both selfish and benevolent actions satisfy us does not mean either that we must equate them or that we must make the mistake of thinking that both are performed *in order to* obtain our own satisfaction. '. . . This is not the language of mankind: or if it were, we should want words to express the difference between the principle of an action, proceeding from cool calculation that it will be to my advantage; and an action, suppose of revenge, or of friendship, by which a man runs upon certain ruin to do evil or good to another. It is manifest that the principles of these actions are totally different, and so want different words to be distinguished by: all that they agree in is, that they both proceed from and are done to gratify, an inclination in a man's self.'[1] Butler is certainly right here at the common-sense level. We distinguish selfish from unselfish actions by trying to discover what the agent was aiming at. It is extremely difficult to defend the view that all actions are consciously aimed at the satisfaction of the agent. For, at the common-sense level, impulsive and benevolent actions are obvious counter-examples. Our ordinary language, our judgements of conduct and legal judgements of intention all reflect this obvious distinction. Without them practical men would be at a loss to assess conduct. And, as Butler pointed out, even if Hobbes' manner of describing the matter were adopted, new words for bringing out this crucial distinction would have to be introduced into his new language. Things are what they are and not some other thing; there are some distinctions of fact which must be reflected in any language that is to be of practical use.

Hobbes' suggestions derived, in part, from his attempt to marry

1. J. Butler, *Sermons on Human Nature*, XI, section 7.

common sense with science, and rather unconvincing science at that. His scientific theory was an attempt to reconstruct rationally the causes of action; men were pictured as natural machines *pushed* towards or away from objects. Every such movement increased or impeded the vital motions, and this was felt as pleasure or pain. The pleasure and pain resulting from action was therefore an integral part of his scientific account. This is not absurd. Most modern theories of behaviour employ some such homeostatic principle of explanation. The *function* of goal-directed behaviour, it is maintained, is to preserve the equilibrium of the organism. But this does not imply that organisms *consciously aim* at attaining an equilibrium state. Hobbes also held an ideo-motor theory of actions which assigns the *cause* of actions to external stimuli which produce phantasms transmitting push. But Hobbes never suggested that as actions bring about an increase or decrease in vital motion they must always be *initiated* by an image of this result. Actions which bring mental pleasures or pains (joy or grief for Hobbes) are initiated by foresight of pleasure to come, together with consciousness of our power to produce something. But this is not the case with *sensual* pleasures. It is true that his account of sensual pleasures is sketchy; but it would be very difficult to conclude that he thought that 'all onerations and exonerations of the body' together with actions directed towards preserving what is 'pleasant, in the sight, hearing, smell, taste or touch' were initiated by anything other than a phantasm of the object to be kept near or pushed away from the body. We have previously remarked on Hobbes' vagueness about the concept of 'end' which he calls the 'fruition' of an action.[1] His lack of clarity about this concept makes it very difficult to decide precisely what his theory was, but it is tempting to suggest that Butler's strictures on Hobbes' theory were not altogether fair. Hobbes was attempting to give a scientific theory about the *causes* of action. It was not a particularly convincing theory in itself because of its ideo-motor bias. But its intrusion into common-sense questions about actions proved disastrous. And one of the disasters occasioned by it was the theory popularly known as psychological hedonism. This point

1. See *supra*, pp. 132–3.

is of such general philosophical importance that it must be briefly explained.

Psychological hedonism is the view, often ascribed too readily to Hobbes, that men can only seek their own pleasure. It need never have troubled moral philosophers very much if questions about actions which are psychologically interesting had been clearly distinguished from those which are ethically relevant. In making moral judgements we are only interested in limited questions about actions; we want to know the point of or reason for them – the *objective* consciously intended by the agent. We are not interested in their psychological function, whether this is put in the old language of increasing or impeding vital motion or in the new language of preserving the equilibrium of the organism, reducing need, or producing satisfaction. Nor are we interested in the cause of actions unless these causes are of such a kind as to make them unavoidable, i.e. to render an agent's intentions ineffective or superfluous. We do not give a man moral marks for his social conditioning or endocrine balance. And when, as moralists, we fasten upon a person's intentions, it is obvious that there are many actions which are not aimed solely at the agent's own pleasure. Butler was obviously right about this; he was the champion of morals and common sense. But the psychologist wants to know more about actions. He is not content to find out a man's intentions; he is intrigued by the causes of actions or what initiates them and often relates their function to some principle similar to Hobbes' pleasure-pain principle. A man may jump into a river *in order to* save a drowning boy. We give him moral marks for his intention. But the action may have been *caused*, in part, by his need for social approval which could be traced back to the nursery years. This is psychologically interesting but morally irrelevant unless he *consciously intended* to obtain social approval or unless the need was irresistible. The same kind of point can be made about the satisfaction derived from the action or its psychological *function*. No doubt the action increased or decreased the hero's vital motions; but this is not ethically relevant unless he saved the boy *in order to* obtain this satisfaction. Unless the psychologist's questions are distinguished from the moralist's we get the typical situation of a seeming clash between a developing science and common sense. We have seen how this collision occurred in Hobbes' account of body.[1] It then requires a Butler or a Berkeley to come to the rescue of common sense. In Hobbes' case the shock to common sense was accentuated because his scientific theory was such a bad one. Nowadays, when theories are much better and much more difficult to relate to common sense because of the discovery of unconscious motives, the need to distinguish scientific questions about causes and function from practical questions about intention is even greater. Butler revived common sense after the shock of Hobbes; but no comparable philosopher has yet emerged to do a similar job after the shock of Freud.

1. See *supra*, pp. 90–1.

CHAPTER 7

MOTIVES AND MORALITY

Introductory

HOBBES explicitly stated in his Preface to the English translation of *De Cive* that his original plan of a trilogy – Body, Man and Citizen – was interrupted because his country was 'boiling hot with questions concerning the rights of dominion and the obedience due from subjects', and that therefore his *De Cive*, which was last in order, 'is yet come forth first time'.[1] Yet he had gathered together its first elements and had 'digested them into three sections by degrees'.[2] Nevertheless the principles on which his political philosophy was based were 'sufficiently known by experience'. We can thus infer that he thought his principles consistent with the sections that had not yet been written, and also that they were self-evident in themselves. He believed that the rules of justice rested on consent and that he could demonstrate how men must come to agree upon them by making explicit the springs of human action and decision.

Thus, Hobbes' theory of motivation was a kind of watershed between his physics and politics. For it was to show what sort of rules and conventions for civil society man as a natural machine must necessarily assent to and need to have supported by the sword of the sovereign. As Bentham was later to put it: 'Nature has placed mankind under the governance of two sovereign masters, pleasure and pain. It is for them alone to point out what we ought to do, as well as to determine what we shall do. On the one hand the standard of right and wrong, on the other the chain of causes and effects, are fastened to their throne.'[3] But to give the

1. E.W. II, xx.   2. E.W. II, xix.
3. J. Bentham, *An Introduction to the Principles of Morals and Legislation* (ed. Harrison, Oxford, 1948), p. 125.

standard of right and wrong or to give moral *reasons* for actions, like giving the meaning of words or images, is to answer one kind of question; whereas to give the *causes* of an action, like giving the causes of imagery or speech, is to answer another kind of question. Hobbes' treatment of motivation, like his treatment of imagery and speech, ignored this distinction and suggested that an adequate answer to both types of question could be provided by answering the second type of question.

It is extremely dubious whether any attempt to substitute psychology for ethics could be made at all plausible; for, as was indicated in our discussion of Hobbes' method, this would involve the fallacy of trying to settle questions about what ought to be by settling questions about what is the case. This logical blemish, however, was not clearly grasped till Hume made it explicit when commenting on the subtle transition from what is to what ought to be,[1] and does not seriously detract from the interest of Hobbes' account.

1. The Transition to Morality

The first step in Hobbes' attempt to bridge the gap between psychology and ethics was his analysis of goodness. 'Whatsoever is the object of any man's appetite or desire, that is it which he for his part calleth good: and the object of his hate and aversion, evil. . .'[2] These words do not name some metaphysical essence; they are 'ever used with relation to the person that useth them: there being nothing simply and absolutely so; nor any common rule of good and evil, to be taken from the nature of the objects themselves'.[3] 'Good', in other words, is a term like 'nice' or 'amusing' which implies a relation to the emotions, desires or interests of the person who uses it. It differs in this respect from a term like 'square'; for when we call a box square it needs considerable ingenuity to suggest that we are implying anything about ourselves.

It should, however, be noticed that Hobbes did not subscribe

1. D. Hume, *A Treatise on Human Nature*, Bk III, Part I, section 1 *ad fin.*
2. E.W. III, 41. 3. E.W. III, 41.

to one version of the subjectivist view, which is that statements about good are psychological statements about ourselves – a species of introspective note. According to Hobbes we always assume certain qualities in the object in virtue of which it pleases us: '. . . nothing is good or evil but in regard of the actions that proceedeth from it, and also of the person to whom it doth good or hurt . . . some herbs are good because they nourish, others evil because they poison us; and one horse is good because he is gentle, strong and carrieth a man easily.'[1] Hobbes here lighted upon an important feature of the term 'good' which many modern writers on ethics have brought out in different ways. In describing something as good we do not refer to any definite properties of the object in the way in which we do when we call something square. But although we do not directly indicate properties we always imply that the object has some in virtue of which the term 'good' is appropriate. Criteria are assumed. Hobbes' horse is good *because* he is 'gentle, strong and carrieth a man easily'. The qualities which are implied vary from context to context, there being, as Hobbes put it, 'no common rule of good and evil, to be taken from the nature of the objects themselves'. The 'common rule' is understood by the speaker and his audience. This explains how an object's goodness is relative to the person who describes it as good without its being introspectively revealed.

There are, however, two major troubles with Hobbes' analysis. The first is that it is difficult to see why we need the word 'good' in our vocabulary in addition to words like 'attractive', 'pleasant', and 'satisfying'. Surely Hobbes' analysis omits the *normative* force of the term. To say that peace is good implies not just that it has qualities in virtue of which it *is* desired; it is to insist that it has qualities in virtue of which it *ought to be* desired and promoted. 'Good' has an impersonal commendatory force about it which is lacking in words like 'nice' and 'attractive', that are used for purely private preferences. There would be nothing surprising about saying 'Peace is good; but unfortunately neither I nor anyone else desires it.' But it would verge on the self-contradictory to say 'Peace is good; but neither I nor anyone else ought to

1. E.W. V, 192.

desire it.' Hobbes' analysis presupposed that 'good' was a word which we use simply to *describe* the relation of the properties of an object to our desires. But this is not the case. For not only are certain impersonal standards or 'common rules' implied; but also the primary function of the word is to advise, commend, prescribe, and indulge in other such practical activities. Plato once described the philosopher as the spectator of all time and all existence. But when he went on to describe the theoretical life as good, he gave up theorizing and commended it to his readers.

This leads on to the second defect in Hobbes' analysis, which was his handling of the relational aspect of 'good'. He thought that part of the *meaning* of 'good' is the relation of certain characteristics of the object to the *actual desires* of the speaker. These desires vary from speaker to speaker, and it is only when talking of peace which, in his view, every man could not help but desire, that he was prepared to speak of something that is absolutely good. But, as we have seen, it would be quite in order to speak of peace as good even though no one in fact desired it. The relational aspect is connected with the commendatory use of the term rather than with its descriptive content. 'Peace is good' is roughly equivalent to saying that peace is something which, because of qualities x, y, z, ought to be chosen, promoted, or pursued, by both the speaker and his audience. The commendatory attitude of the speaker is part of the analysis of 'good', not his actual desires towards the object. Of course one of the most obvious *grounds* for commending something is that it has qualities which we and our audience desire or find satisfying. It would be very strange, too, if something that was called 'good' was not something that could conceivably be desired by anyone. This is surely the point of Mill's often criticized remark that the sole *reason* that can be given for calling something desirable is that people actually desire it. But this is not, surely, the *sole* reason for commending something; still less is it part of what 'good' means. Hobbes was misled by the contingent fact that people often desire what they call good and often call things good *because* they have qualities which they in fact desire, into thinking that there is a necessary connexion between being good and being actually desired by the speaker.

There is another aspect of Hobbes' theory of goodness which is more interesting than the rather crude analysis which we have outlined to date. He often spoke of 'good' in the context of rationality. 'Reason declaring peace to be good, it follows by the same reason, that all the necessary means to peace be good also.'[1] This he contrasted with men swayed by 'irrational appetite, whereby they greedily prefer the present good'. A man may not in fact desire peace at a particular moment; but he *would* desire it if he reflected calmly on what would give him pleasure on the whole and in the long run. Sobered by the fear of death he would see the desirability of peace and of the means necessary to attain it. It is as if a guardian were giving advice to his ward and said, 'I know you *want* to go on the stage, but understanding you as I do, I feel confident that the *best* thing for you to do would be to go to the University.' Hobbes thought that he understood human nature. He therefore thought that peace was what all men *would* desire in so far as they were rational and understood their permanent, long-term interests. And all men were in part rational because of their fear of death. Peace must therefore be good, what any rational man would desire.

This analysis preserves the reference to desire as part of the meaning of 'good', but 'object of desire' is expanded to include what a man would desire if he were rational. The question that arises, however, is whether the addition of 'if he were rational' is a way of covertly smuggling in the impersonal and normative force of the term. To say that something is good implies that it should be chosen or pursued and that there are good reasons which any man would accept for this advice. In Hobbes' case the good reasons derived from an assumed identity of interests on the part of all men. Certainly it would sound odd to say 'The rational thing for you to do would be to seek peace, but you ought not to do so.' Is not 'rational' itself a normative term? Before we deal with this question we must examine the use which Hobbes makes of the concept of rationality in his attempt to provide a psychological foundation for natural law. For his analysis of 'good' is but the gateway to what for him was a far more important task –

1. E.W. II, 48.

the use of psychological postulates to demonstrate 'the absolute necessity of leagues and contracts, and thence the rudiments both of moral and of civil prudence'.[1]

2. *The Justification of Natural Law*

Morality is not concerned simply with the pursuit of good, but with the limitation of its pursuit when it affects that of others. These limitations are imposed by custom and law as well as by moral rules. In primitive communities social controls tend to be undifferentiated. It would be absurd to ask whether a rule was a matter of morality or whether it was merely a custom. These distinctions, like the distinction between mythology and science, took a long time to emerge and presuppose the use of criteria by reference to which rules could be classed as customary, legal and moral.

Historically speaking what we now call morality emerged from custom and law under the name of the law of nature or natural law. It was regarded as a set of rules universally binding on all men and contrasted with the conventions of particular states. The Stoics, who were the first to formulate this conception with explicitness, spoke of man as a citizen of the world as well as of a particular state. He was entitled to this status on account of his reason which he shared with all men. As rational beings all men were equal, whatever their civic status; and as rational beings men could not doubt that contracts ought to be kept, life and property ought to be respected, and justice ought to be practised in the various transactions of life. These were the sorts of rules for which good reasons could be given in *any* society of men. Socrates long ago had insisted on accepting only those rules which the individual himself could justify. It was not enough to adopt traditional standards because they were traditional or authoritatively ordained. The individual must question them and apply to himself only those rules for which a justification could be found. But the Stoics made more explicit the conception of a rationally defensible system of rules which applied universally. They

1. E.W. II, vii.

flourished after the conquests of Alexander and the cosmopolitan tendencies which he fostered. It was therefore possible for them to develop the cosmopolitan implications of the rational individualism of the Socratic tradition.

Stoicism came to Rome, but the Romans were far too practically minded to attempt to implement a set of ideal principles. It so happened, however, that as a concession to those foreign cities with whom their military and commercial expansion was increasingly bringing them into contact, they had developed a simplified system of law called the *jus gentium*, or law of nations. This was a sort of L.C.M. of the legal rules in force in the different cities; it permitted disputes between people of an expanding empire to be settled fairly and efficiently. Although the Roman lawyers kept the ideal law of nature distinct from the law of nations, it is easy to see how the former exerted a simplifying and humanizing influence on the latter. With the coming of Christianity cosmopolitanism and equalitarianism found a more emotional and dynamic form of expression. The system of natural law came gradually to be regarded as a selection from God's rules for man which could be rationally discerned as distinct from being supernaturally revealed. It was appealed to by the more philosophically minded of the clergy to humanize and often to condemn current laws and customs.

The notion of the law of nature, then, was not at all a novel one at the time when Hobbes was writing. But it is very interesting to conjecture why it had assumed such great importance at this period. This was not because of its content – for this changed very little – but because of its status and of the use to which it could be put. The Renaissance, as has often been remarked, focused interest on man as an individual. The law of nature was thought to be rooted in man as an individual, who was in certain respects like all other individuals, rather than derivative from his civic or ecclesiastical status. At a time of acute religious controversy it appeared to those who wanted peace and toleration as a set of rules which were rationally acceptable and unaffected by the revelations of rival religious sects. Also, with the rise of nation states in England, France, and Spain, Kings were beginning to *make* laws instead of declaring the fundamental law of the realm enshrined in its customs. The law of nature therefore was a godsend to those who feared absolutism, as a set of principles binding on Kings as well as on their subjects. Finally, at a time of great commercial expansion, the law of nature appealed to the rising class of traders and business men as a set of rules that could form a basis for international law. The Dutchman, Grotius, coming from a nation as famous for its trade as for its toleration, attempted to use natural law as a scientifically established set of principles on which a system of international law could be erected. He tried to do for law what Galileo had done for physics, to demonstrate that it had an axiomatic foundation in self-evident principles which were clear and distinct to any rational being.

Hobbes, therefore, was not at all original in trying to demonstrate that moral principles could be derived from postulates describing man as an individual. But he differed from Grotius in his account of human nature and in his conviction of the conventionality of civil law. Grotius grounded natural law on man's nature as a rational and *social* being. The maintenance of society was a major need for man irrespective of private benefits. The source of law was to be found in this tendency to maintain some kind of social order. Keeping faith, fair dealing, non-injury to life and property were ways of behaving as natural to man as pursuing his own interests. They gave rise to the civil laws of different states which, though conventional and based on utility, depended on the 'natural obligation' to keep contracts. Natural law, therefore, which comprised all the simple rules for living together which any rational and social being could not help accepting, was the foundation of all systems of civil and international law.

Hobbes, with his eye on Grotius' account, maintained that more or less the same set of principles could be deduced from man's nature as a being who becomes rational through his fear of death. The state of nature was a state of war, not of social co-operation as Grotius taught. 'All society, therefore, is either for gain or for glory; that is, not so much for love of our fellows as for the love of ourselves.'[1] Men are equal enough in body and mind

1. E.W. II, 5.

to render negligible any palpable claims to superior benefits, and even the weakest is able to kill the strongest. So all men have more or less equal hope of attaining their ends. As their basic striving is for power and precedence they live in a constant state of competition, enmity and mutual suspicion. 'In such condition, there is no place for industry; because the fruit thereof is uncertain: and consequently no culture of the earth; no navigation, nor use of the commodities that may be imported by sea; no commodious building; no instruments of moving, and removing, such things as require much force; no knowledge of the face of the earth; no account of time; no arts; no letters; no society; and which is worst of all, continual fear, and danger of violent death; and the life of man, solitary, poor, nasty, brutish, and short.'[1]

Hobbes did not take such a state of nature seriously as a historical hypothesis, though he did mention in passing the plight of 'savage people in many places of America',[2] who in fact had no central government. He was conducting a Galilean experiment of the imaginary sort – a resolution of society into its clear and distinct parts so as to reconstruct the whole in order of logical dependence rather than of historical genesis. He could thus treat men 'as if but now sprung out of the earth and suddenly, like mushrooms, come to full maturity'.[3] Having isolated the underlying movements of men towards each other – their desire for power – he deduced the consequences that followed from this postulate alone. This was the state of war. This analytic exercise was also a way of teaching a lesson; for it showed how men would behave if they had no civil power to restrain them. In such a state there would be no right or wrong, justice or injustice. 'Where there is no common power, there is no law: where no law, no injustice. Force and fraud are in war the two cardinal virtues.'[4]

Having shown the logical consequences of man's desire for power, Hobbes passed to the other clear and distinct component, the fear of death. Man shuns death 'by a certain impulsion of nature, no less than that whereby a stone moves downward'.[5] For Hobbes this aversion was the basis of all virtue and morality. It

1. E.W. III, 113.   3. E.W. II, 109.   5. E.W. II, 8.
2. E.W. III, 114.   4. E.W. III, 115.

brings man up short in his pursuit of power and leads him to reflect about his predicament. In the calmness occasioned by this overwhelming fear man's reason informs him that peace is a necessity for survival and it also 'suggesteth convenient articles of peace, upon which men may be drawn to agreement. These articles are they, which otherwise are called the Laws of Nature.'[1] The first of these is 'that every man, ought to endeavour peace, as far as he has hope of obtaining it; and when he cannot obtain it, that he may seek, and use, all helps, and advantages of war'.[2] From this can be derived the second law 'that a man be willing, when others are so too, as far-forth, as for peace, and defence of himself he shall think it necessary, to lay down this right to all things; and be contented with so much liberty against other men, as he would allow other men against himself'.[3] This is equivalent to the law of the Gospel, 'Whatsoever you require that others should do to you, that do ye to them.' The third law follows 'that men perform their covenants made'.[4] And so Hobbes proceeded with the deduction of the various rules and virtues which seemed to him essential to peace.

But in what sense can Hobbes be said to have *demonstrated* from the maxims of human nature arising from its concupiscible and rational components 'the absolute necessity of leagues and covenants, and thence the rudiments both of moral and of civil prudence'? How can the rule that men '*ought to* endeavour peace' be a *deduction* from postulates which state that men *can* only seek power and avoid death? For there is a crucial transition here of which Hobbes seemed curiously unaware. The science of natural justice, in which the laws of nature were to serve as basic axioms, *prescribed* both that men ought to endeavour peace and ought to follow certain rules in order to obtain it. But this science was to be quite unlike mechanics, physics and psychology, which contain only *descriptions* stating what happens universally under certain conditions. Neither Galileo nor Harvey *prescribed* rules for the behaviour of bodies. Scientists do not advise their subject-matter in the way in which Kings advise their subjects.

There would be no logical objection to Hobbes formulating an

1. E.W. III, 116. 2. E.W. III, 117. 3. E.W. III, 118. 4. E.W. III, 130.

axiomatic system of rules and appealing to people to adopt them as a prescriptive basis for living together. Once accepted, the logical consequences of these rules could be explored and applied to personal life and social organization. This is the parallel between geometry and Hobbes' civil philosophy. The fundamental rules of natural justice would function rather like the aims of an instituted club or association; the details of the ground-plan could be worked out by seeing what followed from the definitive aims. But Hobbes was not trying to institute a new society. He thought that he was making explicit by Galilean resolution the rationale of any existing civil society – deducing the real objectives of its members from their underlying motives. But this more ambitious and more interesting undertaking has, surely, grave logical objections to it. For it presupposes that statements *prescribing* how men ought to behave can be deduced from statements *describing* how they in fact behave. And this breaks one of the first rules of deductive logic, which is that no statement can feature in the conclusions of a valid deduction which is not contained explicitly or implicitly in the premisses. If physics and psychology provide the premisses, then they contain only descriptions. It follows, therefore, that no statement other than a description can feature in the conclusion. It is only if a rule like 'men ought to endeavour peace' is one of the premisses that the principles of natural justice can be deduced from premisses containing *also* physical or psychological postulates. Rules of physical health can be deduced from the science of the human body provided that the prescription 'health ought to be promoted' is included in the premisses. But the science of psychology and physics *alone*, without a basic prescription, will no more yield rules of natural justice than will the science of body alone yield rules of health. Hobbes seems to have thought that the basic prescription 'men ought to endeavour peace' can be deduced from psychology and physics. This seems to be a logical mistake.

There is, too, an absurdity involved in treating these rules as deductions from psychology. For supposing we treat 'men ought to endeavour peace' as a counsel of prudence equivalent to 'it is in the long term interest of men to pursue peace'. This can only be deduced from psychology if our psychological premiss maintains that everywhere and always men can only pursue their own interest. If the premiss were true it would then become superfluous to remind people so forcefully of what they could not help doing anyway. And, of course, Hobbes did not think that this premiss was true. For he laboured the point that men were too often driven by their desire for power to prefer their short-term triumphs to their long-term interest. This gives point to reminding men of their long-term interests but it makes nonsense of the deduction from psychology. For all that could be deduced would be the vacillation of men between the pursuit of their long-term and short-term interest. Hobbes' rules of natural justice, then, if we treat them as deductions from psychology, would either be invalid deductions or they would be logically valid but otiose counsels of prudence for men whose nature was to be prudent anyway.

Suppose, then, that we admit the necessity for a prescriptive premiss. Hobbes' argument is now very interesting and convincing, granted his psychological assumptions. Adopting the Galilean method of resolution he isolated the simple component of man's desire for power and deduced the consequences that followed from this alone – the state of nature. He then isolated man's fear of death and showed that this would lead a rational man (and man, for Hobbes, is rational by definition) to accept certain rules without the observance of which death could not be avoided. These were the laws of nature. If these two components were now put together in the compositive step of the method, men would be demonstrated as poised precariously between civil society, which was the ultimate consequence of accepting the laws of nature and enforcing them by the sword of the sovereign, and the state of nature. At the time when Hobbes wrote *Leviathan* this was a fair enough picture of the conditions which in fact prevailed. The *Leviathan* was tossed into the fray as a grim warning of what would necessarily happen if men allowed their desire for power to get the better of their fear of death. He seems to have thought that only under certain conditions was man's fear of death strong enough to master his desire for power – when a violent death or a death whose exact nature could not be foreseen was imminent. The *Leviathan* would not only help to bring this kind of situation vividly before his readers who were too often lulled into insensitivity to their stark predicament, but it would also provide the science of natural justice in which the rules necessary for making peace a reality instead of a pious hope were demonstrated.

This interpretation of the *Leviathan* only works if Hobbes had laid down as a prescriptive premiss the axiom that men ought to endeavour peace. This he did not do. Nevertheless, as we have previously noted,[1] he did seem to think that the Galilean method, when applied to society, had a normative rather than a purely descriptive function. For the declared intention of his civil philosophy was 'to understand what the quality of human nature is, in what matters it is, in what not *fit* to make up a civil government, and how men must agree amongst themselves that intend to grow up into a *well-grounded* state'.[2] If his civil philosophy had been purely descriptive he could only have deduced the precariousness of man's predicament, poised between civil government and the state of nature. But surely the *Leviathan* rings with prescription. It covertly advises men to damp down their jet of appetite by brooding on the possibility of violent death. It shows men that their nature is 'fit to make up a civil government' and throws in the demonstrable axioms necessary to make their fear of death effective.

3. Rationality and the Law of Nature

There remains for comment the connexion which Hobbes assumed between man's rationality and the acceptance of the axioms of the law of nature. Traditionally these were regarded as the precepts that a rational and *social* being would accept as minimum rules for living peaceably with others. In the thought of the Stoics rationality was linked with respect for others in whom also the divine spark of reason shone. Hobbes assumed that rationality was compatible with egoism and that the law of nature could be defended equally well on a basis of rational self-interest.

1. See *supra*, pp. 70–2.   2. E.W. II, xiv (my italics).

We ought not to keep faith on account of our respect for others but on account of our fear for ourselves.

Now there is no doubt that a defence of these rules can be given in terms of self-interest. Yet Hobbes was at pains to equate the law of nature with *morality*. 'The true doctrine of the laws of nature, is the true moral philosophy.'[1] This, prima facie, does seem a bit startling; for, as Hume pointed out, the question 'What is this to me?', when asked about a rule, seems clearly distinct and different from the question 'Is this right?' Why do we have different forms of words if the two questions mean the same? The moral criterion does not require the disregarding of our own interests but considering them *impartially* with the interests of others who may also be affected by the rule. To ignore the interests of others, or to consider them only as a means to our own is, surely, to refuse to adopt a moral standpoint to a rule. Certainly part of the 'true moral philosophy' lies in the importance of reason, or giving reasons for rules. But moral rules are those for which reasons of a certain sort are given. Indeed, rules *become* moral when looked at from the point of view of the interests affected by them, and with *impartiality* in regard to these interests. This is not to deny that they can *also* be rules of prudence when looked at simply from the point of view of self-interest. Indeed, it is a happy event when a proposal is both moral and in our best interests. It is only to deny the *equation* of the moral defence with that of self-interest.

This criticism of Hobbes' account of course presupposes the validity of the criticisms levelled against his psychological hedonism. But the case for Hobbes' neglect of the principle of impartiality can be strengthened by raising an even more fundamental query about the consistency of rationality itself with thoroughgoing egoism. To use our reason implies, surely, not just the ability to solve intellectual conundrums in our heads; it implies also the willingness to decide questions on the basis of the reasons advanced rather than by reliance on authority or revelation. The rationalist movement was an attempt to break away from authority and to accept only those assumptions or rules the

1. E.W. III, 146.

reasons for which were clear to any thinking man. This pre-supposes discussion, the raising of objections to suggestions, and all the intellectual climate of criticism which Hobbes revelled in while a member of Mersenne's circle. If a man was refuted by his peers he had to go away and remodel his theory to meet objections. Descartes published a celebrated volume of answers to objections raised against his theories. In other words being prepared to abide by reason implies a certain minimum of *impartiality* towards our own theories; we must be prepared to admit that we may be wrong and we must respect other people at least in so far as they too have theories and may make telling objections to ours. We must bother about arguments and disregard the personal and social idiosyncrasies of the men who propound them. Wallis' reference to Hobbes' West-country accent was quite irrelevant to the truth of his contentions. This rule of impartiality must be applied also to ourselves. Now it is notorious that we become very much attached to our own theories, and often it is very much in our interest that we should not be refuted. But if we are to abide by the canons implied by being reasonable or using our reason we must be prepared to *disregard our own interests* and bow before the force of argument. Respect for truth must come before regard for our own interests. To use our reason, therefore, is inconsistent with being *completely* self-interested. Hobbes, therefore, cannot consistently hold that men are both rational and complete egoists.[1]

Hobbes, of course, held no such explicit view of rationality. Being rational, for him, amounted to following out the implications of definitions and being able to frame clear and distinct ideas. It may, too, be objected that in his practice Hobbes treated argument rather like a wrestling bout in which the point was to throw the other fellow and glory in his discomfiture. But even wrestling is conducted according to certain rules, and whether or not the norm of impartiality was implied in Hobbes' rather didactic method of argument depends on the extent to which he regarded argument as a method of arriving at truth or as a process of imposing his will (or definitions) arbitrarily on another man. This brings us back to his vacillation between a self-evidence

1. The substance of this argument I owe to Professor Popper.

and conventionist theory of truth and the part played by what he called 'evidence'.[1]

4. Causes and Reasons

Hobbes' attempt to found the law of nature on psychology looks like a further example of the tendency already noted in his theory of imagery and speech to answer causal questions and to think that he was thereby answering other sorts of questions. The issue he was grappling with was that of the *justification* of or giving *reasons* for the precepts enjoined by the law of nature. Hobbes exhibited the desire for power and fear as the *causes* of everything we do and presumed that he was thereby making clear the reasons for accepting the law of nature. But if we are trying to justify a rule like 'men perform their covenants made' does it matter what causes us to accept it? A man may believe firmly in the sanctity of covenants because of his childhood upbringing, his unconscious need of security, or because of the discomfort generated by an uncompleted task; but all such speculations seem irrelevant to the reasons that can be given for keeping covenants. It is only when beliefs are held in the faces of reasons or when they are the sorts of belief for which no reasons can be given, that we seem justified in passing from the question of validity to the question of causes. If, for instance, a man is convinced that his hands are covered in blood or that a room is occupied by an invisible friend, and if, as in the first case, all the evidence seems to point against it, or, as in the second case, there seems to be no evidence which *could* count against it, then it seems legitimate to ask 'What causes him to believe this?' But it is only the *absence* of reasons that makes the causal question seem relevant.

The ingenuity of Hobbes' theory was that his account of the causes of action ruled out the possibility of any reason other than that of self-interest being effective. To use a modern term, all other reasons were rationalizations, a façade to render pride and fear socially respectable. It is as if the human machine had only two gears. Unless the reasoning engaged one of them it would

1. See *supra*, Ch. 2, sect. 4.

move neither forwards nor backwards. But this presupposed the tenability of his analysis of our basic motives, of psychological hedonism, and of the ideo-motor theory of action. And, as has been indicated, there seem to be good reasons for rejecting all these presuppositions. Indeed, there is a sense in which the tables can be turned on Hobbes. For much of what purports to be causal analysis in Hobbes' attempt to fit all the passions into the desire-aversion model[1] was in fact merely indicating the typical objectives of (reasons for) a man's action. There is therefore a strong case for saying that in a great number of cases he was really giving the reasons for actions when he thought that he was giving their causes.

Nevertheless, in spite of its psychological and logical defects, there is much to be said in favour of Hobbes' ambitious attempt to deduce the necessity of covenants and rules from principles of human nature. His theory provides a refreshing contrast to those which postulate mysterious unobservable qualities described by ethical terms or which suggest transcendental sources of obligation. Hobbes believed both that it is idle to ask what is good for man without a thorough understanding of human nature and that there is a close connexion between man's needs and purposes and what he ought to do. By making the connexion one of logical deducibility he made it *too* close. He was mistaken in thinking that psychology or any other science can of itself tell us what is good; a prescriptive premiss is required to make such advice relevant. Similarly he was mistaken in thinking that what we ought to do can be *deduced* from a theory of human nature; for there is a gap between empirical facts about human nature and what ought to be done about them. But facts about human nature are indispensably *relevant* to our decisions. One of the main problems of moral philosophy is to get clearer about the *ways in which* they are relevant. Hobbes may have been over-optimistic and dogmatic in his claims for his science of human nature. Philosophers, in fact, have ever since been fastening on the logical flaws in naturalistic ethics. But Hobbes never made the opposite mistake, encouraged by so many critics of naturalism, of thinking that the good for

1. See *supra*, pp. 135–8.

man and his palpable duties can be intuited with a cavalier disregard for psychological findings.

5. Free-Will

Hobbes' transition from psychology to ethics was made easy by
his belief in determinism or 'necessitation' as he usually called it;
indeed, on his assumptions the transition was a way of expressing
this belief. For the causes of a man's thoughts or actions determined the reasons which he found acceptable. Hobbes' views on
free-will emerged, in the main, as defined against Bishop Bramhall's in his brief *Of Liberty and Necessity*, drawn up in 1646 at
Newcastle's request, and in his lengthier *The Questions concerning
Liberty, Necessity and Chance,* which gave Bramhall's version of their
discussion together with his own animadversions.[1] We shall, however, only mention Bramhall's views in so far as he exposed possible weaknesses in Hobbes' position.

Hobbes' first important contribution to the controversy was on
the subject of the will. The Bishop's talk of reason representing
things to the will was unintelligible;[2] for there is no special entity
or faculty in a man's mind called 'will' . . . 'as it is absurdly said,
that to dance is an act allured or drawn by fair means out of the
ability to dance; so is it also to say, that to will is an act allured or
drawn out of the power to will, which power is commonly called
the will.'[3] To speak of 'will' was a shorthand way of referring to
the last desire in a process of deliberation.[4]

Secondly, Hobbes claimed that it is not, according to this
'proper and generally received' meaning of the word, the desire
or will of a man that can be said to be free, but the man. For 'free'
is a word that is applied properly only to bodies. Thus 'from the
use of the word free-will, no liberty can be inferred of the will,
desire, or inclination, but the liberty of the man; which consisteth
in this, that he finds no stop, in doing what he has the will, desire,
or inclination to do.'[5] The definition of liberty is 'the absence of
all the impediments to action that are not contained in the nature

1. See *supra*, pp. 36–7.   2. E.W. V, 48.   3. E.W. IV, 266.
4. For discussion, see *supra*, pp. 133–4.   5. E.W. III, 197.

and intrinsical quality of the agent'.[1] A person is thus 'free to do a thing, that may do it if he have the will to do it, and may forbear if he have the will to forbear'.[2] 'Proper and generally received meaning' presumably refers to the ordinary language of educated people. Hobbes was pointing out that, if this criterion of usage is adopted, to speak of liberty is not to make any suggestions about whether or not a person's will or desire is caused; it is rather to suggest that a man is not *constrained* in the pursuit of certain interests that he may have. Theologians, with their mystifying talk of free-will, had obscured this important point which was implicit in the language of common-sense people. Certainly this was an important point that Hobbes made and it is not surprising that both Locke and Hume followed Hobbes in maintaining that 'free' is a term which is appropriately used of men or bodies that lack some kind of constraint on their actions.

The consequence that Hobbes drew from this definition of 'liberty' is also acceptable. For he claimed that if, by calling a man free, we are referring to the absence of external constraint on his action, there is nothing inconsistent in saying that actions that are free are also determined or necessitated. The opposite of 'necessitated' is 'contingent', not 'free'. People, of course, do distinguish 'free from compulsion' from 'free from necessitation'. But a man who is not compelled to do something is one who does not do it out of terror. For 'a man is only said to be compelled when fear makes him willing to it: as when a man willingly throws his goods into the sea to save himself, or submits to his enemy for fear of being killed.'[3] But people who do actions out of love or revenge and are thus free from compulsion (in Hobbes' peculiar sense) do actions which are as necessary as those done out of fear. For all actions have causes and are thus necessitated. It is therefore pointless to use 'free' in the sense of 'free from necessitation'; for there are no such actions. 'That which, I say, necessitateth every action is the sum of all things which being now existent, conduce and concur to the production of that action hereafter, whereof if any one thing now were wanting, the effect could not be produced.'[4] And all human actions are caused by motions

1. E.W. IV, 273.   2. E.W. V, 38.   3. E.W. IV, 261.   4. E.W. IV, 246.

external to them. We only think that contingency exists because we are ignorant of the causes of actions and mistake our ignorance of them for their absence. 'A wooden top that is lashed by the boys, and runs about sometimes to one wall, sometimes to another, sometimes spinning, sometimes hitting men on the shins, if it were sensible of its own motion, would think it proceeded from its own will, unless it felt what lashed it.'[1]

The question remains, however, whether Hobbes' recommended use of 'liberty' as 'an absence of the lets and hindrances of motion'[2] disposes of the objections which Bramhall and many others have raised against determinism. For the issue still remains whether *all* actions are 'necessitated' however we decide to use the word 'free'.

Bramhall did not object to this doctrine in so far as Hobbes spoke only of the actions of animals or of the spontaneous actions of human beings. What he could not stomach was that voluntary actions, which follow on election and deliberation, should also be necessitated. 'The will is moved by the understanding, not as by an efficient having a causal influence into the effect, but only by proposing and representing the object. And therefore, as it were ridiculous to say that the object of the sight is the cause of seeing, so it is to say that the proposing of the object by the understanding to the will is the cause of willing: and therefore the understanding hath no place in the concourse of causes. . . .'[3] Election is a rational act proper only to man. This objection, in a certain way, goes to the heart of the matter, though Hobbes was very quick to deride the unfortunate language of faculties in which Bramhall couched it. However, before we discuss the issues raised, it will be as well to set out shortly Hobbes' reply, which was really nothing more than a reiteration of his theory of motivation.

Hobbes replied that children and animals deliberate as they are moved by the hope of good and fear of evil; that bees and spiders exhibit election, art, prudence, and policy; and that, in fact, *all* human actions proceed from election. For habitual actions like setting the foot in the correct posture for walking were once deliberate. When a man has not time to deliberate, the doing of

1. E.W. V, 55.   2. E.W. II, 120.   3. E.W. V, 73-4.

the action necessarily follows the thought he has of the good or evil consequence thereof to himself, as the thought of revenge in sudden anger or of escape in sudden fear. The imagining of good or evil consequences in deliberation is the same thing as being moved alternately by hope and fear. The last in this succession of contrary appetites is the will. Actions done upon choice and election are therefore as easily explicable in terms of antecedent causes as the motions of anything else in the world. 'The last dictate of the judgement, concerning the good or bad, that may follow on any action, is not properly the whole cause, but the last part of it, and yet may be said to produce the effect necessarily, in such manner as the last feather may be said to break a horse's back, when there were so many laid on before as there wanted but that one to do it . . . the will itself, and each propension of a man during his deliberation, is as much necessitated and depends on a sufficient cause, as anything else whatsoever. As for example, it is no more necessary that fire should burn, than that a man or other creature, whose limbs be moved by fancy, should have election, that is liberty, to do what he hath a fancy to do.'[1]

There are two major issues raised by Hobbes' claim which are derivative from two possible meanings of 'necessitated'[2] or 'determined' which are not always clearly distinguished. 'Determined' may mean simply 'causally explicable'. For an event to be causally explicable we must have established causal laws together with statements describing initial conditions from which two together the event can be predicted. For instance, given that under conditions x, y, z, if heat is applied to iron then it expands, and given, secondly, that here is a case of heat being applied to iron, then it can be predicted that the iron will expand. We have,

1. E.W. IV, 247.
2. Hobbes spoke of events being 'necessitated' when a causal explanation could be given of them because he thought that the causal relation was like that of ground and consequent in logic or geometry. He held that all scientific knowledge was demonstrative and that therefore it resulted in necessary truths. In order to avoid referring again to the difficulties raised by this view, which were discussed in Chapter 2, the term 'determined' is used in this discussion which Hobbes sometimes used as a synonym for his more usual term 'necessitated'.

therefore, to ask about actions proceeding from choice whether Hobbes was right in saying that they are always causally explicable. Of course, there were not the causal laws in psychology in Hobbes' time which would permit this; there still are not such laws. But it is often said that this is a matter of time only and that eventually psychology will have its laws just like physiology and physics. This is the attitude of the scientific optimist. There are, however, doubts which insinuate themselves when we consider the problems raised by Bramhall's elective actions.

Deliberation which precedes human choice may often be of the animal sort – a rehearsal of the alternatives before us. But there may enter in to it something which is unparalleled in the animal world, our consciousness of what we are likely to do. This is a development of self-consciousness made possible by the advance of the sciences of man. A scientist may discover a causal law connecting the properties of clover with certain effects on the digestive organs of sheep. But if he publishes his findings the sheep cannot take cognizance of it and modify their behaviour accordingly. But with men it is different. For many causal connexions discovered by psychologists may only hold good provided that the people whose actions are predicted in accordance with the law remain ignorant of what it asserts. And it is practically impossible to ensure that this is the case. Thus in the case of actions preceded by deliberation, in so far as the causes are known which will enable our actions to be predicted, it is always possible that our knowledge of the causes may intervene and prevent us from doing what we would have done had we not known what we were going to do. Dr Gallup would probably have been correct in his prediction that the majority of voters in the U.S.A. would vote against President Truman had not the voters known that they were going to vote against him. There is thus a case for unpredictability in human affairs in those spheres where action is preceded by informed deliberation.

There is also the problem of giving a causal explanation of actions done after deliberation of a mathematical or logical sort, which proceeds in accordance with certain logical *criteria*. The kind of thinking, which involves the use of symbolic systems, was admitted by Hobbes to be peculiar to man. Was his thinking determined when he deduced the laws of nature as theorems necessary for peace? Hobbes said that 'it is the consultation that causeth a man and necessitateth him to choose to do one thing rather than another'.[1] But the man who manipulates mathematical symbols and eventually makes an atomic explosion, which he could not have made unless he had done the preliminary mathematics, is 'determined' by the rules of logic and mathematics; such 'consultation' is an odd kind of efficient cause. In cases like this the gulf between the causes of an action such as writing something on a piece of paper and the reasons for it seem to be enormous. Similarly, a chess-player may deliberate for hours on how to checkmate his opponent in three moves. There may be antecedent causes for his move – appetites and aversions of one sort and another – but most of us would think it much more important to know the rules of chess without which his action would have no point or reason. Deliberation involving rules, criteria, standards, and so on, is insufficiently explained by reference to antecedent causes, unless, of course, the concept of 'cause' is extended to cover 'reasons' – i.e. notions like that of 'insight', 'understanding', and 'intentions'. The problem, then, is transferred to that of the differences between the types of 'causes' involved. This was the sort of difficulty about Hobbes' view which Bramhall was raising in his talk about 'the understanding'.

So much, then, for the first meaning of 'determined' – that an action is causally explicable. But Hobbes also implied that if a causal explanation can be given of an action, then it could not have happened otherwise than it did. 'Determined', in other words, has often meant, for those who have shared his scientific optimism, inevitable as well as causally explicable. 'This concourse of causes, whereof everyone is determined to be such as it is by a like concourse of former causes, may well be called (in respect they were all set and ordered by the eternal cause of all things, God Almighty) the decree of God.'[2] Many chains of causes stretch from God Almighty, some of them being motions impinging on

1. E.W. IV, 254.   2. E.W. IV, 246.

the sense organs and moving us to and fro in deliberation. We only think that things could be otherwise than they are because of our limited knowledge of causes.

Now this assumed coincidence of inevitability with causal explicability is surely simply a mistake occasioned by the peculiar circumstances of the rise of science. It so happened that the scientific advance, which consisted in the discovery of far-reaching causal laws, coincided with the widespread theological doctrine of predestination and with the metaphysical picture of the universe as a vast piece of clockwork in which human beings were like cog-wheels, pushed onwards in a set pattern of movement. God, as it were, constructed the clock and set it going. If we could see the clock as a whole we would be able to see what our fate would be for years ahead and see also what movements determined that it would be this and no other. There was also the fact that astronomy was taken for centuries as the paradigm of all sciences; and in astronomy, because of the peculiarity of the solar system as a relatively closed system, events like lunar eclipses are both predictable for a long time ahead and unavoidable. For what can we do to prevent them? The tacit assumption therefore developed that wherever a causal explanation could be given of an event, then that event was also inevitable. Thus, with the advance of psychology and the social sciences, which so fired the imagination of Hobbes and Spinoza, shades of the prison house have come increasingly to descend upon the growing boy as more and more details have been filled in by those like Pavlov and Freud who shared the scientific optimism of the seventeenth century.

In human affairs this alleged coincidence of inevitability and causal explicability is so manifestly lacking that almost the reverse is the case. For knowing the causes of what we tend to do is often a necessary condition of preventing ourselves from doing it. If we know that irritability at breakfast is caused by late nights, we know how to prevent irritability at breakfast. Of course, what we say about its inevitability depends very much on our temporal position as an observer. If we look back on our choice of a wife and see the causes that led up to the scene in the registry office, we may often reflect that the course of events was inevitable. But if we approach a courting couple with a battery of psychological laws at our disposal (if such laws existed) and ask ourselves whether, knowing the couple as we do, there are grounds for saying that their marriage is unavoidable, the position is very different.

There are, however, some cases where actions can be shown to have causes of such a kind that they are rendered inevitable, within a certain range of circumstances. For instance, it is claimed that the 'lack of opportunity for forming an attachment to a mother-figure during the first three years', or 'deprivation for a limited period – at least three months and probably more than six – during the first three or four years' (of maternal care) not only causes traits like 'unfriendliness', 'distractability', 'lack of self-inhibition',[1] but also that the cause is of such a kind as to render that sort of behaviour unavoidable. Deliberation by the delinquent, good resolutions, change of foster-home – all these remedial devices are no good. Knowledge, too, of what he is likely to do makes no difference to what he in fact does in the given circumstances. But causal hypotheses of this kind in psychology are extremely rare and the evidence for them is still very tenuous. Unfortunately it has often been assumed by those who have inherited the outlook of the seventeenth century that there is a similar inevitability about conduct wherever the ingenuity of the psychologist has unearthed a cause. But it has yet to be shown that the man whose pipe-smoking is a continuation of biting his mother's nipples cannot give up his expensive habit or that a man can do nothing about his parsimony, pedantry and petulance which were all caused by the way he reacted to the frustration of being potted in his early years. Indeed, the whole practice of psycho-analysts belies this assumed coincidence of causal explicability and inevitability. For a necessary condition of curing patients or changing their behaviour is bringing them to understand and relive the early experiences which caused their later behaviour.

So it appears that in the case of what Bramhall called elective actions a case can be made against determinism in both senses of

---

1. J. Bowlby, *Maternal Care and Mental Health* (Geneva, 1951), p. 47. These findings, however, have been subjected to severe criticism.

the word. Whether this means that a case can be made for free-dom depends entirely on whether it is thought advisable to re-strict the use of 'freedom' to absence of external constraint as Hobbes recommended.

Hobbes, however, spoke much sense on the subject of the ethical consequences of his doctrine which Bramhall so much feared. Bramhall argued that if human actions are determined, then praise and blame, reward and punishment, are both unjust and vain. To the charge of their being vain Hobbes replied that praise and blame, reward and punishment introduce additional cause factors which direct choices. 'If there be necessity that an action should be done, or that any effect shall be brought to pass, it does not therefore follow, that there is nothing necessarily requisite as a means to bring it to pass.'[1] Praise and blame, reward and punishment 'do by example make and conform the will to good and evil'.[2]

To the charge of injustice Hobbes replied that 'the law re-gardeth the will and no other precedent causes of action'.[3] This is quite correct. For the law is only interested in a person's *intentions*; it is not interested in the causes of his actions unless they are of such a kind to make his action unavoidable – e.g. the much debated irresistible impulse. Also, said Hobbes, the punishments annexed to breaches of the law function as deterrents and thus necessitate justice; and consequently it is no injustice to make such a law. 'The intention of the law is not to grieve the delinquent, for that which is past, and not to be undone; but to make him and others just, that else would not be so, and respecteth not the evil act past, but the good to come.'[4]

This is a more questionable position; for punishment *means* pain inflicted on a person by an authorized agency as a consequence of his past acts. Perhaps legislators, in attaching a range of punish-ments to breaches of the law, can look at punishment mainly from the point of view of prevention and deterrence. And, of course, the justification of law should not be confused with the justification of punishment for breaches of the law. But a judge, when it has been established that a person is guilty of a breach of the law, cannot

1. E.W. IV, 255.   2. E.W. IV, 256.   3. E.W. IV, 252.   4. E.W. IV, 253.

help but be influenced by the degree of responsibility of the law-breaker. He will surely be influenced by the deliberateness and cold-bloodedness of the crime in deciding upon the severity of the sentence and will not think of punishment purely from the point of view of its effects on the criminal and on society. Hobbes, it seems, saw that punishment was by its nature retributive as it is pain inflicted on account of a past offence, but that its justification is to be sought along Utilitarian lines. In *Leviathan* he defined it as 'an evil inflicted by public authority, on him that hath done, or omitted that which is judged by the same authority to be a transgression of the law; to the end that the will of men may thereby the better be disposed to obedience'.[1] He went out of his way to distinguish punishment from acts of hostility and to stress the Utilitarian purposes of punishment.[2] But the punishment of the innocent was not to be deplored solely on Utilitarian grounds; it was against the law of nature.[3] If the retributive element is lacking, punishment is not punishment but an act of hostility.

This is sound enough. But surely the underlying assumption of punishment is that people could have *avoided* doing what they did. This is more or less what we mean when we say that a person is responsible for his actions. When a judge imposes a light sentence for a crime committed under great provocation or in the heat of the moment, it is surely because he thinks that a man's responsibility for his action is thereby diminished. Hobbes was right only in maintaining that the 'necessity' of actions makes no difference to the operation of law, if he meant only by 'necessity' causal explicability. For we may be able to give a perfectly adequate and complete causal explanation of a person's intentional behaviour in stealing from his employer. But this is irrelevant. For showing that the behaviour was caused does not also show that his behaviour was unavoidable or that his intentions were redundant. But if the type of cause revealed was *also* of the sort to render his behaviour unavoidable, if it could be established that reflection on the consequences of his action, his resolutions and his attempts to escape his overmastering impulse, could make no difference to what he in fact did; then the 'necessity' would surely affect the

1. E.W. III, 297.   2. E.W. III, 297–301.   3. E.W. III, 304.

176

operation of law and moral judgement. Whether this was the case about the operation of the legal system in the seventeenth century is dubious. But it certainly is the case about the operation of our present legal system.

We have here the same kind of clash between the common-sense practical judgement of judges and the theoretical speculations of a developing science which we noted in our discussion of Hobbes' psychological hedonism.[1] Moralists and judges are concerned primarily with the reasons for actions or people's intentions; psychologists, on the other hand, are interested in their causes and function.[2] Hobbes assumed that reasons can be explained in terms of causes. We have repeatedly questioned this assumption. But the practical consequences of psychological discoveries for our judgements of praise and blame have yet to be adequately assessed. Certainly the Erewhonian period, when crime was likened to disease, and when all reasons were regarded as rationalizations, is passing, together with the fatalism which was the heritage of the seventeenth century. There is a cautious return to the pre-evolutionary view that the possession of reason distinguishes men from brutes, and enables us to counteract the influences of early childhood and economic conditions which were once thought to provide rails along which we ran towards the buffers of our destiny. There is, perhaps, increasing acceptance of Kant's view that man is distinct from the rest of nature in being able to regulate his conduct because of his understanding of scientific laws, and, in the normative sphere, in being able to live in accordance with rules that he himself creates. But the consequences of this insight in terms of the detailed empirical discoveries of psychology and the social sciences have yet to be exhibited. This is one of the main tasks of social philosophy in our generation.

1. See *supra*, pp. 143–9.   2. See *supra*, pp. 135–8.

CHAPTER 8

THE STATE

Introductory

PHILOSOPHERS have tended to ask themselves the question, 'What is the nature of the state?' Some of them, like Plato, have assumed that because we have a word like 'state' there must be some entity which is *properly* designated by the word. Hobbes, however, was a radical nominalist and he cannot be accused of this approach. But he was like many other philosophers in not being concerned purely with a sociological inquiry, the point of which would be to distinguish an association of men called 'state' or 'commonwealth' from other associations like clubs, families, and villages. Nearly all philosophers who have argued about the nature of the state have never questioned the minimum criteria assumed by most sociologists – that it is a non-voluntary institution extending to people in a given geographical area for maintaining internal order and external defence against aggressors. They have usually assumed such minimum criteria and have gone on to liken the state to an organism or to a machine; or they have said that it exists to make the best life possible or to facilitate class-coercion. What kind of question have they been trying to answer by putting forward these rather puzzling pictures?

It is significant that the question about the nature of the state or the proper foundations of commonwealth has only tended to emerge as an important one at certain periods of history. Edmund Burke once remarked that one sure symptom of an ill-conducted state was the propensity of its people to resort to theories and that it was always to be lamented when men were driven to search into the foundations of commonwealth. We may discount Burke's bias against change; but it remains true that people tend to ask themselves about 'the foundations of common-wealth' at a time of insecurity and social change. The philosopher's question, when asked *seriously* rather than just as an academic exercise, is indicative of stresses and strains in the social fabric. For philosophy is intellectual unrest made explicit.

What then has been the worry made explicit in the question about the nature of the state? Surely it has been a worry about what attitude to adopt and what policies to pursue masquerading as a worry about the reality behind the appearances. When Plato suggested that the state was really an organism in which there was specialization of function for the common good, he was constructing a model for rejecting and counteracting the growing tendencies towards individualism and equalitarianism in fourth-century Athens. Philosophers have tended to wave words instead of flags. Their abstract accounts of the nature of the state have had very obvious valuative implications. Now Hobbes compared his *Leviathan* to Plato's *Republic* in so far as he thought that a knowledge of his theory would help a ruler to grapple with contemporary unrest and bewilderment. What were the problems to which he could have been providing answers in picturing the state as an artificial machine based on a contract between individuals? Quite briefly, they were problems thrown up by the development of two complementary, but opposed tendencies – individualism and absolutism. In order to explain this we must say something of the great social changes which had led to these problems.

Societies cannot continue without some form of social control; but they can change gradually as one form of social control takes the place of another. Under the feudal system the predominant social control had been that of tradition. This prescribed a man's status and the roles he had to play in the various departments of life. Economic life was static and secure, regulated by the Guild system which blocked undue competition and self-assertion. There was little social mobility. And the world-view propagated by the Church assigned a proper place to everything in the divine order of things. But in the fourteenth and fifteenth centuries, with the rapid growth of international commerce, a new economic order began to emerge. Large commercial companies were formed.

Work was decreasingly regulated by Guilds, and men who had previously worked for themselves had to hire out their labour to the growing class of ambitious employers. Time became valuable and clock-faces began to show the quarter hours; thrift, efficiency and hard work became virtues; social life became more and more characterized by acquisitiveness, the desire for power, and desire for honour. Life indeed became rather like a race as Hobbes pictured it. And just as motion came to be regarded as normal in Galileo's universe, so too was social mobility increasingly taken for granted. Individual effort as well as traditional status were coming to determine a man's place. In the religion of Protestantism all believers were priests; the individual was alone before God; and he had to make his lonely way in the quest for salvation by his own individual effort. The great gains of this movement were in the field of individual liberty, self-discipline and personal responsibility. But they were won at a cost, and the cost was the loss of security.

The economic, social and religious ties of a traditional society cannot be shaken off without a threat to security. Indeed, this was a time of great individual and social insecurity; this need for a new kind of security to replace the ties of a traditional society was almost universally met by the development of another form of social control – the strengthening and extension of the powers of the King. The nation state was emerging. Machiavelli lamented at the start of the sixteenth century that Italy, divided into five warring city states, was not abreast of the movement towards strong central government in France, Spain and England. Although these two tendencies, the one towards individualism and the other towards the centralization of executive power, were in a sense complementary to each other, they were also obviously opposed. Direct conflict was partly averted by the King winning the support of the more wealthy of the new middle class. Trade and strong government go well together. Henry VII and Elizabeth, for instance, made great use of this class of new men who made money by ability and achieved social status by buying land with it. Hence the great disposal of Crown lands during the sixteenth century, which admirably met the monarch's need for money and the new men's need for social status. In England, however, the tendency towards absolutism did not swamp the tendency towards individual liberty as it did in France and Spain. This may well have been because in England, which is an island, the King could not justify the need for a standing army to defend the country against external aggressors; he had a standing navy. Now a navy cannot be used for internal suppression in the same way as an army can. Thus the King suffered under the perpetual handicap of not having a standing army to stem the rising tide of liberty. The tradition of civil liberty in this country may well owe much to geography.

Thus in England there was a long period in the seventeenth century when no equilibrium resulted from the mutual impact of the forces of absolutism and individual liberty. This state of continued social tension occasioned great intellectual unrest, as is manifest in the volume of political tracts and treatises which were the intellectual threshings accompanying the physical struggles of the antagonists in the Civil War. But theorists were not simply trying to reconcile the competing claims of liberty and security. They were also trying to make explicit how they, as individuals, stood in relation to this new system of centralized social control that had gradually emerged from the more secure and understandable social structure of the Middle Ages. It is significant that Hobbes called the state Leviathan. The problem was to catch the monster with an adequate description which would stress how the individual stood in relation to it. Why should he obey the commands of its magistrates? On what conditions was he justified in resisting its claims? What spheres of private interest could the magistrate legitimately invade? These were the burning questions which theories of the state had to face. These so-called theories incorporated decisions and valuations as well as factual assumptions. Hobbes, as is well known, pictured the state as an artificial machine based on a social contract and controlled by an absolute monarch with unlimited, perpetual, and indivisible sovereignty. How was this macabre model of the state arrived at and what sort of an answer did it give to the questions which gave rise to it? We are now in a position to look at the main details of Hobbes' theory.

1. The Social Contract Theory

The view to which Hobbes subscribed, that civil society was based upon some kind of a contract or covenant, was a commonplace at this period. Two sorts of contracts were suggested. There was the *pactum unionis* which was thought to account for the institution of civil society. Men as individuals made a contract with each other which turned them into citizens. They agreed to accept majority decision in the regulation of their affairs or some other such condition of combination. A model for this was the Pilgrim Fathers who made a declaration in 1620 solemnly covenanting and combining themselves together into a civil society. This kind of contract is to be distinguished from the *pactum subjectionis* which was an agreement on the part of a civil body to submit to a particular form of government. Magna Carta was the stock example of such a conditional acceptance of government. Some thinkers treated this account of the institution of commonwealth as a quasi-historical hypothesis. For others it was purely a vehicle for the expression of certain basic demands. Hobbes' account was unusual in that he fitted the contract into his 'resolution' of civil society and deduced a most ingenious form of *pactum unionis* which made the acceptance of a sovereign the condition of membership.

It is usual for philosophers nowadays to deride the social contract theory and to dismiss it as a strange aberration perpetrated by our forebears who were rather careless about verbal usage. But this rather cavalier attitude is only possible if the historical context of ways of speaking is disregarded. Before examining the ingenious use to which Hobbes put the theory, it will therefore be as well to consider why it seemed such a natural and appropriate vehicle for making the points that required to be made.

In the main those who resorted to a contract theory of society were voicing the demands of individualism in its conflict with absolutism. Kings tended to argue in defence of their increasing arbitrariness that their authority was divinely sanctioned and that patriarchalism was the natural order of society deriving from the Old Testament. The theory of contract was a device for denying these claims. Individuals were presumed to be born free and equal in the sight of God or under natural law, with an identity of interests. Civil society itself, as well as the appointment of an executive, was merely a device for furthering and protecting these interests. The King's authority stemmed purely from popular consent. Civil society itself had been *instituted*; it was not a natural growth like a family or a tree or a bee-hive. Kings, like other men, were limited by natural law or God's commands and by the terms of a contract presupposed by their instituted authority. This was a pictorial way of saying that their authority was conditional, not absolute. Protestants, with their eye on the Bible, even pointed out that the origin of the Jewish state could be traced to a covenant between God and his chosen people.

But why was the model of a contract used for making these points? For there are such obvious objections to its appropriateness. The supposed *pactum unionis* was obviously absurd as an attempt to account for the origin of civil society with its legal system and constitutional framework. For 'contract' was primarily a legal term imported from Roman law into philosophical theorizing. In legal history law antedates and is presupposed by contract. For a contract was a pact plus a *legally* created obligation. A vendor signified his intention, for instance, of conveying a piece of land to a purchaser who signified his intention of paying for it. This pact became a contract when an obligation to complete the conveyance was annexed by law. It was only later that a special form of *consensual* contract (as distinct from earlier forms of verbal, written, and real contracts) grew up in which consent alone was regarded as sufficient to create an obligation without additional legal formalities. This type of contract was associated with the *ius gentium*, and, because of its simplicity and universality, was often thought to be the original and archetypal form of contract. In it intention was regarded as paramount and external acts merely symbolical. This sort of contract, which was in fact a late and streamlined version of older and more complicated ritual procedures, was taken as the paradigm and original form of contract and used to explain not simply the relationship between King and people but also the origin of civil society itself, including its legal system. This was absurd; for historically speaking, contracts presupposed a legal system. As a matter of history, too, the *pactum subjectionis* was just as fictitious. For, as Hume argued, it ascribed a degree of calculation and sophistication to earlier people that was unwarranted by the evidence; it overlooked the enormous importance of habit, tradition and prejudice in the growth of institutions; and it was not supported by historical evidence which suggested that existing forms of government originated in usurpation and that the device of central government itself was a war-time habit carried over into peace.

As an analytic device, too, both types of contract were inappropriate. For a promise is a form of words and a necessary condition of making a promise is to utter the words. How could members of a civil society be regarded as having made a contract with each other, or with a King, if they had never used a form of words to signify an intention which itself was hypothetical? Also, as Hume pointed out, the contract theory assumed the logical priority of the obligation to keep a promise. By why should this obligation be prior to civil obligation? There are no better reasons for keeping a promise than there are for the more general duty of upholding the social order. Finally, membership of a civil society and submission to government are not voluntary undertakings like those of a promisor entering into a conveyance and submitting to fines if he fails to honour his obligation. How could we bind our descendants to accept a legal system and obey a government even if we were the Pilgrim Fathers? Yet they *are* bound without having to make any explicit promise when they come of age.

What, then, made the model of the contract seem so appropriate in spite of these obvious objections? For it is not enough to say that the social contract theory was embedded in Greek thought and that, after the Renaissance, it was popularized together with many other muddles initiated by Greek thinkers. For why was this particular theory seized on and used so universally rather than others? The general point must first be made that just because these objections seem obvious to us, it does not follow that they were obvious then. Thinkers of this period did not conceive either of man or society in evolutionary terms. They supposed that men and social institutions had always been much the same.

After all, did the Kings in the Old Testament behave very differently from their Kings? Were money-lenders at the time of Christ much different from their own? Were governmental forms described by Aristotle so different from those with which they were familiar? Machiavelli perused the pages of Livy to find maxims which could be used by a ruler to set sixteenth-century Italy once more on the road to greatness. It did not occur to him that the social and economic order in which his prince would have to manoeuvre was vastly different from that of ancient Rome. Men, it was true, were beginning to realize that society was not a natural growth, that institutions were to a certain extent arbitrary and alterable by human decision. The role of arbitrariness in Hobbes' writings is most significant. And Machiavelli himself was one of the first to see clearly the role of human *intervention* in the shaping of history and institutions. But this insight was crudely expressed without adequate grasp of the development of social and economic forces. Indeed, the social contract theory was one way in which this insight into the arbitrariness and artificiality of human institutions found expression.

The model of the contract, however, was much more than a way of exhibiting the artificiality of human institutions. It was a device which gave expression to a shift in attitude towards *authority* whose significance was not then properly appreciated. The momentous social changes which were then in full swing could be graphically described as the rise of the fatherless society. Patriarchalism, as a system of authority spreading beyond the family to all institutions, was on the wane. And even with regard to the family itself there are most interesting discussions in the works of writers at this period, including Hobbes, about the proper extent of parental authority. But in the wider context of civil authority men were coming slowly to realize that patriarchalism was a system incompatible with human dignity and responsibility, that men are responsible themselves for the institutions which shape and stunt their lives. After all, the Colonists were founding new states and moulding constitutions by common consent. Why should the mother countries submit to the patriarchal pretensions of monarchs?

To the medieval mind a king or a baron was not an individual with various interests and functions; he was a total person whose status and roles were prescribed by traditions stretching back into time immemorial. Obedience was a matter of personal loyalty within an area of accustomed obligations. But with the rise of self-made men whose wealth bought status and equipped the King's navy, the old pattern of authority made decreasing sense. Men like the Cecils, who wielded such enormous power under the Tudors, could claim no authority stretching back into the distant past. Neither could Samuel Pepys who did so much to re-organize the navy. They owed their authority to their brains and to the wealth which royal patronage enabled them to acquire. A pattern of authority was emerging with which we are much more familiar. Max Weber called it legal-rational authority.[1] When we want to insult it we call it bureaucracy. But Weber himself regarded bureaucracy as the most crucial social phenomenon in the development of the Western world, as it is the most efficient way of exercising power over human beings that has yet been developed. Under this pattern of authority men exercise authority because of their recognized ability rather than because of their traditional ties. They are accountable to their fellows for the proper exercise of their authority, and they are not able to rely on patronage to escape the consequences of their incompetence or disregard for their proper sphere of competence. Under this type of authority obedience is not to a person so much as to a legally established order. Authority is only wielded by individuals in so far as they occupy an 'office' with powers limited to a 'sphere of competence'. Officers are elected or appointed in some agreed manner; they do not emerge like status holders trailing clouds of the immemorial past. The basis of their claim to legitimacy lies in common consent.

The emergence of this pattern of authority was symptomatic of an age when wealth, power and the chance of salvation depended increasingly on individual effort and competence. What was more natural than that the King himself should come to be regarded as

1. M. Weber, *Theory of Social and Economic Organization* (ed. T. Parsons, W. Hodges Co., 1947), Ch. III.

an officer, as the chief executive of the government rather than as a divinely instituted status-holder? The talk of the covenant between King and people in the social contract theory was a pictorial way of stating the agreed conditions on which he held his office and his proper sphere of competence, of *rationalizing* the concept of authority. Of course the old conception of kingship had its own ways of looking after similar points. The King was regarded as being limited by the 'fundamental law' embodied in the customs of the realm which guaranteeed common-law rights to his subjects; similarly the sphere of his 'prerogative' was limited by tradition. But these were ill-defined as under all forms of traditional authority; there were endless controversies about cases like ship-money and monopolies which were on the border-line between the rights of the subject and the sphere of the King's prerogative. The Declaration of Rights of 1689 was an attempt to tidy up these flexible traditions on a solid legal-rational basis. The social contract theory was the theoretical justification of such concrete endeavours to end the spell of tradition; it was symptomatic of a new conception of authority which was compatible with the growing demands for liberty and equality.

And what was more natural than for those whose power derived mainly from the proceeds of commercial transactions to use the model of a contract to intellectualize their relationship to each other as members of a civil society, and of civil society, as a legally constituted person, to its chief executive? In their daily lives they were at this period 'bound' or 'obliged' much more by contractual agreements with each other than by governmental enactments. Contractual obligations honeycombed their lives. The great problem with which thoughtful men were grappling was that of the compatibility of individual liberty with the social control necessary for public security To what extent could an individual admit himself to be bound or obliged if he was, at the same time, to remain free to pursue his paramount interests as an individual and to preserve his dignity as a child of God? Now a contract provides a model for dealing with just this sort of problem. For in a contract free and equal individuals voluntarily enter into a relationship which imposes obligations on them. And the conditions on which they are obliged can be written into the contract. So the contract provides a model for *justifying* the acceptance of social control in a way which is compatible with human dignity and individual liberty. Of course, the model is inappropriate in many respects as has already been indicated. But is not the social contract theory a good example of the typically philosophical device of taking a concept from a limited context and generalizing it to do much more work than it can adequately manage? It was a logical device for stating certain typical demands for liberty, limited government by consent, and the end of traditional forms of authority. It was a way of stressing that the state, like other human institutions, is alterable and to a certain extent arbitrary; that human beings are responsible for its structure which, unlike nature's regularities, can be moulded according to human demands and aspirations; that human beings may have to have fathers by nature but that there is no need to institutionalize their infantile dependency in their attitude to a monarch. The device was widespread and popular because of its usefulness to the rising forces of individualism, commercialism and Protestantism. Hobbes' great ingenuity consisted in taking over this logical weapon and slewing it round so that its broadsides were directed against those who had fashioned it. He used it to show that absolutism was the logical outcome of consistent individualism. To this masterstroke we must now turn.

2. *Hobbes' Version of the Social Contract Theory*

Hobbes' account of the social contract, as has already been suggested, was an attempt to apply the resoluto-compositive method of Galileo to civil society, to reveal the basic principles presupposed by its existence in terms of which a rational reconstruction of its apparent features could be made. In this imaginary experiment its characteristics like law and justice were first of all thought away and later reintroduced as deductions from psychological postulates. The crucial transition was from psychological descriptions of human nature to the normative rules commonly known as the law of nature. The legitimacy of this transition has already been discussed. We have now to explain and discuss the further deduction of the institution of government. For Hobbes prided himself on grounding the authority of sovereigns as well as the liberty and duty of subjects upon axioms of human nature rather than on tradition or supernatural authority. In his attitude to tradition and authority he was at one with the advocates of a new basis for legitimacy. He differed from the Parliament men only in putting the claims of security higher than those of liberty and in trying to show in a way that was compatible with their premisses that there can be no legitimacy without power.

When the institutions of civil society are thought away in an imaginary experiment we have a state of nature. Hobbes maintained that in such a state man has an unlimited right to 'protect his life and members' and 'to use all the means, and do all the actions, without which he cannot preserve himself'.[1] But he also has a right to all things 'to do what he would, and against whom he thought fit, and to possess, use and enjoy all that he would, or could get'.[2] Hobbes was anxious to distinguish 'right' from 'law', 'because RIGHT, consisteth in liberty to do, or to forbear; whereas LAW, determineth and bindeth to one of them'.[3] 'Right,' he said in *De Cive*, means 'that liberty which every man hath to make use of his natural faculties according to right reason'.[4] This is surely a strange use of the term 'right'. Hobbes believed that men avoid death by a natural necessity, like a stone rolling down a hill. 'It is therefore neither absurd nor reprehensible neither against the dictates of true reason, for a man to use all his endeavours to preserve and defend his body and the members thereof from death and sorrows.'[5] This is an understandable point of view, though rather a long-winded way of labouring the obvious. For if men can't help avoiding death there is obviously nothing unreasonable in their taking steps to do what they can't help doing anyhow. But to say that men have a *right* to preserve themselves and furthermore a right to do what they think fit to others in the process, is to make quite a different sort of observation. For it is to say

1. E.W. II, 9.
2. E.W. II, 10.
3. E.W. III, 117.

4. E.W. II, 9. See also E.W. III, 117.
5. E.W. II, 8.

either that, given the need to preserve themselves, there is a rule prohibiting others from interfering, or that, assuming such a need, there ought to be such a rule. The analysis of the term 'right' implies the existence of or demand for a rule enjoining non-interference. Yet Hobbes was most anxious to separate right from law, right being what was *not* legally prohibited. Right is equated with liberty. But, as we shall see later, one of the defects of his account of liberty was his equation of it with a sphere of activity which is not legally prohibited. What he did not see was that to talk either of rights or of liberty was to imply the existence of or demand for some kind of rule enjoining non-interference, though not necessarily a *legal* rule. He *could* have said that natural rights were spheres of activity of the individual which were proclaimed as inviolable by natural law. But it is clear that he did not take this view. For though he spoke little of natural right in his later work, *Leviathan,* in what he did say he contrasted the state of affairs when men had a natural right to all things with the state of affairs which ensued when men accepted the law of nature.[1] So there seems to have been an explicit contrast in his thought rather than a connexion between natural right and natural law.

Whatever Hobbes meant by rights of nature, they play a crucial part as the deduction proceeds. For the second law of nature prescribed that every man should lay down his right to all things 'and be contented with so much liberty against other men, as he would allow other men against himself'.[2] Laying down a right meant standing out of the way of another man enjoying his right – i.e. non-interference. This could be done either by simply renouncing the right in question without worrying about who benefited or by transferring it to another. In the case of a transfer a specific person or persons benefited and the transferrer of the right was said to be bound or obliged not to hinder the recipient of the right. Injustice consisted in hindering a person whom it was a duty not to hinder; it was to perpetrate a kind of logical inconsistency as it consisted in voluntarily undoing what in the beginning had been voluntarily done. Thus, when the state was created by handing over natural rights to the sovereign, interference with his actions

1. See E.W. III, 117.　　　　2. E.W. III, 118.

constituted injustice. For justice was what the sovereign commanded on the individual's behalf; to disregard his commands was logically inconsistent. There were, however, some rights which could not be transferred – that of resisting those that make attacks by force, or of resisting imprisonment. For in such cases the individual could not be said to be aiming at any good to himself. The mutual transferring of rights is called *contract*. When one of the contractors delivers the thing contracted for on his part and leaves the other person to perform his part at some determinate time, or when both postpone completion, it is called a *covenant*, or pact. The third law of nature, as we have seen, is 'that men perform their covenants made'.

Hobbes deduced this transfer of rights from his postulate that men are led by the fear of death to act reasonably and to accept the law of nature which prescribed such a transfer of rights. But men are not really safe yet. For in a state of nature there may be danger in keeping covenants. Men, too, may decide not to keep their contracts because of their belief that some greater advantage may accrue to them by breaking them. If men are to be really consistent in their determination to avoid death, they must make some arrangement whereby it would never be in anyone's interest to break a covenant or transgress any of the other laws of nature. For the laws of nature were only theorems that any rational man would accept. They needed the backing of the sword to ensure peace. 'And covenants, without the sword, are but words, and of no strength to secure a man at all.'[1] Men are not like ants or bees which live sociably together and work for the common good. They agree by contract only, and to make their agreement constant and lasting they need a 'common power to keep them in awe, and to direct their actions to the common benefit'.[2] This is the only hope for strong and undivided action against external aggressors and disturbers of the peace at home.

The social contract therefore follows as the only logically consistent step to take to ensure lasting peace. The contract is a *pactum unionis* 'that may reduce all their wills, by plurality of voices, unto one will'.[3] They constitute themselves a civil society

1. E.W. III, 154.   2. E.W. III, 157.   3. E.W. III, 157.

by appointing a sovereign to act for them in their corporate capacity. It is as if every man should say to every man 'I authorize and give up my right of governing myself, to this man, or to this assembly of men, on this condition, that thou give up thy right to him, and authorize all his actions in like manner.'[1] This contract unites the multitude into one people and marks the generation of a commonwealth, of 'that great LEVIATHAN, or rather, to speak more reverently, of that mortal God, to which we owe under the immortal God, our peace and defence'.[2] Thus the underlying basis or essence of the state consists in the alienation of rights to a person or assembly who acts on behalf of all. The definition of commonwealth is therefore 'one person, of whose acts a great multitude, by mutual covenants one with another, have made themselves every one the author, to the end he may use the strength and means of them all, as he shall think expedient, for their peace and common defence'.[3] The person that results is called sovereign and everyone else his subjects. He is created by the contract but is not a party in it, the contract being a *pactum unionis* between individuals. Thus the people rule in all governments. For the people, as distinct from the multitude with their individual wills, rule even in monarchies. For to refer to the people rather than to the multitude is to indicate an entity which can be said to be one, to have one will, and to perform one action. Commonwealths are treated as distinct entities; for they can be said to take action against each other. This must presuppose some device by which a multitude becomes a people. Some such covenant is surely implicit in what we call a commonwealth or people. For it is nonsense to speak of something as one without concrete ways of ascertaining what its decisions and actions are. If the multitude severally can be regarded as setting up a sovereign to be their representative, all his actions and decisions, because taken on behalf of all, can be regarded as being theirs in their capacity as a people.

Whatever the merits of Hobbes' analysis of the logical presuppositions of civil society, he certainly can be credited with considerable insight into the important problem of what it *means*

1. E.W. III, 158.   2. E.W. III, 158.   3. E.W. III, 158.

to refer to a collection of individuals by a term like 'common-wealth'. For commonwealths are not *natural* wholes like potatoes or penguins in which the relations making the skin or the wings 'parts' are not difficult to discern. Social wholes are to a large extent constructions out of individuals according to a variety of different criteria. An individual may be a member of a group like a family and of an institution like an army. But being a *member* of such social wholes is quite a different kind of relation from that of being a *part* of a body. Hobbes saw this clearly when he insisted that commonwealths are artificial wholes. He saw, too, that the historical question of how commonwealths are in fact formed – e.g. by acquisition – is different from the logical question of the criteria implicit in calling a collection of individuals one people instead of a multitude. For in a commonwealth, he said, it is *as if* every man who desired security said 'I authorize and give up my right . . .' By commonwealth we *mean* individuals who accept an authority with a view to securing peace. A commonwealth is an institution and by 'institution' we mean something like 'indivi-duals with a common aim and standardized methods of attaining it'. But all institutions are not consciously instituted like clubs, and the problem is to explain what an institution is, if like a commonwealth, it has obviously *not* been consciously instituted. The trouble about the language of covenant and contract is that it implies conscious institution. Hobbes' 'as if' qualification recog-nizes the problem but leans over towards the misleading model of conscious institution by covenant.

For Hobbes, then, the social contract served a double function. It was a device which, so he thought, permitted the deduction of the institution of civil society from postulates of human nature. It was also a logical presupposition of the existence of any common-wealth as one commonwealth, whatever its governmental forms. We must examine the cogency of his argument before passing to his views on sovereignty and forms of government.

3. *The Reasons for and Causes of Political Obligation*

Hobbes said explicitly in his introduction to *De Cive* that he was searching for the 'constitutive causes' of the rights and duties of subjects in the quality of human nature.[1] The basic principle which he discovered by this resolution was 'that the dispositions of men are naturally such, that except they be restrained through fear of some coercive power, every man will distrust and dread each other'.[2] Fear of punishment is the cause of political obedience; were it not for the fact that the sword dangles over the head of every member of a state, no motive would be strong enough to counteract the disruptive passions of men. And because Hobbes assumed that men were driven irresistibly by fear like a stone rolling downhill, he was able to deduce that men must establish the rule of the sword. For, like men under the influence of an irresistible impulse, the only *reasons* that they would accept would be those indicating means to objectives dictated by their fear.[3] Thus, given the *de facto* existence of civil society, Hobbes' analysis revealed fear as its only possible constitutive cause and self-preservation as the only possible reason for its institution. He was also able to deduce that since this is the underlying rationale of civil society, men, in so far as they pursue the logical consequences of the reasons for its institution, must institute a perpetual, undivided, and absolute sovereign. For to divide or limit sovereignty would be illogical. There would be a constant danger of the sovereign speaking with a divided voice and being unable to enforce his commands; and since safety is the sole reason for the institution of a sovereign, and since these limitations on sovereignty would endanger the safety of the subject, individuals could not logically institute a sovereign who would perhaps be unable to perform effectively the functions for which he had been instituted. *Salus populi suprema lex.* And complete safety entails complete submission to a sovereign. Absolutism is the logical consequence of government by popular consent once the real interests of any man in consenting to government are properly realized. The claims of Royalists and Parliament men could be reconciled if it were realized that either Charles or Cromwell could be an absolute ruler by consent. The Royalists would have to give up their patriarchal pretensions and the theory of divine right; the Parlia-

1. E.W. II, xiv.   2. E.W. II, xiv, xv.   3. See *supra*, pp. 165-6.

ment men would have to waive their objections to absolutism. Then peace would reign and all could pursue such private interests as did not endanger the peace – trade, for instance, or mathematical study.

The force of Hobbes' argument depends largely on the truth of his premisses. Reasons have been given for doubting his account both of the causes of actions and of the acceptable reasons for them.[1] But even if we were to accept his starting-point, Locke's objection is surely a good one. 'Are men,' he said, 'so foolish that they take care to avoid what mischiefs may be done them by polecats or foxes, but are content, nay think it safety, to be devoured by lions?'[2] After all, absolute rulers are only men and 'He that thinks absolute power purifies men's blood and corrects the baseness of human nature need but read the history of this or any other age to be convinced to the contrary.'[3] Even supposing that security were the sole reason for the institution of civil society – which it is not – it is not an obvious deduction that absolute sovereignty is the only method of achieving it. Indeed, it might turn out to be a matter of substituting one form of insecurity for another. For the sovereign is not party to the contract. He is appointed simply to keep the peace, and how he does it is his own business. Hobbes did suggest that he was subject to the law of nature, but himself laboured the point that this was a poor deterrent to self-assertion. He could well keep the peace by establishing a reign of terror which would make the state of nature seem like paradise. It is, surely, as Locke saw, the *arbitrariness* of another man's authority which is both terrifying and an insult to human dignity. A legal system, as a form of constraint, is introduced in order to get rid of the arbitrary constraints which would characterize a state of nature. If these are to be ended by setting up an authority that is both arbitrary and backed by overwhelming force, it is questionable whether even the most timid man would choose to venture forth from the state of nature, 'He being in a

1. See *supra*, Ch. 6 and 7.

2. J. Locke, *Second Treatise of Civil Government* (ed. Gough, Blackwell, 1948), p. 46.

3. J. Locke, op. cit., p. 45.

much worse condition that is exposed to the arbitrary power of one man who has command of 100,000, than he that is opposed to the arbitrary power of 100,000 single men. . . .'[1]

Once the inadequacies in Hobbes' psychology are admitted and some allowance has been made for his logical mistake in trying to deduce the justification of obedience to government from a theory about its causes, his contribution to political theory can be seen in a wider perspective. If the issue is one of *justifying* or giving reasons for the institution of civil society surely one of the best reasons is Hobbes' reason – civil society exists in order to protect us. *Salus populi suprema lex.* This is not to say that it was in fact instituted with that aim; it is only to say that this is one of the best reasons that can be given for legal machinery and all the paraphernalia of government. The objection to Hobbes' theory is that he thought it was the *only* reason and that he had a very stringent and short-sighted view of what *salus populi* entailed in the way of sovereign power. Similarly, if the question is asked 'Why should we obey government?' Hobbes' answer is very good. Either we should obey government because it would be logically inconsistent not to do so, the term 'government' implying that men have been appointed to give commands as our representatives. Or, if we are unmoved by the logic of the matter, it is in our manifest interest to do so as the alternative is prison and it is also in our long-term interest to have such a device to guard against anarchy. Of course objections can be made to such *unconditional* obedience; it can also be pointed out that this is not the only reason for obeying government; it may not even be a conclusive reason; but it certainly is a very good reason that carries much weight with most of us if we have ever thought seriously about breaking the law.

If we turn to Hobbes' theory about the *causes* of political allegiance, his account was obviously hamstrung by his psychology. Men obviously do not accept a legal system and a government simply because they are afraid of death. They accept it largely out of habit, what Burke called 'a sort of heavy, lumpish acquiescence in government'. It also satisfies their need for order

1. J. Locke, op. cit., p. 69.

and security which was first generated and satisfied by parental care and control. Hume was extremely puzzled by the adoption of the device of central government. For though the instinct of sex might drive men to band together in patriarchal groups, he could suggest no similar psychological explanation for such an unobvious expedient as the appointment of magistrates with authority delegated from a central government. He suggested that patriarchal groups banded together out of necessity to meet external aggressors and men gradually came to apply to peace the lessons learnt in war. 'Camps are the true mothers of cities.' Central government is to be explained more in terms of the logic of the situation than in terms of psychological causes, which only become operative once central government is set up. Hume's puzzlement illustrates the lack of cogency in Hobbes' causal explanation.

4. Acquisition and Institution

Hobbes himself was prepared to admit that, historically speaking, commonwealth by acquisition and hereditary right preceded or made unnecessary instituted government. But even in the case of such natural forms of dominion he could not rid himself of the notion that even these presupposed some form of covenant. In the case of acquisition the vanquished promised his service and obedience in return for his life and liberty. Only in the case of slaves could there be said to be no contract. In such cases men subject themselves to a sovereign out of fear of the person instituted rather than out of fear of each other.

Hereditary governments, too, where the right of dominion seems to issue from generation, presuppose a covenant. For even a parent's right of dominion over his children derives from their consent rather than from the mere fact of generation. Dominion is indivisible as no man can serve two masters; but two persons, male and female, must concur in the act of generation. How then does being a father entail being a lord? Socrates is a man and therefore a living creature because 'a living creature' is part of the definition of 'man'. But 'Sophronicus is Socrates' father, and therefore his lord' is not a valid deduction; for the word 'lord' is not in the definition of 'a father'.[1] Some kind of contract is necessary for making being a father the ground for being a lord. Anyway, in a state of nature dominion was maternal, as mothers alone could declare who the father of the child was, if there was no marriage system! The mother, too, had the child in her power first to nourish and educate it. No case could be made for paternal right even in the family, save by contract. How much weaker was the case for paternal right in hereditary governments?

The significant aspect of Hobbes' treatment of natural forms of government – apart from his lack of interest in them – was his determination to rid all forms of authority of the appeal to tradition or generation as the justification of legitimacy. His rejection of the divine right of kings was but one facet of a thorough-going rejection of patriarchalism and the modes of thought of a traditional society. Hobbes, like most of the self-made men of this period, regarded hereditary right as a feeble justification for natural forms of dominion. They were founded on inequalities due to irrational accidents of birth or conquest and presupposed a superstitious and mystifying appeal to tradition. It was *institution* that appealed to his way of thinking. This was rationally understandable like laying down definitions in geometry or working out a profit and loss account on a balance sheet. It was something that could be done by clear-headed individuals on an equal footing. In his treatment of natural dominion he tried to extend the new rational way of conceiving legitimacy into the strongholds of traditional authority. He was indeed one of the mouthpieces of the gradual transition from traditional to legal-rational authority.[2]

Was Hobbes' view at all plausible that some kind of contract or consent is implicit in the existence of any civil society whatever? Obviously not in the sense that civil society could not exist if individuals had not actually come together and made promises. But Hobbes' analysis did not require this; for he often spoke of 'tacit covenants'. But if the consensual basis of society is watered down sufficiently to cover even this, then any government must rule by consent when there is not either open rebellion or mass

1. See E.W. II, 115.
2. See *supra*, p. 186.

emigration. And the distinctive feature of contract would be lost; for a society arranged according to status and tradition could equally well be said to be based on 'tacit covenant'. Perhaps this is part of what Hobbes wanted to show. But it is rather trivial in that all it achieves is to make acquiescence in government part of the definition of government. Yet, on the other hand, it may be one of those analytic propositions whose enunciation has considerable recommendatory force. People often say, in a certain tone of voice, that the function of government is to govern. This is trivial in descriptive content; but it is a way of demanding that the government should get on with its main job rather than range round too much for new-fangled legislation and plans for social improvement. Similarly, Hobbes wanted to bring out that it was both illogical and unwise not to obey a *de facto* government. For a government is a body appointed to be obeyed.

Another way of looking at Hobbes' ubiquitous covenant is to suggest that he was attempting an analysis of representation. A multitude can only become one person or commonwealth if there is a device which gives them a voice and a will and which enables them to deal collectively with breaches of the peace and external aggression. This device presupposes not that, historically speaking, individuals had alienated their rights and appointed a sovereign, but that they must at least *see the point* of a sovereign authority. They behave *as if* a contract had been made in which they said each one individually, 'I authorize and give up my right . . .' To think of government is to think of magistrates and others *representing* the individual wills of all. For how else could a people be one or magistrates have legitimate authority? The model of institution is introduced and extended, with the 'as if' qualification, to lay bare the rationale of the magistrate's authority. For consent or contract implies granting permission to someone to do something which he would have no *right* to do without such permission. Now if this is interpreted as implying something concrete about the minds of actual subjects, unpalatable consequences follow. For it could only be decided whether a magistrate had legitimate authority by conducting a Gallup Poll. But Hobbes, we must remember, was conducting an imaginary experiment. This was his resolution of society into its logically prior principles. His individuals were therefore ideal constructions like the straight lines of the geometer or Galileo's frictionless surface. Gallup Polls would have appalled him even more than the Common Law.

But the danger of the geometrical method is precisely that it need not apply to anything that exists. Surely the cardinal question to ask about representation is not what is presupposed about the minds of imaginary individuals, but what is entailed about the ways in which actual minds must exhibit themselves on earth. This means actual procedures for appointing representatives; it means also actual procedures for ascertaining whether acts done in a representative capacity meet with approval; and so on. The mistake is to treat terms like 'government by consent' and 'representation' as only implying certain things about the minds of individuals, whether real or imaginary. It is only when their *institutional* implications are also brought out that they have any cash value as distinctive terms about government.

It is interesting that Hobbes' declared intention was 'to understand what the quality of human nature is, in what matters it is, in what not, *fit* to make up a civil government, and how men must be agreed amongst themselves that intend to grow up into a *well-grounded* state'. 'Well-grounded' is surely a normative term; it meant, for Hobbes, the sort of state he believed in – absolute monarchy. Human nature was 'fit' to make up such a civil government because he laid down definitions of human nature which enabled him to get to the desired conclusion. The social contract theory became in his hands an ingenious method for presenting his political demands which were cunningly concealed by the deceptive lucidity of the resoluto-compositive method. The geometrical method is a godsend to dogmatists and the insecure; for it dresses up dubious opinions as necessary truths. By fitting the social contract theory into this analytic framework Hobbes was able to present his uncompromising demand for security as the sole reason for the species of promise that was alleged to underlie the 'well-grounded' state; but the method, when applied to society, is as specious as the promise which the existence of the state is alleged to presuppose.

CHAPTER 9

SOVEREIGNTY, LAW AND FORMS
OF GOVERNMENT

Introductory

THE notion of sovereignty within a nation state, first popularized by Bodin and developed by Hobbes to its logical conclusion, was foreign to the political thought of the Middle Ages. Yet it was assumed by Hobbes that there must be in every state a supreme authority issuing and enforcing commands to all subjects and receiving none; creating law but not itself subject to it. The existence of a commonwealth presupposed such an authority. The sovereign might be a King, a parliament, or the people; but sovereignty must be located somewhere. This is a strange assumption. In Hobbes' case it can perhaps be most easily understood in the context of the traditional assumptions of the English about constitutional authority. For it was an ingenious attempt to rationalize an ambiguous tradition by the application of the geometric method.

Many have described the Civil War in England as a contest between the Common Law and the King's prerogative. In the disputed cases of ship-money and monopolies, both sides quoted long-standing precedents for the legality of their claims. They were able to do so because there had always been a fundamental ambiguity in the tradition about the ultimate source of authority. This can be traced right back to Bracton, the fountainhead of English constitutionalism, who maintained that the King had no peer on earth and that no subject, not even a judge, could question the legality of any of his acts; nevertheless the King's will was not law except in the form of a definition to which the assent of the magistrates was essential. Had the King, then, a master who could 'put a bridle on him'?

The answer to this crucial conundrum was both negative and affirmative. For there were two distinct but overlapping spheres of authority which have been called those of gubernaculum and jurisdictio.[1] The sphere of gubernaculum was that of the King's prerogative. It concerned rights touching the crown like the King's marriage, the keeping of the peace, and external defence. In such matters the King was the sole authority. But in the sphere of jurisdictio, which concerned the traditional rights of the subject – e.g. to property – the King's discretion was limited by precedents of the Common Law. He was bound by oath to proceed by law and not otherwise, and the judges, though appointed by the King, were bound by their oaths to determine the rights of the subject not according to the King's will but according to law. The case against a subject must be made out by due process of law before the King could proceed against him by force.

In the constitutional struggles of the seventeenth century the Royalists were trying to extend the precedents for the King's prerogative into the sphere of jurisdictio. The Parliamentarians, on the other hand, sought to apply the limitations imposed on jurisdictio to acts of gubernaculum as well. So it is easy to understand how both were convinced of the legality of their claims; for the disputes were about cases where the spheres of gubernaculum and jurisdictio overlapped. The Royalists could argue that ship-money, for instance, was necessary for external defence which was in the sphere of gubernaculum where the King's authority was unconditional. As Hobbes put it: 'Mark the oppression; A Parliament-man of 500*l.* a year, land-taxed at 20*s*!'[2] Hampden was simply refusing to contribute to his own defence. The Parliament men, on the other hand, could argue that property was a matter of their Common Law rights which could not be touched without their consent.

It is true that the King could always ignore the dividing line between jurisdictio and gubernaculum by claiming a national emergency or the pretext of 'reasons of state'. But a wise monarch

1. For these terms and for the details of this explanatory exposition I am indebted to C. H. McIlwain, *Constitutionalism Ancient and Modern*.

2. E.W. VI, 209.

used this pretext very warily. Elizabeth, for instance, was very sensitive to the feelings of Parliament on such matters and, as in the case of monopolies, gave way on occasion to their demands. But James I, who came from Scotland where the dual tradition was not firmly established, was not so sensitive. He maintained that the 'fundamental law' guaranteeing authority applied only to himself. Not only had Parliament no business to meddle with affairs of state; but also the liberties of the subject were purely the gift of the King, deriving from his supreme authority. The King's silence on matters of custom simply denoted his assent. The duality of the tradition was a fundamental illusion. No wonder Coke replied that 'When the King says he can not allow our liberties of right, this strikes at the root. We serve here for thousands and for ten thousands.' This explicit rejection of the dual tradition helped to precipitate the struggle. For Parliament in its turn insisted on its right to discuss matters of the King's prerogative. The intellectual outcome was a spate of theories claiming the supreme authority either of Parliament or of the King. Milton, for instance, voiced demands for the absolute and undivided sovereignty of Parliament. Hobbes inclined towards absolute monarchy. The significant feature of such theories was the determination to break away from authority guaranteed by tradition and precedents and to *institute* a clear, rationally understandable, and unambiguous chain of command.

1. Hobbes' Theory of Sovereignty

Little theoretical mischief would have been done if Hobbes had argued in a straightforward way that the time had come to tidy up an ambiguous tradition and to institute a more rational and effective form of authority. But he did not put forward his demands in such an explicit manner. For he held that in every commonwealth there *must* be a sovereign authority. And the 'must' was meant to be a logical 'must', though there are grounds for interpreting it as a normative 'must' dressed up as a logical one. There could, on his view, be reasonable dispute about the advisability of the sovereign authority being wielded by an individual or by a body of men. But there could be no dispute about the logical necessity for the existence of such a sovereign authority if a multitude was to become a people.

This conclusion is acceptable enough if it meant simply that the existence of a commonwealth entails the existence of *authority* as distinct from the exercise of naked power. For 'authority' as distinct from 'power' presupposes that power is exercised legitimately or in accordance with certain rules of authorization *accepted* by those affected by it. The claim to legitimacy is substantiated in different ways in different societies – it may be by appeal to supernatural signs, to traditionally transmitted rules, or to definite procedures of institution – but a man cannot exercise authority unless approval is extended to his actions, whatever the accepted criteria of authorization may be. Now according to Hobbes a commonwealth or people differed from a mere multitude in that in the former wills were represented. Approval was extended in advance to the actions of the people's representative in that they *authorized* his actions on their behalf; he was given authority. The mere exercise of power by one individual over others characterized the state of nature but did not constitute a commonwealth. In this sense there cannot be a commonwealth without someone having authority.

But authority is one thing, *sovereign* authority quite another. For Hobbes held that the type of authority to keep the peace and defend subjects against external aggressors *must* be perpetual, unlimited, and indivisible. By 'sovereignty' he meant not simply authority in certain spheres but authority in all spheres of state activity. And in every commonwealth there must exist such an authority. For authority presupposes individual approval and these features of sovereignty were alone compatible with the 'known inclinations' of men which led them to institute such an authority, and with the logical needs of being *one* people.

Hobbes, therefore, like a geometer, deduced what he thought to be the logical consequences of the type of authority that had been instituted. It was created to provide for the safety of the people. This meant, primarily, the making and interpreting of law and the punishment of injustice which was simply breaches of the law. It followed that the sovereign could not be impeached in his own courts or put to death for actions in his capacity as sovereign; for how could *injury* to a subject come about if he did what every subject had authorized him to do? Iniquity he might commit, 'but not injustice, or injury in the proper signification'.[1] This was logically impossible. Similarly he had been authorized to do anything necessary 'for the preserving of peace and security by prevention of discord at home, and hostility from abroad'.[2] And this meant *anything*; for 'although of so unlimited a power, men may fancy many evil consequences, yet the consequences of the want of it, which is perpetual war of every man against his neighbour, are much worse.'[3] There was no place for jurisdictio in Hobbes' scheme. All was gubernaculum. Civil liberty lay 'only in those things, which in regulating their actions, the sovereign hath praetermitted'.[4] Subjects might buy and sell, choose their abode, diet, and wives, ply whatever trade they liked, and educate their children as they saw fit. It is unlikely that laws would be necessary to regulate these aspects of life. But that was entirely up to the sovereign. Anything might turn out to be prejudicial to security. Any limitation on sovereignty – Common Law rights, for instance – would be logically inconsistent with the type of authority set up.

There were, however, certain rights, whose peculiarity we have already noted,[5] which it was psychologically impossible for any individual to surrender – e.g. the right to preserve himself or to resist imprisonment. The liberty of the subject, therefore, consisted in those acts which it would be vain for the sovereign to forbid as well as in those which he had not in fact forbidden. But this, surely, is a very thin analysis of the relationship between law and liberty. For the question of the liberty of the subject only arises when attempts are made to *prevent* people doing what they want to do. It is odd to talk about our liberty to choose our own diet because it has rarely occurred to anyone in this country, except during a food-shortage, to prevent us eating what we want. And it may be true that we are free to dream what we like, because

1. E.W. III, 163.   3. E.W. III, 195.   5. See *supra*, pp. 189–90.
2. E.W. III, 164.   4. E.W. III, 199.

no one has yet found a way of stopping us; but it is only in senti-
mental lyrics that questions of our liberty to dream arise. Talk of
our liberties seems out of place in cases where interference is a
matter either of indifference or of impossibility.

There is a very good reason for this triviality in Hobbes' talk
about liberties of the subject, which can be brought out by a more
thorough analysis. When we speak of liberties we presuppose (a)
that people have certain interests or things that they might want
to do; (b) that other people have made or are likely to make
attempts to interfere with them in the pursuit of these interests;
(c) that there is a law (or perhaps a custom) that prescribes non-
interference with these interests. Now Hobbes spoke of liberties
in the sense of absence of legal constraints on interests like the
choice of wife and diet. But he failed to deal with the more
important function of law in relation to liberty in providing a
levelling constraint on all to get rid of the arbitrary constraint of
the weak by the strong. Under our present system, for instance,
political liberty consists largely in being able to vote without
arbitrary constraint for the candidate of our choice. But in order to
rid ourselves of the constraints of employers, land-owners, and
political agents, a mass of electoral laws are necessary. It is true
that there is no law forbidding us from voting for the candidate of
our choice; but it is also true and far less trivial that there is a
network of law preventing other people from imposing constraints
of an arbitrary kind on our choice. Liberty may well *mean* the
absence of constraint on doing what we might want to do; but
it is essential to emphasize the role of law as one form of constraint
which saves us as a matter of empirical fact from others of a more
arbitrary sort. Locke, as often, put the matter in proper perspective
when he said: 'So that, however it may be mistaken, the end of
law is, not to abolish or restrain, but to preserve and enlarge
freedom. For in all the states of created beings capable of laws,
where there is no law there is no freedom. For liberty is to be free
from restraint and violence from others; which cannot be where
there is no law: and is not, as we are told, a liberty for every man
to do what he lists.'[1]

1. J. Locke, *Second Treatise of Civil Government* (ed. Gough), p. 29.

There was a third sense in which Hobbes spoke of the liberty of the subject which connected it in another way with law. He held that 'in the act of our submission, consisteth both our obligation, and our liberty'.[1] For both the obligation and the liberty of the subject were to be derived from the words 'I authorize all his actions' which he was imagined to have expressed in instituting a commonwealth. Thereby men made themselves 'artificial chains, called civil laws, which they themselves, by mutual covenants, have fastened at one end, to the lips of that man, or assembly, to whom they have given the sovereign power; and at the other end to their own ears'.[2] These laws are made to promote internal peace and security from external aggressors. Therefore, in obeying them the subject was submitting to laws that he had taken part in instituting. He therefore was exercising his liberty in obeying laws that were conducive to these ends; but he had liberty to refuse to do what went against the intentions implicit in the institution of commonwealth. Thus his obligation to obey the sovereign lasted 'as long as, and no longer, than the power lasteth, by which he is able to protect them'.[3]

This is surely a redundant and specious sense of 'liberty'. For it merely brought out that Hobbes' ideal construct of a subject became such by *choosing* to authorize a representative. What is added by saying that such a choice was an exercise of liberty? Not that there was no law constraining his choice; for law itself came about by his choice. Who, then, or what was not constraining his choice in deciding to accept the constraint of law? For talk of liberty in general is vacuous talk. It means too little because it means too much. It is like the terms 'same' or 'equal', which convey little information until the respects are specified in which people are being compared. Until we know what constraint is presumed to be lacking in preventing a person from doing what he wants, little is conveyed by speaking of his liberty. Certainly this general type of liberty was not that to which Hobbes referred when he said, 'As for other liberties, they depend on the silence of the law.'[4] This was an informative remark in spite of the inadequacy of his analysis of civil liberties. For he spoke of liberties

1. E.W. III, 203. 2. E.W. III, 198. 3. E.W. III, 208. 4. E.W. III, 206.

rather than of liberty, and he specified the type of constraint whose absence gave point to their being described as such. To speak, on the other hand, of the liberty of an individual in authorizing a representative, through whose agency a legal system is instituted, is vacuous. But it is the sort of vacuous talk which has enabled other theorists to conclude that our liberty consists in obeying the police or being locked up in gaol.

For Hobbes, then, the only limitations on sovereignty were those set by the unalterable tendencies of human nature over which it had to be exercised. Sovereignty, too, was necessarily indivisible as well as unlimited. For if a limit was put on sovereignty that must mean that there was a sphere where there was some other authority. This was precisely the claim of those like Coke who claimed that Common Law rights were outside the sphere of prerogative. 'Prerogative,' he said, 'is part of the law, but "sovereign power" is no parliamentary word. . . . Magna Charta is such a fellow that he will have no "sovereign".' Hobbes' reply was again an appeal to a necessary truth. For if the term 'people' or 'commonwealth' *meant* a multitude who had set up an authority to protect them, how could there be *one* people if there were more than one authority? Their unity *consisted* in having one *instituted* person to represent their collective wills. The sovereign was the soul of an artificial monster with a will issuing in laws executed by its limbs – the magistrates. The Civil War showed the danger of dividing the rights of the sovereign. Politics was not tennis; practice and precedent should be surrendered in favour of the safer skill of the geometer.

There is indeed a certain sort of safety in geometry which Hobbes exploited in his geometrization of politics. For little is risked, the conclusions arrived at being merely consequences of the definitions from which a start is made. And it was the *artificiality* of commonwealths that made Hobbes' use of the geometric method seem so appropriate and plausible. For as a commonwealth is not a natural whole like a man or a rabbit, if we wish to speak of a collection of individuals as one, we must institute or lay down criteria. And these are more or less arbitrary. A club, for instance, could be defined as a collection of individuals who accept a constitution and rules and pay a subscription in order to further some interest which they all have. They are separate individuals but can be regarded as 'one' in so far as they combine for certain purposes and accept some authority structure in the process. They can be said to have a 'voice' and to perform 'acts' in so far as they define what constitutes their voice and acts. They act as one in so far as they define what constitutes collective action. This, perhaps, is a necessary fiction in order to get things done effectively and in order to save breath. For it is quicker to say 'The club has decided . . .' than a long rigmarole about individuals acting in accordance with agreed procedures. But it remains figurative talk. Hobbes pictured individuals agreeing to accept an unlimited sovereign as a necessary device for protection. They become one because they institute him as their collective will, voice and limbs. But, of course, they have not really got any of these properties collectively at all; for these are the sorts of things that only individuals have. But if they decide that their one-ness consists in his coercive efforts on their behalf, they become one – in a figurative sense – by *definition*. Once, however, the fallacies have been uncovered in Hobbes' attempted deduction of this sort of totalitarian monster from psychological postulates,[1] other criteria for 'one-ness' could be laid down. For the cogency of Hobbes' argument depends on his deduction from psychology that the business of commonwealth was purely '*salus populi*, the people's safety'.[2] This, on his view, entailed that there must be in every state an ultimate and recognized wielder of coercive power to keep the peace. This could not be done effectively unless the *same* authority made laws. For anything can come in the sphere of gubernaculum; jurisdictio is but one branch of gubernaculum. But this is surely an empirical requirement rather than a logical necessity unless law is interpreted as being commands concerned only with the provision of safety.

Locke, who did not subscribe to Hobbes' deduction of the reasons for commonwealth from psychological postulates, was very cautious in his acceptance of the maxim *Salus populi suprema lex*. And understandably so; for he held that the main business of

1. See *supra*, Ch. 8, sect. 3.   2. E.W. III, x.

government was to safeguard the inviolable rights of the subject. In his account the Common Law rights of Englishmen appeared in the guise of natural rights to life, liberty, and estate. Gubernaculum must never violate jurisdictio. The institution of government made no difference to the subject's indefeasible rights; it only helped to protect them. This implied the existence of an authority other than the will of the sovereign, even if the sovereign were Parliament. Indeed, if we are talking of instituted states, it is possible for a constitution to be framed, as in the U.S.A., with the express intention of there being no overall sovereign in Hobbes' sense. If we say that no commonwealth exists where there is an explicit division of authority, then we are ruling out a great number of forms of commonwealth by definition. For there is no reason why individuals should not decide that a necessary condition of being one people is that no one person or body should exercise supreme authority over them. Their unity could be defined as consisting in decisions and actions issuing from compromises between their representatives in different departments of state.

Of course, very few commonwealths have in fact been instituted in such a clear-headed way. This is the illusion about states popularized by the model of the social contract. Authorities develop in different spheres; often they clash and intellectual confusion as well as more overt forms of conflict develop. Then a geometer like Hobbes comes along and tries to work out a logically consistent structure of command. But there is little reason why his proposals for calling a collection of individuals 'one people' should be accepted rather than anyone else's. For they were deductions from his convictions about the proper business of government. But government has no business except that which those who practise it and suffer from it assign to it. And this is a matter of political preference rather than of dispassionate analysis.

Is there, then, almost nothing to be said for Hobbes' conviction that the existence of a commonwealth entails the existence of a sovereign? This, as has been stressed, depends on what criteria we are going to use for calling a collection of individuals a commonwealth. Most people would maintain that a necessary condition would be the existence of a common legal system, and there is a sense in which sovereignty is indispensable for the working of a legal system. For legal authority necessitates a hierarchical structure of rules. We can only make use of rules or legal principles if we have higher order principles for interpreting and deciding between rules of a lower order. An umpire, for instance, interprets a number of rules at cricket. But part of what is meant by an *umpire* is the rule that his decision is final on the interpretation of rules of a lower order. Similarly a legal system cannot work unless there is a source of final reference. Hobbes wanted to substitute for the Common Law principle, that custom, as interpreted by the judges, is the arbiter of law, the principle that the commands of a determinate body are the final source of legal authority. He was writing at a time when statute law was increasing in importance; and it is intolerable for lawyers to work with two inconsistent higher order principles for ascertaining what the law is. In this respect any workable system of law requires the sovereignty of a supreme legal principle like the principle, in this country, that the principles of constitutional law shall determine what is or is not an act of Parliament which in its turn provides lower order principles which the courts will recognize. But the supremacy of a legal principle does not entail the supreme authority of any determinate body; still less does it entail that the supreme law-making body shall also be responsible for wielding coercive power. Indeed, the empirical necessity and advisability of this is hotly denied by those who advocate the separation of the legislature from the executive as in the U.S.A.

It may well be the case, again, that most people would say that a necessary condition of a collection of individuals being a commonwealth is the existence of a central and supreme authority for coercion. This is another sense in which people speak of sovereignty. But it surely is not a necessary condition that the *same* body should be the supreme authority both for law and for coercion as Hobbes insisted. An army is the sort of organization that can only work if there is a final authority in the chain of command. But the commander-in-chief need not be concerned at all with making the law of the land.

When we consider soberly Hobbes' demands for perpetual, unlimited and indivisible sovereignty, 'there is,' as Aristotle said of Plato's proposals, 'another matter which must not be ignored – the teaching of actual experience.'[1] It is surely inadvisable to propose a form of authority that no one can ever have the actual *power* to exercise. In theory a monarch can be given unlimited authority; but in practice he is limited in what he can command by the major interests of his subjects and their deep-rooted traditions, and by those without whose religious or economic power his political power is precarious. A ruler cannot exercise authority indefinitely by sole reliance on the sword; he must cajole and bargain with those who wield other sorts of power; he must provide incentives for his subjects and bend them to his will by propaganda. Hobbes saw the great importance of religion as an instrument of state propaganda and insisted on the sovereign having supreme authority in this sphere.[2] He also saw the importance of economic matters. For all the land and its resources were to belong to the sovereign. Private property was simply that which the sovereign had declared to belong to an individual. The individual was given a right to exclude other individuals from his property, but not the sovereign who had distributed land 'in order to the common peace and security'.[3] A sovereign might act inequitably in regard to property; but he could never act unjustly, and his actions in this respect could never be a legitimate occasion for rebellion. So much for ship-money. The sovereign, too, was to have authority over matters of trade and of exchange of property. 'And therefore it belongeth to the commonwealth, that is to say, to the sovereign, to appoint in what manner all kinds of contract between subjects, as buying, selling, exchanging, borrowing, lending, letting and taking to hire, are to be made; and by what words and signs they shall be understood for valid.'[4] The concoction of commodities in the body of commonwealth was done by means of money which was 'as it were the sanguification of the commonwealth: for natural blood is in like manner made of the fruits of the earth; and circulating, nourisheth by the way every

1. Aristotle, *Politics*, II, 5.   3. E.W. III, 235.
2. See *infra* Ch. 10.   4. E.W. III, 237.

member of the body of man'.[1] Collectors and receivers were the veins gathering the money into the public coffers; treasurers appointed for public disbursements were the arteries.

But such a vast structure of authority could not be wielded competently by one man; it must be delegated; there must be experts in the different spheres of authority. Hobbes envisaged the appointment by the sovereign of viceroys, governors, prefects – the nerves and tendons which move the limbs of the monster; then there were to be military commanders, public ministers for education and instruction in civil duty. Religious instructors, too, were to receive their power *dei gratia et regis*; the sovereign alone taught religion *dei gratia*. Judges, too, and all public ministers for execution who supported them, were to be ministers of the sovereign. The sovereign, however, would do well to rely on advice from counsellors in the various spheres of state.[2] This reliance on 'many and prudent counsellors, with every one counselling apart, in his proper element'[3] was better than not having any counsellors at all. For to try to rule alone would be like trying to play tennis without seconds. But a ruler foolish enough to rely on the counsel of a democratic assembly would be like a man carried to hit the ball in a wheelbarrow! But, surely, as soon as such a vast structure of delegated authority became well established and as soon as the sovereign began to rely increasingly on expert advice in different spheres, the indivisibility of his authority would become somewhat of a fiction in practice; for others would come to share his actual power. Henry VIII found this out to his cost with his succession of Chancellors. But for Hobbes, political science was concerned with an ideal experiment – the construction of a logically consistent pyramid of authority; it was not concerned with the actual determinants and distribution of power.

2. Law as Command

That Hobbes' doctrine of sovereignty was primarily intended to clarify confusion in the field of law – the stronghold of the

1. E.W. III, 238.   2. E.W. III, 246.   3. E.W. III, 249.

opposition to the Stuarts – can be seen from his writings on legal theory. In *Leviathan* he declared his interest in law to be that of an analytic philosopher inquiring into the nature of law rather than that of a legalist looking into the details of particular legal systems.[1] Nevertheless, in spite of his considerable contribution to legal theory, his treatment of law at a theoretical level had very obvious practical consequences for the English legal system. These were most explicit in his *Dialogue between a Philosopher and a Student of the Common Laws of England* – a sustained attack on the theory of law held by Sir Edward Coke and other champions of the Common Law against the Stuarts.

Law in feudal times had been regarded as a *declaration* of existing custom. *The law* was there to discover – a sort of property belonging to the people – as it applied to particular circumstances. With the development of Common Law or the King's Law this view still persisted. The King and his Courts never *made laws*; he declared what the law was. Some maintain that this legal fiction still holds good of Common Law in so far as it has not been changed by statute.[2] Up to the time of the Long Parliament of the seventeenth century legislation was a very minor function of Parliament, which was regarded as a kind of court.[3] Specific provisions of law might be altered from time to time; but the law itself unfolded as generation replaced generation. It assigned to every man his rights and duties, his liberties and obligations; it imposed limitations on King and subjects alike. It included not simply principles for deciding private disputes, but conventions of the constitution and rights of both King and subjects. It was this fundamental law which was thought to bestow authority in the spheres of gubernaculum and jurisdictio to which we have already referred.

The law, which was made explicit by the decisions of judges which constituted precedents for future cases falling in similar categories, was presumed to be in accordance with reason, though the lawyers like Sir Edward Coke held that it required the special

1. E.W. III, 251.

2. See, e.g. H. Maine, *Ancient Law* (Everyman Ed.), pp. 18, 19.

3. See C. H. McIlwain, *The High Court of Parliament*, New Haven, 1910.

sort of 'artificial reason' which only a lawyer with a long training could acquire, to interpret it. And if the system of precedents, on which the Common Law proceeded, resulted in a gross wrong being done for which there was no redress in law, then the subject could appeal to the Court of Chancery where the Chancellor had authority to settle the claim according to general considerations of equity.[1] The Chancellor was traditionally an ecclesiastic and therefore deemed to be an authority on matters of conscience. The Court of Equity became increasingly important during the sixteenth century and there was constant friction between the Chancellor and the Common Law Courts. Matters came to a head with the accession of James I. For he, believing in the Divine Right of Kings, held that his untrained reason was a better judge of the law than Coke's 'artificial reason' and that, anyway, as God's vicar on earth, he was above the law. Law was his command; customary law was only valid because he condoned it. He also supported his Chancellor, Lord Ellesmere, against Sir Edward Coke, the Chief Justice, in a great quarrel about the respective spheres of Equity and Common Law.

With the coming of the Long Parliament, also, which indulged in an unprecedented amount of legislative activity, it became more and more obvious that *laws* were being *made*; the law was not being declared. For where was the precedent for a Parliament prolonging its own life by statute? Legislation came gradually to take precedence over all other Parliamentary business and Common Law came more and more to be superseded by Statute Law. Precedent and immemorial custom were no longer completely binding on legal decisions; large parts of Common Law in fact came to be abolished by Acts of Parliament. We are so used, in this country, to the legislative sovereignty of Parliament that we find it difficult to realize that there is no logical or practical necessity for the supremacy of the statute-making authority and that in the seventeenth century it was still thought that there were principles of Common Law that could control Acts of Parliament. This transitional state of confusion with regard to legislative

1. In actual fact it developed an elaborate system of precedents as time went on, just like the Common Law Courts.

authority was the context of Hobbes' view that law is the command of the sovereign – 'the word of him that by right hath command over others'.[1] He was an uncompromising advocate of the supremacy of Statute Law over the Common Law.

Hobbes' political objections to the Common Law were obvious enough; for it imposed a limit on sovereignty and hence endangered the peace. But more interesting was his theoretical attack on its presuppositions. Common Law was an attempt to make explicit the customs of the realm; this, thought Hobbes, was tantamount to perpetuating the stupidity of ignorant men ill-versed in the science of natural justice. 'The skill of making and maintaining commonwealths, consisteth in certain rules, as doth arithmetic and geometry; not, as tennis play, on practice only.'[2] The philosopher remarked acidly to the defender of the Common Law: 'Now as to the authority you ascribe to custom, I deny that any custom of its own nature can amount to the authority of a law. For if the custom be unreasonable, you must, with all other lawyers, confess that it is no law, but ought to be abolished; and if the custom be reasonable, it is not the custom, but the equity that makes the law.'[3] The alternative would be a regress of judgements depending upon precedents terminating in some ignorant man's decision.

Although Hobbes stressed the character of civil law as command – for it was authority, not wisdom, that *made* a law – he nevertheless contrived to hang on to the accepted presumption that law could not be unreasonable. In effect he wished to do away with the Common Law and the 'artificial reason' necessary to interpret its precedents and in its place to put Statute Law which could be interpreted and amended by the judges in accordance with equity.[4] Presumably Hobbes had his eye on the Court of Chancery; but his case for Equity, especially in *Leviathan*, was formulated in terms of the relationship between the civil law and the laws of nature. 'The law of nature, and the civil law, contain each other, and are of equal extent.'[5] Nevertheless he remained clear about the distinction. The laws of nature were 'but conclu-

1. E.W. III, 147.　　3. E.W. VI, 62–3.　　5. E.W. III, 253.
2. E.W. III, 195–6.　　4. See E.W. VI, 68.

sions, or theorems concerning what conduceth to the conserva-
tion and defence of themselves'.[1] Civil law, on the other hand, 'is
to every subject, those rules, which the commonwealth hath
commanded him, by word, writing or other sufficient signs of the
will, to make use of, for the distinction of right, and wrong; that is
to say, of what is contrary, and what is not contrary to the rule'.[2]
Laws properly so called were rules issuing in writing from a determinate source which were enforced by the sword; we are obliged
by them. Justice in a commonwealth was simply what was commanded by law. The only sense in which a law could be unjust
was if it were abrogated by another law. Of course, a law could
be unequitable; but this must be distinguished from being unjust
in a strict sense of 'unjust'. This should rarely happen; for the
sovereign and his appointed judges were guided by the laws of
nature or considerations of equity in making and interpreting
laws. Indeed, in Hobbes' ideal experiment a commonwealth was
created when the theorems of natural law were converted into
the commands of the civil law by being officially issued in statutes
and supported by the sword of the sovereign. Yet there was a
reciprocal connexion. For men were imagined as having coven-
anted to obey the civil law and the third law of nature was
that men should keep their covenants made. Thus, 'Civil, and
natural law are not different kinds, but different parts of law;
whereof one part being written, is called civil, the other unwritten,
natural.'[3]

So Hobbes gleefully shook hands with the lawyers in agreeing
with the presumption 'that law can never be against reason'.[4]
But, he remarked savagely, 'the doubt is of whose reason it is,
that shall be received for law'.[5] It could not be any private reason;
for that would make as many contradictions in the law as there
were in the Schools. Neither could it be 'as Sir Edward Coke
makes it, an artificial perfection of reason, gotten by long study,
observation, and experience, as his was'.[6] For long study might
only serve to increase and confirm erroneous sentences. So it is
not that *juris prudentia*, or wisdom of subordinate judges; but the

1. E.W. III, 147.   3. E.W. III, 254.   5. E.W. III, 256.
2. E.W. III, 251.   4. E.W. III, 256.   6. E.W. III, 256.

reason of this our artificial man the commonwealth, and his command, that maketh law.'[1] The subordinate judges should have regard to the reason which moved the sovereign in making the laws; for though they were written, they had to be interpreted not by the letter but by their 'intendment or meaning'.[2] Equity was to enter in at all stages of the making and interpreting of law. And the sovereign was ultimately the sole judge of equity. In fact, of course, his Chancellor was, and Hobbes staunchly resisted Coke's claim that the Chancellor should be a lawyer and supported the traditional view that he should be an ecclesiastic well-versed in the law of nature.[3]

It is not clear what Hobbes' proposals amounted to in institutional terms. Presumably he meant the King's courts to remain but to cease working according to the traditions of Case Law. Instead their function would be simply to interpret Statutes according to general principles of equity – 'from it I conclude, that justice fulfils the law, and equity interprets the law, and amends the judgements given upon the same law.'[4] Presumably, also, the Court of Chancery would remain and assume great importance as an institutional device for dealing with consequences of the law which seemed unequitable, though there was no legal redress.[5] But whatever institutional provision Hobbes had in mind, it is quite clear that his main proposal was to do away with the appeal to custom as interpreted by the 'artificial reason' of the Common Law judges and to substitute the authority of actual Statutes which would be made and interpreted according to general principles of equity. And the sovereign would be the final authority on the interpretation of equity or laws of nature. He would be the geometer presiding over the science of natural justice. Plato claimed that God everywhere did geometry; Hobbes assigned a similar role to the sovereign of his mortal God.

It would be out of place here to enter into the long-standing

1. E.W. III, 256.   2. E.W. III, 262.   3. E.W. VI, 64–8.   4. E.W. VI, 68.

5. Whether Hobbes definitely linked in his own mind general principles of equity with the Chancellor's Court is not clear. Neither is it clear whether Hobbes realized that this court also had developed its own system of precedents. See E.W. VI, 63–8.

debate on the advantages and disadvantages of Common Law; and it would be superfluous to comment further on Hobbes' pious hope that an absolute monarch and his appointed judges would make and interpret laws strictly in accordance with principles of equity. But it is worth while to pick out one or two points which he made as an avowed analytic philosopher of law which justify his claim to be the precursor of the analytic school of jurisprudence which came to the fore in the nineteenth century.

Firstly, Hobbes made a very good beginning in clarifying the question of what we mean when we talk about law. It is difficult for us to realize that in the seventeenth century thinkers were only beginning to get clear about the criteria by means of which the different social codes and rules could be distinguished from each other. Common Law was an interesting blend of what we now call custom and law in which the supreme legal principle was that custom should be the determinant of law. Hobbes attempted to distinguish law both from custom and from the laws of nature, or what we now call morality. The law is simply those rules which have been promulgated explicitly in writing by an authority having power to enforce them. It is not the content of rules that makes them laws; it is their authoritative source, their determinate character, and their predictable coercive sanction. General considerations of custom and equity may influence those who make and interpret laws. But the question 'What is the law?' should be clearly distinguished from the question 'Is the law right or reasonable?' Similarly, justice in the strict sense is what the law commands; this precise sense of 'justice' should be clearly distinguished from general notions of equity stemming from the application of ideal principles or 'theorems'. Words like 'duty', 'conscience' and 'obligation',[1] are used in at least two senses. One refers to the demand of an external authority on us; the other to our own reasoned conviction, often after we have weighed

1. Hobbes' view of 'natural obligation' felt 'in foro interno', and of its distinction from legal obligation, is one of the most difficult and controversial subjects in Hobbesian exegesis. See Warrender, H., *The Political Philosophy of Hobbes* (O.U.P., 1957) and articles by Plamenatz, J., and Wernham, A. G., in Brown, K. C., *Hobbes Studies* (Blackwell, 1965).

the claims on us of our duties and obligations in the first sense. Hobbes held that the law-maker should be guided by ideal principles (laws of nature); but he did well to point out that there is no necessary connexion between law and ideal principles. Those who think that law is an expression of the moral consciousness of a people can be at best stating a contingent truth about laws in some countries. To regard it as a necessary truth is to betray a certain insularity of thought; for it is the sort of assumption that could only be made by one who has lived in England or some other country where most laws are not obviously immoral.

Secondly, Hobbes saw that a system of law cannot work efficiently without some kind of legal sovereignty. He interpreted this as implying the sovereignty of a determinate person or body who must also be the supreme authority for coercion. It has been maintained that all that in fact is required is the sovereignty of a legal principle.[1] The necessity of such a principle is implicit in Hobbes' attempt to dispense with the authority claimed for custom in Common Law and to substitute that of statutes issuing from a determinate sovereign. His doctrine of the necessity of legal sovereignty in this sense is but one example of many possible supreme legal principles.

Thirdly, Hobbes is famous for his contention that law is *command*. The historical context of this view has already been explained. But it is also interesting from a logical point of view. It is attractive because it points to the prescriptive character of legal language which distinguishes it from statements of fact. The trouble, however, about the view is that 'command' is too strong a word, which suggests the picture of a sergeant-major rather than of a judge or a legislator. So many laws obviously do not command – e.g. enabling statutes and laws conferring franchises. The law does not command a man to sell a house; rather it lays down rules or directions for selling a house if he wants to do so. Law, logically speaking, is much more adequately classed as a system of *rules* or as a record of *decisions* taken by judges, legislative bodies, and so on, rather than as a collection of commands. Some, indeed, would go so far as to regard the law as a kind of costing system in

1. See *supra*, pp. 210–11, and Kelsen, H., *General Theory of Law and State*.

which the function of statements is mainly predictive. The law, it is claimed, *states* what will probably happen *if* the subject decides to act in a certain manner. But this, surely, is to run too far away from the view that law is command; for it omits the normative force of legal language in laying down standards to *guide* people's choices.

So much, then, for Hobbes' doctrine of sovereignty and for his analysis of the chains stretching from the lips of the sovereign to the ears of the subject. There remains only to consider his views on the most suitable occupant for the office of sovereign.

3. *Forms of Government*

Hobbes claimed no demonstrability for his conclusion that monarchy was the best form of government. He admitted in his Preface to *De Cive* that it was the one thing 'in this whole book not to be demonstrated, but only probably stated'.[1] However, his first contention that there can only be three types of commonwealth was incontrovertible as it followed from the definition of commonwealth. For differences could be due only to the differences in the person or persons representing all and every one of the multitude. This could be one man, some men, or all men. There were no further possibilities. Thus the classification of commonwealths into monarchies, aristocracies and democracies was exhaustive as sovereign power was indivisible. Words like 'tyranny', 'oligarchy' and 'anarchy' were only emotive descriptions of monarchy, aristocracy and democracy by people who did not like them; they did not refer to logically distinct types of commonwealth.

It followed, also, from his definition of commonwealth that it was ridiculous to talk of the people's representatives under a monarchy unless reference was being made to the monarch. For it was as absurd to think of a body of men representing the opinions of all to the monarch as it would be to think of a sovereign assembly inviting the people of their dominion to send up deputies, with power to make known their advice or desires, and

1. E.W. II, xxii.

then regarding these deputies rather than themselves as the absolute representatives of the people. This necessary truth had lately been blatantly neglected by those who never considered their King as their representative in spite of an unquestioned claim to his title stretching back for six hundred years. Yet they bestowed the title of 'representatives' on those men 'which at his command were sent up by the people to carry their petitions, and give him, if he permitted it, their advice'.[1] Pym and Hampden were not geometers.

The differences between these forms of government were not, therefore, due to differences in power 'but in the difference of convenience, or aptitude to produce the peace, and security of the people; for which end they were instituted.'[2] Democracy might well be the rationally prior form of government; for the coming together of men to institute a commonwealth is a kind of democratic act, which requires only fixed prescription as to time and place of assembly for democracy in its full sense to emerge. Aristocracy and monarchy arise from such a democratic act when the people give up their habit of assembly and hand over to a limited section or to one man the uncontrolled exercise of sovereign rights on their behalf. But, in spite of the logical priority of democracy, its inconveniences for promoting the peace and security of the people are so manifest that monarchy is infinitely to be preferred.

In the first place, members of a sovereign assembly have always the conflict between public and private interest, whereas in a monarchy the private interest is the same as the public interest, the riches, power and honour of a monarch arising only from the riches, strength and reputation of his subjects. Secondly, a monarch has constant access to secret and expert counsel; whereas matters have to be debated openly in a sovereign assembly by those versed more in the acquisition of wealth than of knowledge. Thirdly, the resolutions of a monarch are subject only to the inconstancies of human nature, whereas in an assembly there is inconstancy due to number as well as to nature. Fourthly, a monarch cannot disagree with himself out of envy or interest; but the

1. E.W. III, 173.   2. E.W. III, 173.

disagreements of an assembly may produce a civil war. Fifthly, though it is an undoubted inconvenience that under monarchy a subject may be deprived of his possessions for the enriching of a favourite (e.g. Buckingham), the same may well happen under a sovereign assembly with additional inconvenience proportionate to the numerical difference. Democracies, too, cannot attend continuously to public business and have to appoint executive committees; this tends to make them aristocracies in practice. Monarchies may be notorious for their problem of succession; but democracies are as contentious as children and always resort to a protector in time of trouble.

If Hobbes' case for monarchy seems rather shaky, so was the England in which he had lived and from which he fled. But he did at least, in the indemonstrable part of his political writings, ask the right sort of questions about forms of government. Some Utopians like Plato have fixed their gaze on the ideal state and the ideal ruler, and have dismissed democracy because of its failure to conform to such an ideal. Hobbes never did this. He shared with Plato a general distrust of his fellow men; but he thought that institutional control rather than the breeding and training of a ruling class of philosophical shamans was the only effective safeguard against the depravity of man. He assumed quite sensibly that the first thing to get clear about in politics is not what is the ideal state but what is the worst thing that can befall a man. His unhesitating answer was civil war. His case against democracy was that it was less likely than monarchy to avert this ultimate disaster. He was very conscious of the inconveniences of monarchy and paid scant attention to the character and training of the monarch. Sovereignty was for Hobbes an *office*. He assumed that anyone who occupied it would be no better and no worse than anyone else. The *office* was the thing; he bothered little about the conscience of the King.

If we believe that the threat of civil war is more of an evil than the threat of arbitrary and overwhelming interference with the liberties of the subject, then Hobbes' preference for monarchy is not unreasonable. The case for democracy in no way rests on its being an ideal form of government. It rests solely on its being less likely to be intolerable to the individual than other forms of government. For it provides institutional methods for getting rid of rulers without a revolution if they turn out to be even worse than was expected. All that the convinced democrat can say in answer to Hobbes is that the worst evil of all is, as Locke put it, 'to be subject to the inconstant, uncertain, arbitrary will of another man'.[1] The possible risk of civil war under a sovereign assembly is preferable to the probable risk to individual liberty under an absolute monarch.

1. J. Locke, *Second Treatise of Civil Government* (ed. Gough), p. 13.

CHAPTER 10

RELIGION

Introductory

FOR those unfamiliar with the atmosphere of the seventeenth century one of the most surprising features of its literature is the ubiquity of religious controversy and quotations from the Scriptures. For the politician nowadays religion is something which he perhaps introduces at the end of a speech to add a touch of inspiration to a drab economic analysis. In the seventeenth century such detachment from or indifference to religion was almost impossible. Political passions were fanned by religious arguments; democratic movements expressed themselves in religious forms. Even the Royal Society was founded by men who believed that science would reveal more and more of God's creation and thus enhance our worship. Religion was so connected with the customs and practices of ordinary life that to be called an atheist was tantamount to being called a rogue or a brigand. Every man practised some form of religion and the impact of Luther's doctrine of the priesthood of all believers reverberated round the land with the recent translation of the Bible into English. Reasons from the Scriptures for most diverse forms of conduct were thus the property of all who could read or listen to the multitude of preachers who were only too willing to expound the word of God. The seventeenth century in England was the great period of various forms of individualism it was from the many sects and splinter groups which broke away from the Established Church that the Nonconformist movement in this country developed. But these movements were not simply religious movements in the limited sense of the word; they were manifestations of the wider revolt against patriarchalism and of the striving for individual liberty to which we have already referred[1]. If we were to consider the beliefs and conduct of men like Cromwell, Rainborough, John Wildman and George Fox, it would be impossible to separate their opinions on politics and morals from their religious convictions or to give a clear-cut religious, moral or political reason for any of their major decisions.

Indeed, as we have already explained, these distinctions were only in process of being made explicit by those who reflected in a more abstract way on the assumptions of their fellows.[2] And Hobbes was one of the few with the detachment necessary to attempt this. He rigorously excluded theology from philosophy and tried to map the proper domains of knowledge and faith. He outlined a theory of the causes of religion and superstition and discussed the grounds of religious belief. He also conducted an elaborate inquiry into the use of various crucial terms in the Scriptures in order to decide on their proper use – 'proper' implying not at variance with the new science of motion! But all his theorizing about religion was subordinate to his main interest in it as a possible source of civil discord. It is seldom realized that 371 out of 714 pages in *Leviathan* deal with religious matters. They are packed with detailed arguments and quotations drawn from the Scriptures in which he defended what he called 'true religion' against the twin threats of Catholicism and the priesthood of all believers. His attitude was not quite like that of Machiavelli, who was quite unmoved by religious problems and regarded religion simply as a useful form of social cement to restrain the multitude and to enhance their patriotism. Hobbes felt passionately about religion – other people's religion. His astonishing knowledge of the details of the Scriptures and his insight into the follies and superstitions which accumulate around the nucleus of faith were like the mental card-index and merciless penetration of a malevolent village gossip. His was the attitude of the insecure intellectual who sees the social fabric threatened by the absurd vapourings of ignorant, credulous and passionate men. And he had good cause to be afraid. For the main enemies of the sort of absolutism which he envisaged were indeed those whose belief in individual

1. See *supra*, pp. 179–81.   2. See *supra*, p. 155.

liberty assumed predominantly religious forms or those who, because of their Catholic convictions, could never give the kind of undivided allegiance to a sovereign which he demanded of them.

We have no intention of following Hobbes into the minutiae of Scriptural exegesis, but will be content to deal with his general views on the subject of religious belief and his use of the Scriptures to justify his demand for absolute sovereignty. We shall also raise the problem of Hobbes' own religious convictions. For 'religion', he said in an Epistle Dedicatory to Charles II, 'is not philosophy, but law.'[1] From the point of view of a man laying out the foundations of commonwealth, the important thing was to look into the authority by which religious doctrines became law, and were publicly taught, rather than to indulge in abortive speculations about the supernatural credentials of the doctrines. But that did not prevent Hobbes from writing with scorn and irony about the source and content of most people's religious convictions. In view of this obvious lack of sympathy with religious men it will not be amiss to conjecture where he himself stood on these matters.

1. The Causes of Religion

Religion being peculiar to man, there must be some peculiar quality in human nature, which the beasts lack, from which it springs. This is man's curiosity, his desire to know the causes of things, especially of good and evil fortune. Often this desire cannot be completely satisfied. But in such cases man is not content to confess his ignorance. Instead he tends to invent causes as his fancy suggests, since experience has convinced him that things do not happen without causes. Man, too, is haunted by fear of 'death, poverty or other calamity' which his capacity for prudence aggravates. 'This perpetual fear, always accompanying mankind in the ignorance of causes, as it were in the dark, must needs have for object something.'[2] Recourse is therefore had to powers or invisible agents to explain good or evil fortune. In this sense the old poets were right when they said that the gods were first created by human fear. At least this was true of the gods of the

1. E.W. VII, 5.   2. E.W. III, 95.

Gentiles; belief in the one God, eternal, invisible and omnipotent, on the other hand, was more likely to have arisen from 'the desire men have to know the causes of natural bodies'.[1]

Gods cannot remain metaphysical blank cheques. They have to be filled in with some kind of substance, and man has usually thought of this as like his own soul. The conception of the soul's substance is derived from appearances in dreams, reflections in a looking-glass and other such creatures of the fancy. These are taken for 'real and external' substances or ghosts. The gods, therefore, are favoured with thin aerial bodies, differing from apparitions only in their ability to appear and vanish when they please. These invisible agents are thought to operate by means of signs, omens and other phenomena which often precede happenings, though they have no obvious connexion with them. They are approached and honoured by man in ways which are appropriate to dealings between man and man. 'And in these four things, opinion of ghosts, ignorance of second causes, devotion to what men fear and taking of things casual for prognostics, consisteth the natural seed of religion.'[2]

Hobbes, however, did not make the mistake of thinking that, because we can assign a psychological cause to religion, religious belief is necessarily undermined. He went to considerable lengths to explain the different ways in which this seed of religion could be cultivated – either according to natural invention which led to the superstitions and nature worship of the Gentiles[3] or according to God's commandments and direction. In his account of the passions he put his view succinctly: 'Fear of power invisible, feigned by the mind or imagined from tales publicly allowed, RELIGION; not allowed, SUPERSTITION. And when the power imagined is truly such as we imagine, TRUE RELIGION.'[4] This remark was really rather startling in its candour if we consider coldly its implication when taken in conjunction with Hobbes' other contentions. For he held that we can have no *idea* of God though we might give names to 'things supernatural'. How then can we ever *imagine* the required power? Truth, also as we have

---

1. E.W. III, 95.   3. E.W. III, 98–105.
2. E.W. III, 98.   4. E.W. III, 45.

seen, can only be affirmed of propositions, not of our imagining;[1] and Hobbes elsewhere laboured the point that nothing could be rationally asserted of God's attributes; religious beliefs were not true or false like the propositions of geometry but were expressions of devotion resting on our trust in the person propounding them. In view of these implications it is difficult to judge whether Hobbes was here indulging in irony or expressing himself somewhat carelessly.

What, then, constituted 'true religion' for Hobbes? For if there are grounds or reasons for religious beliefs, then speculations about their causes, however interesting in themselves, do nothing to undermine the beliefs themselves. It is only if there are no good reasons for what is asserted in religious beliefs that those who suggest causes for them are justified in regarding them *only* as projections of our fears and infantile wishes. It is interesting to note that Freud himself in his *The Future of an Illusion* defined illusions as beliefs which we very much wish to be true like Columbus' belief that he had discovered a new sea-route to India. But they may be true. When beliefs are held in flat contradiction to what is known they are to be called delusions. Therefore, maintained Freud, though the grounds for religious belief are very flimsy, they are not to be dismissed solely because, psychologically speaking, they spring from some of the oldest, strongest and most insistent wishes of man.[2] Hobbes seems implicitly to have held some such view; for he used his theory of causes mainly to expose superstitions. But it is difficult to disentangle what he thought the grounds of religious belief to be and more difficult still to gauge how convincing he thought them.

2. The Grounds of Religious Belief

In Hobbes' system God played a role rather like a supreme civil servant; he issued orders which the privileged could decipher, but he obscured his person in an enigmatic anonymity. He declared himself to man by laws in three ways 'by the dictates of natural

1. See *supra*, pp. 59–60.

2. See S. Freud, *The Future of an Illusion*, Ch. VI (Hogarth Press, 1928).

reason, by revelation, and the voice of some man, to whom by the operation of miracles, he procureth credit with the rest. From hence there ariseth a triple word of God, rational, sensible and prophetic: to which correspondeth a triple hearing: right reason, sense supernatural, and faith.'[1]

To reasonable men capable of understanding Hobbes' principles of natural justice, God's commands amounted to the laws of nature. God's function here was mainly to enable Hobbes to say that theorems conducive to peace could be regarded as laws properly so called in so far as they were the commands of God. There were also rules with a divine source enjoining worship and honour of God which a rational man could understand. God's nature, however, was a much more baffling matter for a rational man. There was first of all existence which, in this context, Hobbes seems to have taken as an *attribute* of God in spite of his interesting remarks elsewhere about the ambiguities of the verb 'to be'. 'For no man can have the will to honour that, which he thinks not to have any being.'[2] Secondly, Hobbes held, at least in his *Leviathan*, that God was the cause of the world. 'For he that from any effect he seeth come to pass, should reason to the next and immediate cause thereof, and from thence to the cause of that cause, and plunge himself profoundly in the pursuit of causes: shall at last come to this, that there must be, as even the heathen philosophers confessed, one first mover; that is, a first, and an eternal cause of all things; which is that which men mean by the name of God.'[3] In his later *De Corpore*, however, he indicated the difficulties in the notion of an unmoved mover. For though it could be affirmed that nothing is moved by itself, it followed also that nothing could move something else which was not itself moved. Philosophers therefore could not determine questions about the creation of the world which were to be handed over for decision to the lawful authorities.[4] Thirdly, Hobbes was convinced of God's irresistible power which gave him sovereignty over all men and the right of afflicting men at his pleasure. The problem of why evil men often prosper and good men suffer adversity could be decided only from arguments drawn from

1. E.W. III, 345.   2. E.W. III, 351.   3. E.W. III, 95–6.   4. E.W. I, 412.

God's power. Did not God reply to Job, 'Where wast thou, when I laid the foundations of the earth?' Job had not sinned; his suffering was an unfortunate consequence of God's manifestation of power.

The main function of reason, however, in the realms of religion was to suggest what God cannot be – at ease, finite, figured, having parts, occupying a place, moved or at rest, plural, having passions, rational appetite, sight, knowledge and understanding. If we rely on natural reason we must either qualify God in a negative manner by adjectives like 'infinite', 'eternal', 'incomprehensible'; or superlatives, as 'most high', 'most great' and the like, or indefinites like 'good' and 'holy' which are not really descriptions of his nature but expressions of our admiration. Thus rational disputation about the nature of God is pointless and is a dishonour to him; 'for in the attributes which we give to God, we are not to consider the signification of philosophical truth; but the signification of pious intention, to do him the greatest honour we are able.'[1] Worship, however, in a commonwealth must be public and uniform as a commonwealth is but one person. The attributes of God, therefore, which are words by means of which we worship him, must be settled by agreement. For 'whatsoever may be done by the wills of particular men, where there is no law but reason, may be done by the will of the commonwealth, by laws civil.'[2] It follows therefore that the sovereign must decide on God's attributes.

The comparative helplessness of reason in deciding on God's attributes must not, however, lead us to abandon it. For it is a gift of God for our use till the Second Coming of Jesus. It is therefore not 'to be folded up in the napkin of an implicit faith, but employed in the purchase of justice, peace and true religion'.[3] For though many matters connected with God cannot be rationally demonstrated, yet there is nothing in God's word contrary to reason. If we think that there is, then usually we are at fault in our reasoning. We must therefore be prepared, to a certain extent, to 'captivate our understanding to the words; and not to labour in sifting out a philosophical truth by logic, of such mysteries as are

1. E.W. III, 354.   2. E.W. III, 355.   3. E.W. III, 360.

not comprehensible, nor fall under any rule of natural science. For it is with the mysteries of our religion as with wholesome pills for the sick; which swallowed whole, have the virtue to cure; but chewed up, are for the most part cast up again without effect.'[1]

Hobbes did not play down the use of reason in religious matters in order to exalt the inner light of the individual. Indeed, some of his scathing comments were reserved for those who claimed individual intimacy with the will of God, or what he called immediate revelation by sense supernatural. The favoured individual, he pointed out, may understand well enough how God spoke to him; but how are others to understand this? 'For if a man pretend to me, that God hath spoken to him supernaturally and immediately, and I make doubt of it, I can not easily perceive what argument he can produce, to oblige me to believe it.'[2] And a private individual has not the argument of the sword by which a sovereign can compel at least outward conformity to the authorized religion. And how seriously are we to take this talk of supernatural sense? For if a man says that God spoke to him in a dream, this 'is no more than to say he dreamed that God spoke to him'.[3] Anyone who understands the causation of dreams and who has marked men's conceit of their own godliness, cannot help but be sceptical of such claims; for visions and voices are explicable as dreams that occur in the intermediate state between sleeping and waking. Inspiration, too, is psychologically suspect; for 'to say he speaks by supernatural inspiration, is to say he finds an ardent desire to speak, or some strong opinion of himself, for which he can allege no natural and sufficient reason.'[4]

Nevertheless dreams, visions, voices and inspiration are not to be dismissed; for this is the means by which the prophets have been informed of the will of God which has been recorded in the Scriptures. These mediate revelations to prophets being the foundation on which Hobbes thought religious belief was built, the crucial question was how true prophets could be distinguished from false ones. Hobbes suggested two criteria; the working of miracles and not teaching religious doctrines at variance with those already established. Both criteria must be satisfied, neither

1. E.W. III, 360. 2. E.W. III, 361. 3. E.W. III, 361. 4. E.W. III, 362.

being in itself sufficient. But as miracles had now ceased there was no sign left whereby to acknowledge the pretended revelations or inspirations of any private men. Since the time of Jesus the Holy Scriptures had supplied the place of and sufficiently recompensed the want of all other prophecy. From these 'by wise and learned interpretation, and careful ratiocination, all rules and precepts necessary to the knowledge of our duty both to God and man, without enthusiasm or supernatural inspiration, may easily be deduced.'[1]

Reliance on the authority of Scripture is, as Hobbes saw, rather hazardous. For which books of the Bible are to be taken as authoritative and what does the doctrine therein enunciated mean? Hobbes subjected the books of the Bible to scrutiny and suggested, amongst other things, that the books ascribed to Moses must have been written after his death. The authority of the Old Testament could be traced back only to the time of Esdras. However, most of the Old Testament could be accepted as genuine; so also could the New Testament, though the authority for it could not be traced back before the Council of Laodicea. With regard to the authentic texts there could be no dispute about the genuineness of the revelation therein incorporated. For who could know that they were God's word save the prophets themselves? The question of authority was not suitably raised in connexion with the authenticity of their divine source, but in connexion with the authority by which they were made law. And to this there could only be one answer for those who themselves were not favoured with supernatural intimations – the authority of the commonwealth whose commands had already the force of laws. For how else could agreement be established about the implementation of God's commands?

3. The Concepts of Scripture

There was, however, the further problem of agreement about the meaning of what was asserted in the recognized books of the Scripture. This depended on the constant signification of words

1. E.W. III, 365.

'not as in natural science, on the will of the writer, nor, as in common conversation, on vulgar use, but on the sense they carry in Scripture.'[1] In fact, this 'sense' was very much refined by Hobbes' mechanical theory of nature; the writers of the Scriptures would have been somewhat surprised to learn what their terms meant.

Hobbes started with the terms 'body' and 'spirit'. A body is that which occupies 'some certain room' and as it is subject to change it is also called 'substance' which means 'subject to various accidents'. As 'body' and 'substance' signify the same thing, 'substance incorporeal' is a contradiction in terms. This usage of 'body', however, is more general than that of common people who call only those parts of the universe 'body' as 'they can discern by the sense of feeling, to resist their force, or by the sense of their eyes to hinder them from a farther prospect.'[2] Therefore, in the common language of men, air and aerial substances are not taken for bodies but are called wind, breath or spirits – the Latin word *spiritus* signifying all these. For instance, the aerial substance, which gives life and motion to the bodies of living creatures, is called vital and animal spirits. Ignorant men, however, often use the term 'bodies' or 'spirits' to refer to 'those idols of the brain, which represent bodies to us, where they are not, as in a looking-glass, in a dream, or to a distempered brain waking'.[3] The term 'spirits' is favoured by such credulous folk because these apparitions have no resistance to touch. So 'the proper signification of spirit in common speech, is either a subtle, fluid, and invisible body, or a ghost, or other idol or phantasm of the imagination.'[4] There are, of course, metaphorical significations like 'spirit of contradiction' where 'spirit' is taken for a disposition or inclination of mind, or for an eminent ability, extraordinary passion or disease of the mind – e.g. 'the spirit of wisdom', 'possessed with a spirit'. Hobbes has been hailed by some modern philosophers as one of the founders of the method of solving philosophical problems by paying attention to the ordinary use of words; he can certainly be credited, too, with another modern habit – that of giving meaning to the words of others by reading his own theories

1. E.W. III, 380.   2. E.W. III, 381.   3. E.W. III, 382.   4. E.W. III, 382.

into them, instead of attempting to reconstruct the theoretical framework of beliefs in which the words occur.

Where these senses of 'spirit' fail us in Scriptural interpretation we must realize the limits of human understanding and rely on faith. For instance, when God is said to be a spirit or where by the spirit of God is meant God himself, 'our faith consisteth not in our opinion, but in our submission. . . . For the nature of God is incomprehensible; that is to say, we understand nothing of what he is, but only that he is.'[1] Hobbes then proceeded to cite strings of passages from the Scriptures in which reference was made to the spirit of God and tried to show how his various senses of 'spirit' could take care of them. 'Holy Ghost' and 'Holy Spirit' were rather a trouble to him. For 'Jesus was full of the Holy Ghost.'[2] Hobbes took this as meaning zeal to do the work for which he was sent by God the Father! For '. . . to interpret it of a ghost, is to say, that God himself, for so our Saviour was, was filled with God; which is very improper and insignificant.'[3] The translation of 'spirits' by the term 'ghosts' was a bad lapse. For 'ghosts' is a word that signifies 'nothing, neither in heaven nor earth, but the imaginary inhabitants of man's brain'. 'Spirit' is a respectable rendering; for this means either a real, if aerial, substance, or some extraordinary affection or ability of mind or body. When the disciples saw Jesus walking on the water, they took him to be a spirit or aerial body, and not a phantasm; 'for it is said, they all saw him; which cannot be understood of the delusions of the brain (which are not common to many at once, as visible bodies are; but singular, because of the differences of fancies) but of bodies only.'[4]

It is possible that God created angels to act as his messengers and to execute his will in extraordinary and supernatural ways. But if he did, they must have been substances endued with dimensions, taking up room, and moving from place to place. Very often, however, where angels crop up in the Scriptures 'there can be nothing else understood by the word *angel*, but some image raised, supernaturally, in the fancy, to signify the presence of

1. E.W. III, 383. 3. E.W. III, 386–7.
2. St Luke, iv, 1. 4. E.W. III, 387.

God in the execution of some supernatural work.'[1] Indeed, if we are to take account only of the Old Testament and of dreams and visions that happen in the ordinary course of events, it could be held that angels are nothing but 'supernatural apparitions of the fancy, raised by the special and extraordinary operation of God'.[2] But many passages in the New Testament and Jesus' own words 'have extorted from my feeble reason, an acknowledgement and belief that there be also angels substantial and permanent.'[3]

The term 'inspiration' can only be used metaphorically in the Scriptures. For literally it means 'blowing into a man some thin and subtle air or wind, in such manner as a man filleth a bladder with his breath'.[4] If it says in the Scriptures, therefore, that God inspired into man the breath of life, it can only mean that God gave him vital motion. Similarly the word 'infused' can only be employed metaphorically to describe the way God's graces are imparted to man: 'for those graces are virtues, not bodies to be carried hither and thither, and to be poured into men as into barrels.'[5] The term 'word of God' is used properly to refer to the words spoken to prophets; but it is also used metaphorically to designate God's wisdom, power and eternal decree in making the world. It can be used as well for the effect of his word, that which by his word is affirmed, commanded, threatened, or promised – e.g. the word was made flesh, where Jesus was what was promised. Finally, 'the word of God' can mean such words as are consonant with reason and equity.

Miracles interested Hobbes. They are works that cause wonder in virtue either of their strangeness or of their production by other than natural means. 'Therefore, if a horse or cow should speak, it were a miracle; because both the thing is strange, and the natural cause difficult to imagine.'[6] But we do not call reproduction a miracle; for though we don't know by what means men and animals manage it, there is nothing unusual about it. The first rainbow was a miracle, and served its purpose as a sign from God. But nowadays, whether or not we know their causes, rainbows have ceased to be miracles because of their frequency. Con-

1. E.W. III, 389.   3. E.W. III, 394.   5. E.W. III, 395.

2. E.W. III, 393–4.   4. E.W. III, 394.   6. E.W. III, 428.

versely rare works produced by human industry are not miracu-
lous. Furthermore, as men differ in their capacity for admiration
and wonder, so what is a miracle to some may not be so to others.
That is why events like eclipses of the sun and moon have been
taken as miracles by the common people. But these two criteria,
though necessary, are not sufficient; for a miracle is always
wrought for the procuring of credit to God's messengers, ministers
and prophets. Strictly speaking, therefore, the creation of the
world and the destruction of all living creatures in the deluge were
not miracles; for no prophet was thereby provided with impeccable credentials. But the works of God done by Moses in Egypt
were miracles because they established Moses' divine mission.
This method of providing divine testimonials was only employed
for the benefit of the elect; the lesser breeds were passed over by
what was essentially a device for increasing and consolidating
church membership. Nowadays, however, under Christian sovereigns, there is nothing that a man 'endowed but with a mediocrity
of reason would think supernatural'.[1] The question, therefore, to
ask is not whether a reported action is a miracle, but whether the
report is true or false. This cannot be settled simply by the private
conscience, but rather by the public one residing in the sovereign.
Of course, thought being free, a private man has always the liberty
'to believe or not believe in his heart those acts that have been
given out for miracles. . . . But when it comes to confession of that
faith, the private reason must submit to the public; that is to say,
to God's lieutenant.'[2] This treatment of miracles was typical of
Hobbes' technique with religious questions. It resembled Euripides' treatment of his religious heritage.[3] Radical probing was
mingled with subtle irony and when the lid seemed about to blow
off the traditional teaching, the sovereign appeared as a kind of
deus ex machina to dish up the mixture as before.

The notions of eternal life and eternal torment deserved attention; for they might provide incentives more potent than those
which Hobbes thought would keep men from civil war. Adam had

1. E.W. III, 436.   2. E.W. III, 437.

3. See A. W. Verrall's classic exposition of this technique for saying what it
is dangerous to say in his *Euripides the Rationalist.*

lost the gift of eternal life by his sin, but Jesus had recovered it for believers – to enjoy, however, at the resurrection of the dead. There was no Scriptural evidence for saying that this boon would be experienced 'in another higher heaven, called *caelum empyreum*'.[1] Jerusalem and Mt Zion were singled out by Isaiah as the dwelling place for the people of God. Christians must keep their feet on the ground. For those not fortunate enough to rise again, no situation was promised in the Scriptures – only rather depressing company, e.g. deceased giants. Predictions of hell fire were to be taken metaphorically, and terms like 'Satan' and 'Devil' were appellations of an office rather than proper names of persons; they were variables whose values were the earthly enemies of the Church. To be saved was the same as to enjoy eternal life 'when God shall reign at the coming again of Christ in Jerusalem'.

Hobbes in fact interpreted the Scriptures in such a way that there was little danger of his readers thinking with his Jewish contemporary, Spinoza, that 'blessedness is not the reward of right living; it is the right living itself.' By making terms like 'eternal life', 'heaven' and 'hell' concrete, and by postponing their relevance till the Second Coming, he effectively removed one of the most potent grounds for sedition and saintliness – the belief that eternal life is something to be enjoyed here and now as an anticipation of a future state, and that the kingdom of heaven is a state of mind which can be achieved in this life when two or three are gathered together in the name of Jesus. Maybe the notions are rather mystical – especially when judged by the yardstick of Hobbes' mechanical theory – but there are such good Scriptural grounds for withholding a completely eschatological interpretation from much of Jesus' teaching on the subject of eternal life and the kingdom of heaven,[2] that Hobbes' interpretation was either a superb piece of irony or a case of very special pleading. As the issue at stake was the relationship between church and state it is not surprising that Hobbes glossed over in

1. E.W. III, 441.

2. See, for instance, C. H. Dodd's case against a thorough-going eschatological interpretation in his *The Parables of the Kingdom*.

the Scriptures passages which sectaries and Catholics brought so prominently to his notice when he left his study.

4. Church and State

Hobbes defined a church as 'a company of men professing Christian religion, united in the person of one sovereign, at whose command they ought to assemble, and without whose authority they ought not to assemble'.[1] There is therefore no universal church which all Christians are bound to obey; for there is no power on earth to which all other commonwealths are subject. A church is the same thing as a Christian commonwealth consisting of Christian men. It is called a civil state in so far as its members are men and a church in so far as they are Christians. 'Temporal and spiritual government, are but two words brought into the world, to make men see double, and mistake their lawful sovereign.'[2]

Hobbes had already demonstrated from the law of nature that the chief pastor of the church must be the civil sovereign; he now had to show that this rational conclusion was in accordance with the will of God as revealed in the Scriptures. And the ingenuity with which he manipulated the Scriptures, in order to provide a divine sanction for his *Leviathan*, was astonishing.

Most divines, he admitted, took the phrase 'kingdom of God' to refer to eternal felicity or for the earnest of it which they termed 'kingdom of grace'. But a study of the Scriptures would reveal that in most places 'kingdom of God' signified 'a kingdom properly so named, constituted by the votes of the people of Israel in peculiar manner'.[3] God was thus their chosen king by covenant as well as ruling over them naturally, as over all men, by his might. This covenant was first made by Abraham and renewed by Moses on Mount Sinai, making the Jews into a peculiar people. Therefore, Hobbes concluded, 'by the kingdom of God, is properly meant a commonwealth, instituted, by the consent of those which were to be subject thereto, for their civil government, and the regulating of their behaviour, not only towards God their king, but also towards one another in point of justice, and towards

1. E.W. III, 459.　　2. E.W. III, 460.　　3. E.W. III, 397.

other nations both in peace and war; which properly was a kingdom wherein God was king, and the high-priest was to be, after the death of Moses, his sole viceroy or lieutenant.'[1] The civil and ecclesiastical powers, in other words, were united in Abraham, Moses and subsequent high-priests. 'Whosoever had the sovereignty of the commonwealth among the Jews, the same had also the supreme authority in the matter of God's external worship, and represented God's person.'[2]

Whatever the correct interpretation of the relationship between the spiritual and temporal powers amongst the Jews, most people would say that the situation was rather transformed by the coming of Jesus and the spread of Christianity to the Gentile world. But Hobbes had his story pat to deal with this obvious rejoinder. Jesus was certainly called King of the Jews, but as he himself said, his kingdom was not of this world. By the pact of baptism his followers undertook to accept him as King at the appointed hour of the Second Coming. His mission on earth was 'to restore unto God by a new covenant, the kingdom, which being his by the old covenant, had been cut off by the rebellion of the Israelites in the election of Saul'.[3] It was also to proclaim himself the Messiah, the King promised by the prophets, when he should come again to take possession of his father's kingdom. His preaching on earth was not contrary to the law of the Jews or of Caesar; for he preached only of his kingdom to be and advocated the payment of tribute to Caesar. Christians should therefore submit unquestioningly to the civil sovereign until the Second Coming when institutional arrangements would be somewhat different.

Jesus and his Messianic mission having been accommodated comfortably and innocuously in the entrails of *Leviathan*, Hobbes turned his attention to the church which he founded – probably somewhat inadvertently. Hobbes divided the time between the Ascension and the Second Coming into two main periods – before and after civil sovereigns embraced the Christian religion. During the former period 'power ecclesiastical' was with the apostles and those to whom the Holy Spirit was transmitted by the laying on of hands. They were left no coercive power by Jesus; only authority

1. E.W. III, 400.   2. E.W. III, 475.   3. E.W. III, 479.

to proclaim the kingdom of God to be and to persuade men to prepare themselves for it. They were thus schoolmasters rather than commanders, and their precepts were not laws but wholesome counsels. The time between the Ascension and the Second Coming was a regeneration, not a reigning. The non-coercive character of ecclesiastical authority was evidenced also by Jesus' comparison of apostles to fishers of men, by the nature of faith which is not to be coerced, and the instructions of Jesus and St Paul advocating submission to princes, who enforce outward conformity but not inner faith.

The sole content of the message of the early church was 'that Jesus was the Christ, that is to say the King that was to save them, and reign over them eternally in the world to come'.[1] None of the early ministers regarded himself or anyone else as an authority on the Scriptures of such a sort that all should take his interpretation for law. Indeed, difficulties about interpretation were dealt with in church assemblies. The Old Testament had not been made law for the Jews until the renovation of the covenant with God at the return from captivity and the restoration of their commonwealth under Esdras; and that was done by the sovereign civil power. Every convert might have made the New Testament canonical for himself until the coming of Christian sovereigns; but for others such individual interpretations were counsels, not laws. Jesus did not in fact leave new laws to oblige us in this world but new doctrines to prepare us for the next. They only became obligatory canons when 'obedience to them was commanded by them that God had given power to on earth to be legislators'.[2] Consequently the Scripture was only law where the lawful civil power had made it so. Councils like that of Laodicea, which first settled the canonical Scriptures, were purely meetings for agreeing about what was to be taught; they did not establish canons or laws in the strict sense. There was no Scriptural authority for setting up 'canons against laws, and a ghostly authority against the civil'.

Hobbes went on to show how pastors and ministers of the early church were elected by the congregation, how economic provision was made, and how this voluntary body for regeneration was

1. E.W. III, 511.   2. E.W. III, 519.

organized under an infidel prince. When, however, the prince became a Christian, all was transformed. For conversion to Christianity could not take away from him his right to take the steps necessary to conserving peace. Before conversion he had been pastor of his people in that no subject could lawfully teach the people save by his authority and permission; so too, after conversion, he still retained the right to ordain what pastor he chose and 'to teach the Church, that is, to teach the people committed to their charge'.[1] If, therefore, a congregation elected a pastor in a Christian commonwealth, it was ultimately the sovereign who did so; for this election would have been invalid without his consent. And as teachers taught only on his authority, so pastors were really his ministers like judges in courts of justice or army commanders. 'And the reason hereof, is not because they that teach, but because they that are to learn, are his subjects.'[2] The sovereign, indeed, had the right to perform all pastoral functions like baptism and the laying on of hands; but he was likely to be a very busy man, and, like the Pope, usually would leave such mundane tasks to his ministers. So Christian sovereigns 'have all manner of power over their subjects, that can be given to man, for the government of men's external actions, both in policy and religion; and may make such laws as themselves shall judge fittest, for the government of their own subjects, both as they are the commonwealth, and as they are the Church; for both Church and State are the same men.'[3] If a sovereign, therefore, committed government in matters of religion to the Pope, the latter only exercised that charge in another's dominion in the right of the civil sovereign. He was on a par with supreme pastors, assemblies of pastors, or any other persons charged with the supervision of religion. But this was purely a matter of convenience. The civil sovereign had merely delegated his authority to interpret and teach the Scriptures. No division of sovereignty was thereby implied.

After a lengthy and learned demolition of Cardinal Bellarmine's defence of Rome's challenge to the temporal power in his *De Summo Pontifice*, Hobbes reiterated his recipe for protection against false prophets, whose individualistic and anarchic out-

1. E.W. III, 538.   2. E.W. III, 539.   3. E.W. III, 546.

pourings were just as much a danger to the state religion as the 'ghostly authority' of Rome. 'All that is NECESSARY to salvation,' he maintained, was 'faith in Christ and obedience to laws.'[1] Under obedience came charity and love because they both imply a will to obey: righteousness because it is the will to give every one his own, that is to obey the laws; and repentance which is the same thing as the return of the will to obedience. Faith, of course, was a gift of God. But for those not blessed with private revelation it came by way of teachers appointed by the sovereign. The only article of faith necessary to salvation was that Jesus is the Christ.

Under a Christian sovereign there could thus be no difficulty about reconciling the sword of justice with the shield of faith. The sovereign required obedience to the civil law which contained all the laws of nature or of God, and he allowed belief in the article of faith that Jesus is the Christ and in those conclusions which he deduced from it. If a sovereign drew false conclusions from this article, and commanded 'some superstructions of hay or stubble'[2] to be taught, how could the subject's salvation be imperilled by believing his lawful teacher? Anyway who was to judge whether a deduced consequence was erroneous? 'Shall a private man judge, when the question is of his own obedience?'[3] Under an infidel sovereign resistance was against the laws of nature and in defiance of the counsels of the apostles. Faith, too, was internal and invisible and could not be damaged by such compliance. A man who risked his life for his faith might expect his reward in heaven, but should not complain of his lawful sovereign. Martyrs there could be; the first degree of martyrdom however was reserved for those who were called to preach that Jesus Christ was risen from the dead on first-hand evidence of his resurrection. Martyrs of the second degree were those who were called to preach that Jesus is the Christ. This was the sole message which justified martyrdom – and the sufferer had to be called. 'To die for every tenet that serveth the ambition or profit of the clergy, is not required.'[4] But only a very unreasonable prince would put to death or persecute a subject who was waiting for the Second Coming before he transferred his allegiance, and who, in

1. E.W. III, 585.   2. E.W. III, 601.   3. E.W. III, 601.   4. E.W. III, 496.

the meantime, was obliged by his conscience to obey the civil law. For in the sphere of overt action, at any rate, the claims of the immortal God were indistinguishable from those of the mortal God, Leviathan.

5. Knowledge and Faith

Hobbes concluded *Leviathan* with his famous section on the kingdom of darkness in which he launched a savage attack on superstition and Catholicism as enemies of the true religion. Spiritual darkness descended through misinterpretations of the Scriptures, belief in demons and other relics of the Gentile religion, acceptance of absurdities from ancient philosophers – especially Aristotle, and the promulgation of the doctrines of the Catholic church which were 'contrary to the peaceable societies of mankind'. The Papacy, Hobbes very shrewdly remarked, 'is no other than the ghost of the deceased Roman empire, sitting crowned upon the grave thereof.'[1] The Pontifex Maximus became the Pope. *Aqua lustralis* turned into holy water, saturnalia into carnivals, bacchanalia into wakes, and the Venus-Cupid ensemble into the Madonna with Child. The Latin language employed by the Church was the ghost of the old Roman language. The whole set-up resembled fairy tales told by old wives. The Pope was the counterpart of the king of the fairies. 'The ecclesiastics are spiritual men and ghostly fathers. The fairies are spirits and ghosts. Fairies and ghosts inhabit darkness, solitudes and graves. The ecclesiastics walk in obscurity of doctrine, in monasteries, churches and churchyards.'[2] Both fairies and ecclesiastics snatch away the reason of the young, marry not, and dwell in enchanted castles. Superstition was inevitable; as most men were ignorant and all were fearful. But the Papacy ruthlessly exploited the fear of ignorant men to perpetuate the power of unscrupulous priests as a rival to the secular power.

Hobbes left his readers in little doubt about the types of religious belief which he considered pernicious! He also made it reasonably clear what beliefs he thought it desirable for a subject

1. E.W. III, 698.   2. E.W. III, 698.

to confess publicly. But his own private beliefs on these matters were not so readily apparent. Certainly he held that faith was radically different from knowledge. The object of both faith and knowledge were propositions. But the reasons for accepting them were different. In the case of knowledge we consider the proposition itself and call to mind what its terms signify. For instance we know that two plus two make four because we have agreed about how these symbols are to be used. Truth is a matter of following out the consequences of our definitions. We are thus enabled to settle such problems as whether theft is injury or not; for it depends purely on remembering what we have called 'theft' and what 'injury'.[1] When, however, our reasons for assent derive 'not from the proposition itself but from the person propounding, whom we esteem so learned that he is not deceived, and we see no reason why he should deceive us; our assent, because it grows not from any confidence of our own, but from another man's knowledge, is called faith'.[2] In matters of faith the method of definition is inappropriate; for explication only makes those things which exceed human capacity more obscure and harder to be credited.

Hobbes held, as we have seen, that the one article of faith necessary for salvation was that Jesus is the Christ. On what authority did this belief rest? In *De Cive* he said it was tantamount to belief in Christ. 'To believe in Christ, therefore, is nothing else but to believe Jesus himself, saying that he is the Christ.'[3] But the Scriptures are our authority for this revelation by Jesus of his Messianic secret. Who, then, is to be the authority in interpreting the Scriptures? In *Leviathan* Hobbes raised this problem and attacked the claims of the Papacy and the testimony of the private spirit to infallibility in interpreting the word of God. Talk of infallibility is quite out of place in this sphere. For it is obvious 'that Christian men do not know, but only believe the Scripture to be the word of God'.[4] St Paul said that 'Faith cometh by hearing'.[5] And that means hearing our lawful pastors. It seems therefore that Hobbes thought that ultimately faith that Jesus is the Christ, which was necessary to salvation, depended on our trust

1. E.W. II, 303. See also *supra*, Ch. 2, sect. 4.   2. E.W. II, 304–5.

3. E.W. II, 306.   4. E.W. III, 589.   5. Romans, x, 17.

in teachers appointed by the sovereign who would interpret the Scripture for us. Charles II or Cromwell must have been flattered by the problems referred to them by Hobbes – the creation of the world, God's attributes, and the proper interpretation of the Scriptures!

What, then, did Hobbes himself believe? He went out of his way to attack atheism and quoted divine authority for classing atheists as fools in a footnote on the subject of atheism in *De Cive*.[1] They were to be punished by God and Kings as enemies in a state of nature; for they accepted no laws, either human or divine. In *Leviathan*, too, he gave a rather Platonic description of atheists who believe that God takes no interest in the affairs of men.[2] Such men who took from God the government of the world and man had 'a wretched apprehension of God'.[3] But to be suspected of atheism was very dangerous in those days, as Hobbes discovered when he was sought as a scapegoat for the Great Fire.[4] Nothing much can be assumed about Hobbes' convictions from the evidence of these explicit attacks. Some might say, in fact, that he protested too much. Anyway, he obviously thought, like Spinoza, that atheism was dangerous for those who had not acquired scientific understanding. The Church helped to render peaceable those who had not a clear understanding of the principles of natural justice.

But it was obvious that the existence of God even as rather a remote and incomprehensible first cause did not seem as clear and distinct to Hobbes as some of his postulates of natural and civil philosophy. Indeed, he remarked in the same *De Cive* footnote than the proposition that there is a God was no more likely to be clear to the understanding of the vulgar, who were engaged in worldly pursuits, than was the proportion which the circle had to the square. And we have already noted the doubts he had about the arguments for a first cause in his *De Corpore*.

Did Hobbes, then, like Kant, 'abolish knowledge to make room for belief' in the sphere of religion? But had he himself very strong beliefs that stood in need of this suspense of rational criteria? People who make this move usually have passionate

1. E.W. II, 199.   2. E.W. III, 344.   3. E.W. II, 214.   4. See *supra*, p. 39.

religious beliefs for which they can find no rational justification. But could Hobbes have felt very strongly as a private person about religious issues if he could cheerfully hand over the attributes of God and the interpretation of the Scriptures to a sovereign? Hobbes might say at Court or on his way to church that a man must believe that Jesus was the Christ and that the interpretation of this must be left to the pastors appointed by the sovereign. But what did he think in the privacy of his study? When we read Hobbes' outrageous and impish excursions into Scriptural exegesis we cannot help but feel that his reverence for the word of God was limited – especially if we consider what he had to say about divine inspiration and the causes of superstition.

Probably Hobbes was very confident of his own interpretation of the Scriptures on certain key points – that Jesus' kingdom did not begin till the Second Coming, that in the meantime civil obedience was prescribed both by Jesus and St Paul, that the cardinal article of faith was that Jesus was the Christ, that Jesus only gave authority to his followers to teach and preach, and that there never was a divinely instituted spiritual authority independent of or a rival to the state. Most of his Scriptural exegeses were directed towards establishing these points. He probably thought, however, that a great many beliefs, which were not so politically important, could be substantiated or refuted by appeal to the Scriptures. But these could be merely a matter of inner conviction; Hobbes probably only had convictions on Scriptural matters that were politically important. He was patently not a religious man, and though he stated that belief in Jesus was necessary for salvation, he probably never felt very deeply about the state of his own soul or anyone else's. That was a matter of private conviction when shorn of expressions which might endanger the peace. Certainly no attempt should be made to enforce details of dogma by the Inquisition or any other fanatical device; for the danger to the peace therein contained was a far more potent consideration than the hypothetical benefit which might accrue to the soul of the man who knew all the right answers. Whether Hobbes himself believed in salvation through Jesus, in the divinity of Jesus, or even in the existence of God cannot definitely be settled. And, after all, it would be very difficult to say what believing in such propositions implies.

There were, too, the laws of nature which were God's commands enjoining the rules necessary to peace. They were in remarkable conformity with faith in Christ and obedience to the laws which were all that was necessary to salvation. Within this universally agreed and socially beneficial framework of conformity private men might indulge in private speculation and spin out their own idiosyncratic interpretation of further minutiae of the word of God. What Hobbes thought about these matters as he prepared himself for sleep after singing from his books of prick-song, only God and Hobbes knew. But we can safely infer that there was little consultation on these matters between them.

INDEX